MAO TSE-TUNG

Selected Works

VOLUME FOUR

1941-1945

NEW YORK
INTERNATIONAL PUBLISHERS

CONTENTS

PERIOD OF THE WAR OF RESISTANCE AGAINST JAPANESE AGGRESSION (III)

6 MAO TSE-TUNG

PREFACE AND POSTSCRIPT TO "RURAL SURVEY"

PREFACE

The Party's rural policy now is not one of agrarian revolution as during the ten-year civil war but one of the Anti-Japanese National United Front. The whole Party should execute the directives of the Central Committee of the Party of July 7 and December 25, 1940,[1] as well as those of the forthcoming Seventh National Congress. It is only for the purpose of helping comrades to find a way to tackle problems that the following materials are published. What constitutes a very grave danger is the fact that many of our comrades should have been placed in the position of giving guidance and direction while they have not yet broken off the habit of doing things in a crude, perfunctory fashion with little understanding of their nature and sometimes even in complete ignorance of the conditions prevailing at lower levels. No really good leadership can result from the absence of a real, specific knowledge of the actual conditions of the classes in Chinese society.

The only way to know the conditions is to make an investigation of society, to investigate the life and activities of each social class. For those whose duty it is to give guidance and direction, the most essential method of knowing the conditions is that they should, proceeding according to plan, devote their attention to a number of cities and villages and make a comprehensive survey of each of them from the basic viewpoint of Marxism, *i.e.* by means of class analysis. Only by doing so can one grasp the essentials of China's social problems.

To do this, we should first cast our eyes down and not hold our heads high and gaze skywards. If a person does not care, or does not make up his mind, to cast his eyes down, he can never really learn anything about China.

Secondly, fact-finding conferences should be held. Certainly we can acquire no complete knowledge by looking in all directions and listening to gossip. Of the data I have obtained through fact-finding conferences, those on Hunan and the Chingkang mountains are lost. The materials published here consist mainly of the *Survey of Hsingkuo*, the *Survey of Changkang Township*, and the *Survey of Tsaiki Township*. Holding a fact-finding conference is the simplest, the most practicable and the most reliable method which has taught me a great deal, and which gives me a better education than any university. The attendance of the conference ought to include the really experienced cadres of the middle and lower ranks, or the local people. During my investigation of the five counties in Hunan and the two counties in the Chingkang mountains, I approached the middle-ranking, responsible cadres in the counties, and during the Sunwu investigation I approached a number of cadres of both middle and lower rank, as well as a needy *hsiuts'ai*,[2] an insolvent ex-president of the chamber of commerce and an erstwhile petty official in charge of county revenue. All of them gave me a great deal of information which I had never had before. The man who for the first time gave me a complete picture of the rottenness of Chinese jails was a petty jailer I met during my investigation in Hengshan, Hunan. During my investigation in the county of Hsingkuo and the townships of Changkang and Tsaiki, I approached comrades at the township level and ordinary peasants. All these people—the cadres, the peasants, the *hsiuts'ai*, the jailer, the merchant and the revenue clerk— were my respected and beloved teachers and, in order to learn from them as a pupil, I, as was only proper, was respectful and industrious and adopted a comradely attitude towards them, for otherwise they would have paid no heed to me and would have told me nothing they knew, or at least not everything. A fact-finding conference does not require a large attendance; three to five, or seven or eight persons will be enough. But ample time must be allowed and an outline of investigation prepared beforehand and, furthermore, one must personally put questions to the participants and jot down the answers, and hold discussions with them. Therefore we cannot do it or do it well unless we are full of enthusiasm, determined to cast our eyes down, anxious to learn and ready to become humble pupils by dropping our pretentious airs and graces. It must be understood that the masses are the real heroes, while we ourselves are often ridiculously childish, and, unless we grasp this point we shall never be able to acquire even elementary knowledge.

I should like to reiterate that the present materials for reference are published mainly to show the method of knowing the conditions prevailing down below, and not to request comrades to memorise the specific data and the conclusions drawn from them. Generally speaking, unlike the bourgeoisie of Europe, America or Japan, the Chinese bourgeoisie, still in its infancy, has as yet not been and will never be able to provide us with any comprehensive or even preliminary data on social conditions, and this makes it necessary for us to collect them ourselves. Specifically speaking, people engaged in practical work must at all times endeavour to know the changing conditions—something for which no Communist Party in any country can rely on others. Therefore, all people engaged in practical work must investigate the conditions prevailing at the lower levels. Such investigations are especially necessary for those who know only theory but not the actual conditions, for otherwise they will be unable to link theory with practice. Although my assertion "No investigation, no right to speak" has been ridiculed by some people as "narrow empiricism", yet even now I do not regret having said it and, what is more, I still stick to it. There are many people who, the moment they take office, noisily speechify and criticise, picking faults right and left; yet in fact ten out of ten such people meet with failure. For, not based on comprehensive investigation, their speeches and criticisms are but ignorant and idle chatter. Our Party has suffered incalculably at the hands of this type of "imperial envoys". And the air is thick with such "imperial envoys", who can be seen almost everywhere. Stalin rightly says: "Theory becomes aimless if it is not connected with revolutionary practice." And he rightly adds: "Practice gropes in the dark if its path is not illumined by revolutionary theory."[3] Except for those practical workers who lack vision, perspective and foresight, no one can be labelled a "narrow empiricist".

Today I still feel keenly the need to make a comprehensive study of China and of other countries of the world; this has to do with the scantiness of my own knowledge along these lines and does not imply that I know everything while others are ignorant. It is my wish that, together with comrades of the whole Party, I should continue to be a pupil of the masses and learn from them.

March 17, 1941

POSTSCRIPT

The experiences of the ten-year civil war may serve as our best and most appropriate guidance in the present period of the Anti-Japanese War. But this only refers to the aspect of linking ourselves with the masses and mobilising them to oppose the enemy, and not to the aspect of tactical line. The Party's tactical line at present is different in principle from that in the past. In the past we opposed the landlords and the counter-revolutionary bourgeois, but at present we unite with all the landlords and the bourgeois who are not opposed to the Resistance to Japan. Even in the latter period of the ten-year civil war, we were wrong in not adopting different policies towards the reactionary government and party that launched armed attacks on us on the one hand and, on the other, all the social strata with a capitalist character that were under our régime, or towards the different cliques in the reactionary government and party. At that time, we pursued a policy of "all struggle" towards all sections of society except the peasantry and the lower stratum of the urban petty bourgeoisie —a policy undoubtedly erroneous. In agrarian policy we also made a mistake in repudiating the correct policy adopted in the earlier and middle periods of the ten-year civil war,[4] *i.e.* allotting the same amount of land to the landlords as to the peasants, so that the landlords could engage in farming and would not become displaced or turn to banditry to disturb peace and order. At present the Party policy must be different from those mentioned above; neither one of "all struggle and no alliance", nor one of "all alliance and no struggle" (*e.g.* the *Ch'en Tu-hsiu-ism* of 1927), it is rather a policy of uniting with all social strata opposed to Japanese imperialism and establishing a united front with them, yet waging different forms of struggle against them according to the different degrees of their vacillation and reaction, of their tendency to capitulate to the enemy and oppose the Communists and the people. The present policy is a dual policy, combining "alliance" with "struggle". The labour policy is a dual policy of properly improving the living conditions of the workers without impeding the reasonable capitalist economic developments. The agrarian policy is a dual policy of demanding that the landlords reduce rent and interest and stipulating that the peasants pay this reduced amount of rent and interest. In regard to political rights, the policy is a dual one of granting all the anti-Japanese landlords and capitalists the same personal, political and property rights as the workers and peasants, while guarding against all possible counter-revolutionary activities on their part. State and co-operative enterprises in our economy should be developed, but in the rural base areas today the main economic sector does not consist of state enterprises, but private ones; we ought to give the sector of non-monopoly capitalism in our economy a chance to develop in order to oppose Japanese imperialism and semi-feudalism. This is the most revolutionary policy for China today and to oppose or impede the execution of this policy is undoubtedly a mistake. To preserve strictly and resolutely the communist integrity of Party members, and to protect and develop properly the capitalist sector of social economy that is beneficial, are both indispensable tasks for us in the period of resisting Japan and building up a democratic republic. In this period it is possible that some Communists will be corrupted by the bourgeoisie and that capitalist ideas may arise among Communists; we must wage struggles against such decadent ideas in the Party, but we should not mistakenly transfer the struggle against capitalist ideas inside the Party to the field of social economy and oppose the capitalist sector of economy. We must draw a sharp line of demarcation between the two. The Chinese Communist Party is working under the most complicated conditions, and all Party members, especially the cadres, must steel themselves into fighters who understand Marxist tactics, because to view problems one-sidedly and naïvely will never lead the revolution to victory.

April 19, 1941

REFORM OUR STUDY

This is a report at a cadres' meeting in Yenan. This article and two others, *Rectify the Party's Style in Work* and *Oppose the Party "Eight-Legged Essay"*, are the major works Comrade Mao Tse-tung contributed to the campaign for rectifying the style in work. In these articles a forward step was made in summing up past differences over the Party line from the point of view of ideology and analysing the petty-bourgeois ideology and petty-bourgeois style of work which, masquerading as Marxism-Leninism, were very prevalent in the Party—notably the subjectivist and sectarian tendencies and their form of expression, the Party "eight-legged essay". He urged that a campaign for Marxist-Leninist education, namely, a campaign to rectify the style in work according to the ideological principles of Marxism-Leninism, should be carried out throughout the Party. His call immediately started a great debate inside and outside the Party on proletarian ideology *versus* petty-bourgeois ideology, and consolidated the position of the former, thus raising considerably the ideological level of the broad sections of the cadres and enabling the Party to achieve unprecedented unity.

.   .   .   .   .

I suggest that a reform be introduced in the method and system of study of the whole Party. The reasons are as follows:

I

The twenty years of the Chinese Communist Party are the twenty years in which the universal truth of Marxism-Leninism has daily become more integrated with the concrete practice of the Chinese revolution. We shall see that our knowledge of Marxism-Leninism and the Chinese revolution has now been greatly deepened and enriched, if only we recall for a moment how superficial and meagre it was in our Party's infancy. For a hundred years the best sons and daughters of the woe-stricken Chinese nation have waged struggles and sacrificed themselves in quest of the truth that would save our country and our people, and one no sooner fell than others stepped into the breach; they are not unwept and unsung. But it was only after the First World War and the Russian October Revolution that we have found the truth of truths,

Marxism-Leninism, as the best weapon to liberate our nation, and the Chinese Communist Party has become the advocator, propagator and organiser of the use of this weapon. Once integrated with the concrete practice of the Chinese revolution, the universal truth of Marxism-Leninism has made the Chinese revolution assume a new aspect. Since the outbreak of the Anti-Japanese War, our Party, basing itself on the universal truth of Marxism-Leninism, has gone a step further in the study of the practice of the War of Resistance and the study of the China and world of today, and has also made some start in the study of Chinese history. These are all very good signs.

II

But we still have defects, and very big ones too. In my opinion, unless these defects are corrected, we shall not be able to push our work forward or make further advance in our great undertaking to integrate the universal truth of Marxism-Leninism with the concrete practice of the Chinese revolution.

First, the study of the contemporary situation. In such a large party as ours, although we have had some achievements in the study of the present domestic and international situation, our collection of material is very scrappy and our research very desultory on any aspect of the subject—political, military, economic or cultural. Generally speaking, in the last twenty years we have not done any systematic and comprehensive work in collecting material about the above-mentioned aspects and in studying them, nor have we had a lively atmosphere of investigation and study of the actual conditions. Such extremely bad styles in work as "catching sparrows with eyes blindfolded" or "the blind man groping for fish", crudity and perfunctoriness, boastfulness and satisfaction with scrappy knowledge, are utterly opposed to the basic spirit of Marxism-Leninism; nevertheless, they are still found among many comrades in the Party. Marx, Engels, Lenin and Stalin teach us to study conditions seriously and to proceed from objective reality, not from subjective wishes; but many of our comrades run directly counter to this truth.

Secondly, the study of history. Although a few Party members and sympathisers have taken up this work, they have not done it in an organised way. Many Party members are completely in the dark about Chinese history either of the last hundred years or of ancient times. Many of our Marxist-Leninist scholars are always dragging ancient Greece into their discourses, but as to their own ancestors, I am sorry to say, they have clean forgotten them. There is no lively atmosphere of studying seriously either the present or the past.

Finally, the study of international revolutionary experiences and of the universal truth of Marxism-Leninism. Many comrades seem to study Marxism-Leninism regardless of the practical need of the revolution but simply for study's sake. Consequently, though they have read it up, they cannot digest it. They can only quote words and phrases from Marx, Engels, Lenin and Stalin, but they do not know how to adopt their stand, viewpoint and method in the concrete study of China's present and past or in the concrete analysis and solution of the problems of the Chinese revolution. Such an attitude towards Marxism-Leninism is very harmful, particularly for cadres of the middle rank and above.

The three things I have just mentioned—neglect of studying the present situation, neglect of studying history and neglect of applying Marxism-Leninism—all point to an extremely bad style in work. Spread far and wide, this style in work has ruined many of our comrades.

Indeed, many comrades in our ranks have been corrupted by this style in work. Unwilling to make a systematic and comprehensive investigation and study of the actual conditions inside and outside the country, the province, the county or the district, they issue orders and decrees on the strength of a scrappy knowledge and with the assertion "It must be so because I think so". Isn't this subjectivist style in work still found among a great number of comrades?

There are comrades who feel pride, instead of shame, in their ignorance or scanty knowledge of our own history. A particularly serious matter is that very few really know the history of the Chinese Communist Party and the history of China in the hundred years since the Opium War. As to the study of the economic, political, military and cultural history of the last hundred years, practically no one has taken it up seriously. Ignorant of our own affairs, some people have got only scraps of knowledge about ancient Greece and other foreign countries which, with pitiful industry, they have picked up bit by bit from the rubbish heap of obsolete foreign books.

For several decades, many who studied abroad have had this shortcoming. They come back from Europe, America or Japan, only to talk about the foreign things they have swallowed raw and whole. They play the role of a talking-machine and forget their duty of understanding and creating new things. This shortcoming has also infected the Communist Party.

We are studying Marxism, but the method used by many of us in this study runs directly counter to Marxism. That is to say, they have violated the basic principle repeatedly enjoined by Marx, Engels, Lenin and Stalin: the unity of theory and practice. Having violated this principle, they have invented an opposite one: the separation of theory from practice. In schools and in the spare-time education of cadres, teachers of philosophy do not guide the students to study the logic of the Chinese revolution; teachers of economics do not guide them to study the characteristic features of Chinese economy; teachers of political science do not guide them to study the tactics of the Chinese revolution; teachers of military science do not guide them to study the strategy and tactics fit for China's special conditions, and so on and so forth. The result is that errors are disseminated to the great harm of the people. What a man has learnt in Yenan, he doesn't know how to apply in Fu County.[1] If professors of economics cannot explain the border region currency and the national currency,[2] naturally the students cannot explain them either. Thus an anomalous mentality has been created among a number of our students: they have little interest in studying Chinese problems and take the directives of the Party lightly, but give all their heart to the dogmas, said to be eternally immutable, which their teachers have taught them.

Of course, what I have said above applies only to the worst type in our Party, and it is not the general case. However, people of this type actually exist, in quite large numbers and with a quite harmful influence; we must not treat the matter casually.

III

In order to make the idea clear by reiteration, I shall contrast two antagonistic attitudes.

First, the subjectivist attitude.

With this attitude, one works by sheer subjective enthusiasm, with a blurred picture of the present-day China before his mind's eye, instead of studying the circumstances systematically and comprehensively. With this attitude, one chops up history, strives to know only ancient Greece and not China and remains completely in the dark about the China of yesterday and of the day before yesterday. With this attitude, one studies the theory of Marxism-Leninism in the abstract and without any aim. One studies Marx, Engels, Lenin and Stalin not for the stand, viewpoint and method by means of which one can solve the theoretical and tactical problems of the Chinese revolution, but studies theory purely for theory's sake. This is random shooting instead of aiming one's arrow at the target. Marx, Engels, Lenin and Stalin teach us to proceed from actualities and to derive from them laws which will guide our action. With this end in view, we should, as Marx has said, endeavour to possess data in detail and subject them to scientific analysis and synthetic study.[3] But many of us are doing precisely the opposite. Some, while engaged in research work, are not interested in studying either the China of today or the China of yesterday, but confine all their attention to studying empty "theories" divorced from reality. Others, while engaged in practical work, pay no attention to the study of objective conditions and often, guided solely by enthusiasm, take their personal feelings for policies. Both kinds of people are subjectivist and neglect the existence of objective things. When making a speech, they enumerate items in a long series of A, B, C, D, or first, second, third, fourth; when writing an article, they produce a big screed full of bombast. They do not want to seek truth from facts; they want to impress people by claptrap. They are flashy without substance, brittle without solidity. They are cocksure and will yield to no one in this world, strutting about as if they were "imperial envoys". Such is the style in work of some comrades within our ranks. To adopt such a style in one's own behaviour means the undoing of oneself; to adopt it in educating others means the undoing of others; and to adopt it in directing the revolution, means the undoing of the revolution. In short, this subjectivist methodology, anti-scientific and anti-Marxist-Leninist, is the sworn enemy of the Communist Party, of the working class, of the people and of the nation, a symptom of impurity in Party spirit. Confronted with our sworn enemy, we have to overthrow it. Only when subjectivism is overthrown can the truth of Marxism-Leninism hold sway, Party spirit become strengthened and the revolution succeed. We should make it clear that lack of the scientific attitude, *i.e.* the Marxist attitude of the unity of theory with practice, means lack of Party spirit or deficiency of it.

There is a couplet which portrays the above-mentioned type of people. It runs:

The rushes on the wall—swollen in head, weak in legs, and loose in roots;
The bamboo shoots among the rocks—sharp in tongue, thick of skin, but empty in the belly.

Just look at those who do not take the scientific attitude, who can only say by rote words and phrases from the works of Marx, Engels, Lenin and Stalin, who enjoy fame without real learning to deserve it. Isn't this a fit description of them? If any of them really desires to rectify his defect, I advise him to commit to memory this couplet, or, if he has a bit more courage, to stick a copy of it on the wall of his room. Marxism-Leninism is a science, and science is knowledge come by honestly: absolutely no trickery will do. Let us, then, choose to be honest.

Secondly, the Marxist-Leninist attitude.

With this attitude, one applies the theory and method of Marxism-Leninism in a systematic and comprehensive study of the circumstances. Instead of relying on sheer enthusiasm, one must, as Stalin says, combine revolutionary sweep with practical spirit.[4] With this attitude, one will not chop up history, but will endeavour to know not only ancient Greece but also China, not only the revolutionary history of foreign countries but also that of China, not only the China of today but also the China of yesterday and the day before yesterday.

With this attitude, one will study the theory of Marxism-Leninism with a definite aim, with the aim of integrating it with the practical movement of the Chinese revolution and seeking from it a stand, a viewpoint and a method for solving the theoretical and tactical problems of the Chinese revolution. This is the attitude of "shooting one's arrow at the target". The "target" is the Chinese revolution, and the "arrow" Marxism-Leninism. The reason why we Chinese Communists have sought for this "arrow" is that we wish to hit the "target" of the Chinese revolution and the revolution of the East. This is the attitude of "seeking truth from facts". The "facts" refers to all things existing objectively; "truth" consists in the internal relationship of things, i.e. their laws; and to "seek" means to study. Proceeding from the actual conditions inside and outside the country, the province, the county or the district, we should find out the laws that are intrinsic in them and not merely fancied, i.e. find out the internal relations of the events occurring on all sides, and use them as the guide to our action. In order to do this we must rely not on our subjective imagination or the spur of the moment or on lifeless books, but on facts existing objectively, on the data obtained in detail, and must draw from the data correct conclusions under the guidance of the general principles of Marxism-Leninism. Such conclusions should not be merely a superficial arrangement of items in the order of A, B, C, D, etc., or hackneyed rhetoric full of bombast, but scientific conclusions. Such an attitude is one of seeking truth from facts, and not one of impressing people by claptrap. This attitude is a manifestation of Party spirit; it is the Marxist-Leninist style in work of uniting theory with practice. It is the minimum requirement of any Communist. With this attitude, one will be neither "swollen in head, weak in legs, and loose in roots", nor "sharp in tongue, thick of skin, but empty in the belly".

IV

In accordance with the points stated above, I would like to make the following proposals:

1. Place before the whole Party the task of making a systematic and comprehensive study of our circumstances. Make a

detailed investigation and study, according to the theory and method of Marxism-Leninism, of the economic, financial, political, military, cultural and party activities of our enemy, of our friends and of ourselves, and then draw therefrom the proper and inevitable conclusions. To this end, we should direct our comrades' attention to the investigation and study of such practical matters. We should make our comrades understand that the fundamental task of the leading bodies of the Communist Party lies in two important things, namely, to know the conditions and to grasp the policy; the former is what we call knowing the world, and the latter, changing the world. We should make our comrades understand that one has no right to speak on a subject unless he has investigated it, and that big talk, idle chatter, or a superficial arrangement of items in the order of first, second, third, fourth, etc., is of no use at all. Take our agitation work, for example. If we do not know the actual conditions of the agitation work of our enemy, of our friends, and of ourselves, we cannot correctly decide our own policy of agitation. In any branch of work, we can handle the work well only after we have known the conditions. A fundamental link in changing the Party's style in work is to carry out throughout the Party plans for study and investigation.

2. As to the study of the Chinese history of the last hundred years, we should assemble all qualified persons to take up the work jointly but with a proper division of labour, and put an end to the state of affairs in which each goes his own way. Only after an analytic study of China's economic history, political history, military history and cultural history can we make a synthetic study of her history as a whole.

3. As to the spare-time education for cadres and cadres' training schools, we should make it our central task to study the practical problems of the Chinese revolution under the guidance of the basic principles of Marxism-Leninism, and do away with the method of studying Marxism-Leninism statically and in isolation. In the study of Marxism-Leninism, the *History of the Communist Party of the Soviet Union, Short Course*, is to be used as the principal material. The *History of the Communist Party of the Soviet Union, Short Course*, is the best synthesis and summary of the world Communist movement of the past hundred years, a model of the unity of theory with

practice, and the only perfect model of its kind in the whole world. When we see how Lenin and Stalin integrated the universal truth of Marxism with the concrete practice of the Soviet revolution, and thereby developed Marxism, we shall know how we should work in China.

We have traversed many a tortuous road. Errors, however, are often the precursor of truth. I am confident that, in the present circumstances of the Chinese revolution and of the world revolution, which are so intensely alive and so richly varied, the present reform of our study will certainly yield good results.

May 1941

EXPOSE THE MUNICH PLOT IN
THE FAR EAST

An inner-Party directive written for the Central Committee.

(1) Japan, the United States and Chiang Kai-shek are plotting a new Munich in the Far East against communism and the Soviet Union by bringing about a Japanese-American reconciliation at China's expense. We must expose their plot and fight it.

(2) Now that the Japanese imperialists have concluded their military offensive aimed at forcing Chiang Kai-shek into capitulation, there are bound to be activities to lure him to capitulate. This is a repetition of the enemy's old policy of striking and stroking alternately or simultaneously. We must expose and fight it.

(3) Along with her military offensive, Japan has launched a campaign of rumour-mongering, as witness the allegations of "the unwillingness of the Eighth Route Army to fight in co-ordination with the Central army of the Kuomintang"; of "its seizing every opportunity to expand its territory"; of "its establishment of international connections"; of "its setting up of a rival central government", etc. This is Japan's cunning scheme of fomenting discord between the Kuomintang and the Communist Party in order to facilitate her efforts to lure the Kuomintang to capitulate. But, with dubious intentions, the *Central News Agency* and the Kuomintang press in general have repeated such rumours word for word and spread them without the slightest qualm of echoing Japan's anti-Communist propaganda. We must also expose and fight this.

(4) Although the New Fourth Army has been declared "in rebellion" and the Eighth Route Army has not been supplied with a single bullet or a single coin by the Kuomintang government, they have never ceased fighting the enemy forces. Moreover, in the present campaign in southern Shansi,[1] the Eighth Route Army is of its own accord fighting in co-ordination with the Kuomintang troops; and for the last two weeks it has started an all-out offensive in North China,

where fierce battles are still raging at this moment. The armed forces and the people under Communist leadership are already the mainstay in the War of Resistance. All calumnies against the Communist Party are aimed at undermining the Resistance and paving the way for capitulation. Our Eighth Route and New Fourth Armies should exploit their successes in the war and fight all defeatists and capitulators.

May 25, 1941

ON THE ANTI-FASCIST INTERNATIONAL UNITED FRONT

An inner-Party directive written for the Central Committee of the Chinese Communist Party.

The fascist rulers of Germany started to attack the Soviet Union on June 22. This perfidious act of aggression is directed not only against the Soviet Union but also against the freedom and independence of all nations. The Soviet Union's sacred war of resistance to fascist aggression is fought not only in defence of the Soviet Union itself but also in defence of all nations that are waging struggles against fascist enslavement in order to liberate themselves.

The task of Communists throughout the world now is to mobilise the people of all countries, to organise an international united front and to fight fascism and defend the freedom and independence of the Soviet Union, of China and of all other nations. At present, all strength must be concentrated on combating fascist enslavement.

For the Chinese Communist Party its tasks throughout the country are as follows:

1. Persist in the Anti-Japanese National United Front and the Kuomintang-Communist co-operation, drive the Japanese imperialists out of China and thereby give assistance to the Soviet Union.

2. Resolutely combat all the anti-Soviet and anti-Communist activities of the reactionaries among the big bourgeoisie.

3. In foreign affairs, unite against the common foe with all the people in Britain, the United States and other countries who are opposed to the fascist rulers of Germany, Italy and Japan.

June 23, 1941

SPEECH BEFORE THE ASSEMBLY OF THE SHENSI-KANSU-NINGSIA BORDER REGION

Messrs. Assemblymen and Comrades: The opening of the session of the border region assembly today is highly significant. The assembly has but one objective: to overthrow Japanese imperialism and build up a China of New Democracy or, in other words, a China dedicated to the revolutionary Three People's Principles. There can be no other objective for China at present but this one. Our principal enemies at this moment are not domestic but the Japanese, German and Italian fascists. Now the Soviet Red Army is fighting for the future of the Soviet Union and the whole of mankind and we are combating Japanese imperialism. Japanese imperialism is carrying on its aggression with the purpose of subjugating China. The Chinese Communist Party stands for uniting all anti-Japanese forces throughout the country to overthrow Japanese imperialism, for co-operating with all parties, all classes and all national groups that are willing to fight Japan, *i.e.* for an alliance with all people except the collaborators to wage a common struggle. This has been the consistent stand of the Communist Party all along. For more than four years the Chinese people have waged a heroic War of Resistance, a war kept up through the co-operation between the Kuomintang and the Communist Party as well as between all classes, parties and national groups. But we have not yet won the war, and in order to win it we have to carry on the fight and see to it that the revolutionary Three People's Principles are put into effect.

Why should we put into effect the revolutionary Three People's Principles? Because up to now Dr. Sun Yat-sen's revolutionary Three People's Principles have not yet been realised throughout China. Why shouldn't we put socialism into effect at present? Socialism is of course a better system, which has long been established in the Soviet Union, but conditions are still lacking in China today for introducing it. What has been carried out in the Shensi-Kansu-Ningsia border region is the revolutionary Three People's Principles. In solving any practical problem we have never exceeded the limits of the revolutionary Three People's Principles. For the present moment, of the revolutionary Three People's Principles, the Principle of Nationalism means overthrowing Japanese imperialism, and the Principles of Democracy and the People's Welfare mean working for the interests of all the anti-Japanese people in the country and not merely for those of a section. People throughout the country should have the freedom of person, the right to take part in politics and the right to protect their own property. They should have an opportunity to voice their opinions and should be clad and fed, obtain employment and receive education; in short, everyone should get his due. Chinese society is of a shape tapering off towards the two ends but bulging out in the middle, for the proletariat on the one hand and the landlord class and the big bourgeoisie on the other constitute each only a small minority, while the peasantry, the urban petty bourgeoisie and the other intermediate classes form the broadest sections of the masses. It is impossible for any political party to run the country well unless its policy is formulated in line with the interests of these classes, unless people from these classes can get their due, unless they have the right to voice their opinions. The policies the Chinese Communist Party has put forward aim at uniting all the anti-Japanese people and take into account all the anti-Japanese classes, especially the peasantry, the urban petty bourgeoisie and the other intermediate classes. The policies put forward by the Communist Party, which provide people of all circles with an opportunity to speak their mind, with jobs and with food, are policies of the genuine revolutionary Three People's Principles. In agrarian relations, we see to it that, on the one hand, rent and interest are reduced so that the peasants may have food to eat, and on the other hand, rent and interest at the reduced rate is paid to the landlords so that they can also live. As to the relationship between labour and capital, we on the one hand help the workers so that they may get employment and food, and on the other pursue a policy of developing industries so that the capitalists may reap some profit. In all this our aim is to unite the people throughout the country in a common endeavour to resist Japan. We call such policies the policies of New Democracy. Such are the policies really adapted to the actual conditions of China, and we hope that they will be put into effect throughout the country, just as they have been in the Shensi-Kansu-Ningsia border region and in the anti-Japanese base areas in the enemy's rear.

We have successfully enforced these policies and won the support of the people of the whole country. But we also have our shortcomings. Some Communists are not yet adept at co-operating in a democratic spirit with non-Party people; they still retain the style of narrow *closed-door-ism* or sectarianism and do not understand the principle that Communists are obliged to co-operate with non-Party people who stand for resisting the Japanese, and have no right to exclude them. This principle means that we should listen open-mindedly to the opinions of the masses, keep ourselves in contact with the masses and avoid alienation from the masses. The article in the Administrative Programme of the Shensi-Kansu-Ningsia Border Region, which stipulates that Communists should co-operate in a democratic spirit with non-Party people and must not act in disregard of other people's opinions and monopolise everything, refers exactly to these comrades who have not yet grasped the Party's policy. Communists must listen open-mindedly to the opinions of people outside the Party and must give them an opportunity to have their say. If what they say is right we ought to welcome it and learn from it and, even if it is wrong, we should let them say their say and then patiently explain the matter to them. A Communist should never regard himself as infallible and arrogantly bully others, or think that he is good in everything and others good for nothing; he must never shut himself up in a tiny compartment and brag and boast as if he lorded it over all. With the exception of the collaborators who are in league with the Japanese invaders and the reactionary die-hards who undermine the Resistance and solidarity—these people should of course be deprived of the right to voice their opinion—everybody is entitled to freedom of speech, and it doesn't matter even if what he says is wrong. Affairs of state are the public concern of the whole people, not the private business of a party or a group. Hence Communists are in duty bound to co-operate in a democratic spirit with non-Party people and have no right to exclude them or to monopolise everything. The

Communist Party is a party that works for the interests of the
nation and the people, and it certainly has no private ends to
seek. It should be watched over by the people and should not
run counter to their wishes. Its members should stand *among*
the people and not *above* them. Messrs. assemblymen and
comrades, this principle of the Communist Party for co-
operation in a democratic spirit with non-Party people has
been firmly laid down and will never change. So long as
parties exist in society, people who join party organisations are
always fewer than those who do not, hence our Party members
must always co-operate with non-Party people and should
make a good start right in this assembly. I believe that, under
such a policy, our Communist assemblymen can receive
excellent steeling in the assembly and overcome their *closed-
door-ism* or sectarianism. Since we are not members of a small
sect thinking ourselves infallible, we must learn how to keep
our doors open and co-operate in a democratic spirit with
non-Party people and how to discuss matters with others.
Perhaps even now there are Communists who would say that,
if they must co-operate with others, they will quit. But I
believe that there are very few such persons. I can assure you
that the vast majority of our Party members will certainly
follow the line of the Central Committee. At the same time,
I also ask comrades outside the Party to have a clear idea of
our stand, of the fact that the Communist Party is not a small
sect or clique which seeks only its private ends. The Communist
Party is not like that; it sincerely and honestly wishes to set
the affairs of state to rights. But we still have many defects.
We are not afraid to admit those defects and are determined
to remove them. We must get rid of them by intensifying
inner-Party education and also by co-operating in a democratic spirit with non-Party people. It is only by subjecting
our defects to such a crossfire from both within and without the
Party that we can remedy them and really set the affairs of
state to rights.

Messrs. assemblymen, you have taken the trouble to come
here for the meeting, and I happily greet this distinguished
assembly and wish it success.

November 21, 1941

RECTIFY THE PARTY'S STYLE IN WORK

This is a speech delivered at the Inauguration of the Central Party School of the Chinese Communist Party.

The Party School opens today, and I wish it every success.

I would like to say something about our Party's style in work.

Why should there be a revolutionary party? There should be a revolutionary party because there are in the world enemies of the people who oppress them, and the people want to shake off their oppression. In the era of capitalism and imperialism we need such a revolutionary party as the Communist Party. Without such a revolutionary party as the Communist Party it is simply impossible for the people to shake off the oppression of their enemies. As Communists who are to lead the people to overthrow the enemy, we must keep our ranks in good order, march in step, train our troops well and secure well-made weapons. Without these conditions, the enemy cannot possibly be overthrown.

Now what are the problems that still confront our Party? The general line of our Party is undoubtedly correct and our Party has also made achievements in its work. The Party has a membership of several hundred thousands who are leading the people to fight the enemy amid untold difficulties and with surpassing bravery. This is what we all see and nobody can doubt.

Then is there any problem that confronts our Party? There is, I should say, and what is more, the problem is in a certain sense quite serious.

What is it? It is the fact that a number of our comrades have certain ideas which strike one as not quite correct, not quite desirable.

That is to say, there is still something incorrect in the approach in our study, in the style in our Party work and in the tendency in our literary work. The incorrect approach in study refers to the evil of subjectivism. The incorrect style in Party work refers to the evil of sectarianism. The incorrect tendency in

28

our literary work refers to the evil of the Party "eight-legged essay".[1] These are like ill winds, but they do not sweep the sky like the north wind in the winter. Subjectivism, sectarianism and the Party "eight-legged essay" are no longer dominant in our style in work; they are but a gust of contrary wind, a foul draught escaped from the air-raid shelter. (*Laughter.*) But it is bad that such winds should still be blowing in the Party. We must stop the passage of the foul draught. Our whole Party should take up this job, and the Party School should do the same. These three ill winds, subjectivism, sectarianism and the Party "eight-legged essay", have their historical origin; though no longer dominant in the whole Party, they still do constant mischief and make assaults on us, and we must stop them and study, analyse and explain them.

It is our task to oppose subjectivism in order to rectify the incorrect approach in our study, to oppose sectarianism in order to rectify the incorrect style in Party work, and to oppose the Party "eight-legged essay" in order to rectify the incorrect tendency in our literary work.

In order to accomplish the task of overthrowing our enemy, we must accomplish the task of rectifying our Party's unsound style in work. The approach in study and the tendency in literary work form part of the Party's style in work or Party style. Once our Party's style in work becomes completely right, the people of the whole country will follow us. Those outside the Party who are tainted with such bad style in work will, in so far as they are good people, also follow our example and rectify their own errors and we shall then be able to exercise an influence upon the whole nation. So long as the ranks of us Communists are in good order, our steps in perfect co-ordination, our troops well-trained, and our weapons well-made, we can overthrow any enemy, no matter how powerful.

Let me speak first of subjectivism.

Subjectivism is an incorrect approach in study, opposed to Marxism-Leninism and incompatible with the Communist Party. What we want is a Marxist-Leninist approach in study. The approach we have in mind applies not only to study in the schools but also to study in the whole Party. It is a problem concerning the method of thinking of comrades in our leading bodies, of all our cadres and all our members, a problem concerning the attitude of all our members towards Marxism-Leninism and towards our work. As such, the problem of our approach in study is one of extraordinary importance, indeed, of primary importance.

Certain muddled ideas are now prevailing among many people. There are, for example, muddled ideas about what is a theoretician, what is an intellectual, or what is the integration of theory with practice, etc.

First, we wish to enquire whether the theoretical level of our Party is high or low. Translations of Marxist-Leninist books have lately appeared in greater numbers and found more readers. This is very good. But can we therefore say that the theoretical level of our Party has been greatly raised? True, our theoretical level is now somewhat higher than it used to be. But considering the rich content of the Chinese revolutionary movement, our theoretical front lags far too much behind and the contrast of the two shows up our extreme backwardness in theory. Generally speaking, our theory has not yet kept pace with revolutionary practice, let alone outstripped it as it should. Our practice with its rich variety still needs to be raised to its proper theoretical level. We have not yet examined all the problems, or rather the important ones relating to revolutionary practice, and raised them to the theoretical plane. Just think, how many of us have, on China's economics, politics, military affairs or culture, originated a theory worthy of the name, which can be considered scientific, comprehensive and not crude or sketchy? Especially as regards economic theory, in the hundred years of the development of Chinese capitalism since the Opium War, not a single book has yet appeared that is genuinely scientific and accounts for China's actual economic development. Can we say, then, that the theoretical level is high as regards economic matters in China? Can we say that our Party has already produced some who can pass as real economic theoreticians? Indeed no. We have read a great many books on Marxism-Leninism, but can we claim therefore that we have already got theoreticians? Again no. Marxism-Leninism is the theory formulated by Marx, Engels, Lenin and Stalin on the basis of reality, the comprehensive conclusion derived by them from historical and revolutionary realities. If we only read their works but do not go further and study in the light of their theory the realities of Chinese history and revolution or examine the practice of the Chinese revolution according to the theory, we should not presumptuously claim to be Marxist theoreticians. If, members of the Chinese Communist Party as we are, we do not see the problems of China right under our nose and can only memorise certain conclusions or principles in Marxist writings, then our record on the theoretical front is very poor indeed. If one learns by rote Marxist economics or philosophy, reciting glibly from Chapter I to Chapter X, but is utterly unable to apply it, can one be considered a Marxist theoretician? No, one cannot. What kind of theoreticians do we want? We want theoreticians who, basing themselves on the stand, viewpoint and method of Marxism-Leninism, can correctly interpret the actual problems arising in history and revolution and give a scientific explanation and theoretical elucidation of China's various problems in economics, politics, military affairs and culture. Such are the theoreticians we want. If one wishes to be a theoretician of this kind, one ought to have a true grasp of the essence of Marxism-Leninism, its stand, viewpoint and method, and a true grasp of the theory of Lenin and Stalin on the colonial revolution and the Chinese revolution, and to apply them in a penetrating and scientific analysis of China's actual problems so as to discover the laws of their development—only thus can one be the theoretician we really need.

The Central Committee has made a decision calling upon our comrades to learn how to apply the Marxist-Leninist stand, viewpoint and method in a serious study of Chinese history, of Chinese economics, politics, military affairs and culture, and to analyse every problem concretely on the basis of abundant data and then draw theoretical conclusions. This task rests upon our shoulders.

Comrades in the Party School should never regard Marxist theory as lifeless dogma. You should master Marxist theory and apply it, master it for the very purpose of applying it. If you can apply the Marxist-Leninist viewpoint in elucidating one or two practical problems, you deserve praise and credit. The more things you can elucidate and the more extensively and penetratingly, the better your record. Now it should be made a rule in the Party School that a student is to be marked or graded according to how he looks at China's problems after he has studied Marxism-Leninism, according to whether he envisages them clearly or dimly, whether he can envisage them at all or not.

Next comes the question of the "intellectual". Since China is a semi-colonial, semi-feudal country with a backward culture, the intellectuals are particularly cherished as a great treasure. Two years ago the Central Committee made a decision on the problem of intellectuals[2] that we should win them over in great numbers and welcome all of them in so far as they are revolutionary and willing to take part in the Resistance to Japan. It is entirely right that we should value intellectuals, for without revolutionary intellectuals the revolution cannot succeed. But, as we all know, there are not a few who plume themselves on their intellectuality and give themselves airs and graces for being intellectuals without realising that such airs are bad and harmful and in fact form an obstacle to their progress. They ought to learn the truth that many so-called intellectuals are relatively the least knowledgeable, while the workers and peasants are on occasions more knowledgeable. Some will say: "Ha! You are turning things upside down and talking nonsense." (*Laughter.*) But, comrades, don't get excited; there is some truth in what I have just said.

What is knowledge? Ever since the existence of class society there have been in the world only two kinds of knowledge: that which concerns the struggle for production and that which concerns the class struggle. The natural and social sciences are the crystallisations of these two kinds of knowledge, and philosophy is the generalisation and summary of the knowledge of both nature and society. Is there any other knowledge besides these? No. Now let us look at some students, the students who have been brought up in schools completely divorced from the practical activities of society. How about them? A man proceeds from a primary school of that sort to a university of the same sort, takes his diploma, and is regarded as stocked with knowledge. But all that he has is knowledge of books, and he has not yet taken part in any practical activities or applied in any branch of social life the knowledge he has acquired. Can such a person be regarded as a complete intellectual? Hardly so; because his knowledge is not yet complete. What then is comparatively complete knowledge? All comparatively complete knowledge is acquired through two stages, first the stage of perceptual knowledge and secondly the stage of rational knowledge, the latter being the development of the former to a higher plane. What sort of knowledge is the bookish information of the students? Granted that their information is entirely true knowledge, it is still not knowledge acquired through their own personal experience but only a matter of theories written down by their forefathers to sum up the experiences of the struggle for production and of the struggle between classes. It is entirely necessary that they should inherit this kind of knowledge, but it must be understood that in a certain sense such knowledge is to them still something one-sided, something which has been verified by others but not yet by themselves. The most important thing is that they should be well versed in applying such knowledge in life and practice. Therefore, I should advise those who have only bookish knowledge but little or no practical experience that they should be aware of their own shortcomings and be modest.

How can we turn those intellectuals who have only bookish knowledge into real intellectuals? The only way is to make them take part in practical work so that they will become practical workers and to make those who are engaged in theoretical work study important practical problems. Then our aim can be achieved.

What I have said may put some people out of temper. They will say: "According to your definition, Karl Marx himself would not be regarded as an intellectual." I would answer that they are wrong. Marx not only took part in practical revolutionary movements but also originated revolutionary theories. Beginning with commodities, the most rudimentary factor of capitalism, he made a careful and comprehensive study of the economic structure of capitalist society. A commodity is something that millions upon millions of people see and handle every day, but they are so used to it as to fail to notice it. Marx alone studied it scientifically, made great researches on its actual development and formulated thoroughly scientific theories from what exists universally. He studied nature, history and the revolution of the proletariat; he created dialectical materialism, historical materialism and the theory of the proletarian revolution. Thus Marx became a perfectly developed intellectual representing the peak of human wisdom, fundamentally different from the intellectuals who have only bookish knowledge. Marx made detailed investigation and reasearch in the midst of practical struggles, formed various generalisations and then verified the conclusions he had drawn by testing them again in practical struggles— activities of this kind are called theoretical work. Our Party needs many comrades who will learn to undertake such work. There are in our Party a great number of comrades who can learn to undertake such theoretical study and most of them are intelligent and promising and deserve our high regard. But they must follow a correct direction and avoid the mistakes they have committed in the past. They must get rid of doctrinairism and must not confine themselves to mere words in books.

There is only one kind of true theory in the world, the theory that is drawn from objective reality and then in turn verified by it; nothing else can be called theory in our sense. Stalin said that theory becomes aimless if it is not connected with practice.[3] An aimless theory is useless, incorrect and should be thrown away. We should say, "Fie, for shame!" to those who are fond of theorising in such an aimless way. Marxism-Leninism is the most unerring, scientific and revolutionary truth derived from objective reality as well as verified in it, but many who study it regard it as lifeless dogma, to the detriment of the development of theory, doing harm to themselves as well as to other comrades.

On the other hand, those comrades who are engaged in practical work will also come to grief if they misuse their experience. True, these comrades are often rich in experience which is certainly valuable, but it would be a great danger if they should rest content with such experience. They ought to realise that their knowledge is usually perceptual and partial, and that they lack rational and comprehensive knowledge; in other words, they are not equipped with theory, and their knowledge is thus comparatively incomplete. Without comparatively complete knowledge it is impossible to do revolutionary work well.

Thus there are two kinds of incomplete knowledge: one is

knowledge already contained in books and the other is knowledge which is usually perceptual and partial, and both are
one-sided. Only through an integration of the two can
excellent and comparatively complete knowledge emerge.

In order to study theory, however, our cadres from the
working class and peasantry must first acquire literacy.
Without literacy they cannot learn Marxist-Leninist theory.
When they have acquired literacy they can learn it at any
time. I never entered any Marxist-Leninist school in my
youth, and was taught only such stuff as: "The master said:
'How pleasant it is to learn and practise constantly what one
has learnt.'"[4] Though such stuff is out-of-date as teaching
material, yet it did me some good because it is from this that
I learned to read. However, we now study, not Confucius
any more, but such fresh subjects as the Chinese language,
history, geography and the natural sciences which, once
mastered, will prove useful everywhere. The Central Committee now emphatically demands that our cadres of worker-
peasant origin should acquire literacy so that they can take
up any branch of study, political science, military science or
economics. Otherwise, for all their rich and varied experiences,
they will never be able to study theory.

Thus, to oppose subjectivism we must make the two above-
mentioned types of people each develop the aspect in which
they are deficient and merge the two. Those with knowledge
of books must develop in the direction of practical work so
that they will not stop dead at books or commit the mistake
of doctrinairism. Those with practical experience must turn
to the study of theory and take up reading seriously so that
they can systematise and synthesise their experiences and
raise them to a theoretical plane and will not erroneously take
fragmentary experiences for universal truth or commit the
mistake of empiricism. Doctrinairism and empiricism alike
are subjectivism, each issuing from one of its poles.

Therefore there are in our Party two forms of subjectivism—
doctrinairism and empiricism. Each sees only a part rather
than the whole. If we do not notice this, if we do not know
the defect of such one-sidedness and make efforts to overcome
it, we are liable to go astray.

Of the two forms of subjectivism, however, doctrinairism

constitutes at present the greater danger in our Party. The doctrinaires can easily put on the Marxist mask to bluff, capture and enslave the cadres from the working class and peasantry who can hardly see through them, and they can also bluff and capture the innocent youth. If we can overcome doctrinairism, then the cadres who have knowledge of books will voluntarily unite with those who have practical experience and take to the study of practical things, and then there will emerge many excellent workers capable of integrating theory with experience as well as a number of real theoreticians. If we can overcome doctrinairism, then the comrades who have practical experience will have excellent teachers who can help them to raise their experiences to the theoretical plane and avoid the mistake of empiricism.

Besides muddled ideas about the "theoretician" and the "intellectual", there is the muddled idea current among many comrades about "the integration of theory with practice", a phrase to which they are paying daily lip-service. They talk every day of "integrating" the two, but actually they mean "severing" them, because they make no attempt whatsoever to integrate them. How can we integrate Marxist-Leninist theory with the practice of the Chinese revolution? To put it in common parlance, we should "shoot the arrow at the target". Marxism-Leninism bears the same relation to the Chinese revolution as the arrow to the target. Some comrades, however, are "shooting their arrows at no target", shooting at random, and such people are liable to do harm to the revolution. Others, with the arrows in their hands, are only caressing them, exclaiming ecstatically, "What a fine arrow! What a fine arrow!" but will never let it fly. Such people are connoisseurs of curios, and have almost nothing to do with the revolution. The arrow of Marxism-Leninism must be used to shoot at the target of the Chinese revolution. Unless this matter is thoroughly thrashed out, the theoretical level of our Party can never be raised and the Chinese revolution can never succeed.

Our comrades must understand that we study Marxism-Leninism not for ornament, not because it is a mystery, but because it is a science which will lead the proletarian revolution to victory. Up to now, there are still many who regard certain words or phrases in Marxist-Leninist works as a sort of patent panacea which, once acquired, can cure all maladies with the greatest ease. This is sheer infantile ignorance, and to such people we must give some elementary education. And it is also these ignorant people who look upon Marxism-Leninism as a religious dogma. To them we should say bluntly: Your dogma is of no use at all. Marx, Engels, Lenin and Stalin have repeatedly said that their theory is not a dogma but a guide to action. But of all their sayings, these people choose to forget this one, which is of the highest, utmost importance. Only when they become versed in applying the Marxist-Leninist stand, viewpoint and method, and Lenin's and Stalin's theory concerning the Chinese revolution, and when further they can, through conscientious research into China's historical facts and revolutionary practice, formulate theories to meet China's needs in various directions—only when they do that can the Chinese Communists be described as integrating theory with practice. It is useless if one only talks about "integrating" the two but never really attempts to "integrate" them, even though one goes on talking for a hundred years. As we are opposed to the subjective one-sided way of viewing things, we must destroy the subjectivism and one-sidedness of doctrinairism.

So much for today about opposing subjectivism in order to rectify the incorrect approach in study in the whole Party.

Now I shall take up the question of sectarianism.

Thanks to twenty years' steeling, there is no longer any sectarianism that plays a dominant role in our Party. Remnants of sectarianism, however, are still found both in relations inside the Party and in the relations between the Party and the outside world. Sectarianism in relations inside the Party leads to a mutual exclusiveness among the members, hindering unity and solidarity within the Party; sectarianism in the relations between the Party and the outside world leads to exclusiveness towards non-Party people, hindering the Party's work of uniting the whole of our people. Only by eradicating these two evils can the Party advance unimpeded in its great task of achieving solidarity among all the comrades of the Party and all the people of the country.

What are the remnants of sectarianism in the relations inside the Party? They are mainly as follows:

First, the assertion of independence. Some comrades see only the interests of a part but not those of the whole; they always unduly emphasise the importance of that part of work which is in their charge and wish to subordinate the interests of the whole to those of the part. They do not understand democratic centralism in the Party and do not realise that the Communist Party needs not only democracy but, even more urgently, centralisation. They forget democratic centralism which subordinates the minority to the majority, the lower level to the higher level, the part to the whole and the whole Party to the Central Committee. Chang Kuo-t'ao is one who asserted his independence of the Central Committee, and the result is that he has turned traitor to the Party and become a Kuomintang secret agent. Although the sectarianism now in question is not of such an extremely serious nature, we must still guard against it and must completely remove all traces of disunity. We should advocate the spirit of taking the whole situation into consideration. Every member, every branch of work, every opinion expressed or action taken must start from the interests of the whole Party, and no violation of this principle can be tolerated.

Those who assert their independence often adhere to the view that the individual comes first, and are often wrong on the problem of the relationship between the individual and the Party. Although they pay lip-service to the Party, they actually put themselves in the first place and the Party in the second. Comrade Liu Shao-ch'i once remarked of certain people that they have unusually long arms and are very clever in turning everything to their own advantage, paying little heed to the interests of others and the Party as a whole. "What is mine is mine, and what is yours is mine too." (*Uproarious laughter.*) What are they after? They are after fame, after position, and they want to cut smart figures. Whenever they are in charge of any work, they assert their independence. Towards this end they will ingratiate themselves with some people, ostracise others, resort to boasting, flattery and touting; in a word, introducing into the Communist Party the philistine style in work characteristic of the bourgeois political parties. It is their dishonesty that is the undoing of these people. We ought to be honest and straightforward in doing our work, I think;

without honesty nothing can be accomplished in the world. Who are the honest people? Marx, Engels, Lenin and Stalin to be sure, and the scientists as well. Who are dishonest? Trotsky, Bukharin, Ch'en Tu-hsiu and Chang Kuo-t'ao are all very dishonest; and dishonest are all those who assert independence out of personal or departmental interest. All those who are cunning and do not adopt a scientific attitude towards their work are in reality most foolish persons and will all come to no good end, however much they may be pleased with their ruses and however clever they may fancy themselves. Students in our Party School must pay attention to this question. We must build up a centralised and unified Party and completely get rid of unprincipled factional struggles. In order to make our Party march in step to fight for a common aim, we must oppose individualism and sectarianism.

Cadres native to one locality and those from the outside must unite, and oppose the sectarian tendency. Since many anti-Japanese bases have been established only after the arrival of the Eighth Route Army and the New Fourth Army, and much of the work there has been developed only after the arrival of cadres from other places, we must give good heed to the relationship between the native cadres and those from the outside. Our comrades should understand that, under such conditions, only through the perfect union of the native cadres and those from the outside, and only after a host of native cadres has emerged and been given responsible posts, can our bases be consolidated and our Party take root there; otherwise that is impossible. All the cadres, native to the place or coming from the outside, have their merits and defects, and they can make progress only by acquiring each other's strong points to overcome their own weaknesses. Compared with the native cadres, the cadres from the outside often know less about local conditions or have less contact with the masses. Take myself, for instance. I have been in northern Shensi for five or six years, but as to knowledge of local conditions and contact with the people here, I lag far behind many of the native cadres. Our comrades going to Shansi, Hopeh, Shantung and other anti-Japanese bases must take note of this. Further-more, even within the same base there is the distinction between those sections that are developed earlier and those that are developed later, and between cadres native to the place and those coming from the outside. Cadres coming from a more developed section to a less developed one may also be taken as cadres coming from the outside to that particular section and therefore they, too, should pay attention to the problem of helping the native cadres. Generally speaking, if the cadres coming from the outside who hold responsible positions in a certain place cannot get on with the native cadres, they should bear the principal blame. The comrades who assume leadership are more to blame. At present this problem has not yet received sufficient attention in many places; some people despise the native cadres and jeer at them, saying, "What do the natives know? Clod-hoppers all of them!" Such people utterly fail to understand the importance of the native cadres; they know neither the good qualities of the native cadres nor their own defects, and adopt an incorrect, sectarian attitude. All cadres from the outside should take loving care of the native cadres and give them constant help, and must not ridicule or attack them. Of course, the native cadres on their part should also learn from the cadres from the outside, acquiring their strong points and abandoning their own improper narrow views, so that they may be perfectly united with the cadres from the outside and form an indivisible whole with them, thereby avoiding the tendency to sectarianism.

The same holds good of the relationship between cadres in army service and those in civilian work. They must be perfectly united and oppose the tendency towards sectarianism. Army cadres must help civilian cadres, and vice versa. If conflict arises between them each should forgive the other and make proper self-criticism. Generally speaking, wherever an army cadre is actually in the responsible position, he should principally bear the blame if he cannot get on with the civilian cadres. Army cadres must realise their own responsibility and be modest towards civilian cadres before we can create the condition for both military work and construction work in the base areas to proceed smoothly.

The same applies to the relationship among different armed units, different localities and different departments. We must oppose the tendency towards group egoism which looks after the interests of one's own department to the exclusion of those of all others. Anyone is a group egoist utterly devoid of the spirit of communism who ignores the difficulties of others, who refuses to release the cadres as requested by other units or, by way of dumping rubbish in the neighbour's yard, releases only the incompetent, and who never gives the slightest consideration to other departments, other localities or other persons. Disregard of the whole situation and complete indifference to other departments, other localities and other persons constitute the characteristics of group egoism. We must intensify the education of such persons to make them realise that this is definitely a sectarian tendency which, if allowed to develop, will become a great danger.

Another problem is that of the relationship between old and new cadres. Since the Resistance our Party has grown considerably and a host of new cadres has appeared, which is a very good sign. In his *Report to the Eighteenth Congress of the Communist Party of the Soviet Union* Comrade Stalin said, "There are never enough old cadres, there are far less than required, and they are already partly going out of commission owing to the operation of the laws of nature."[5] Here Stalin is talking about cadres as well as the laws of nature. If there were not large numbers of new cadres working in perfect co-ordination with the old cadres in our Party, our work would be interrupted. All old cadres, therefore, should greet new cadres with the warmest welcome and the greatest interest. True, the new cadres have their defects since, having but lately joined the revolution, they still lack experience and some of them may have brought with them the vestiges of the evil ideology of the old society, namely, remnants of petty-bourgeois individualism. But through education, through steeling in the revolution, these defects can be gradually removed. Their merit consists, as Stalin has pointed out, in that they have a sharp sense for everything new and are therefore highly enthusiastic and active—precisely the quality which some old cadres lack.[6] Cadres, old and new, must respect each other, learn from each other, each acquire the other's strong points to overcome their own weakness, so that both will be perfectly united and work for the common cause, thereby guarding against the tendency to sectarianism. Generally speaking, wherever the old cadres assume the principal leadership, they should bear the chief blame if they cannot get on with the new cadres.

The above-mentioned relations—between the part and the whole, between the individual and the Party, between native cadres and cadres from the outside, between cadres in army service and cadres in civilian work, between different military units, localities and departments and between old and new cadres—are all relations inside the Party. In all these, we should promote the spirit of communism and guard against the tendency to sectarianism, so that our ranks will be in good order and our steps in perfect co-ordination to facilitate our struggle. This is a very important problem, a problem which we must solve in rectifying our Party's style in work. Sectarianism is a manifestation of subjectivism in the matter of organisation and, if we want to get rid of subjectivism and promote the Marxist-Leninist spirit of seeking truth from facts, we must clean up the remnants of sectarianism in the relations inside the Party and start from the principle that the Party's interests are placed above all personal or departmental interests, thereby enabling the Party to attain perfect unity and solidarity.

Remnants of sectarianism in the Party's relations with the outside should be eliminated just as those in the relations inside it. The reason is that, in order to defeat the enemy, it is not enough to unite the whole membership of our Party alone, but necessary for us to unite the whole nation. In the cause of uniting the whole nation, the Chinese Communist Party has done tremendous and difficult work for twenty years, and since the start of the War of Resistance our work has been yielding even greater results. This does not mean, however, that all our comrades have acquired a correct style in work in dealing with the masses and show no sectarian tendency. No. The tendency still exists among a number of comrades and, in some cases, to a very serious degree. Many of our comrades are much given to swaggering before non-Party people, despising and belittling them, and are unwilling to show them respect or appreciate their good qualities. This is precisely a sectarian tendency. Having read a few Marxist books, these comrades become arrogant rather than modest and habitually dismiss others as no good without knowing that they themselves are really mere tyros and smatterers. Our comrades must realise the truth that the Party members are always a minority as compared with non-Party people. Suppose there were one Communist in a hundred Chinese, then among China's population of 450,000,000 there would be 4,500,000 Communists. Yet, even if our membership reached such a colossal figure, the Communists would still form only one per cent of the whole population, while 99 per cent of our countrymen would not be Communists. On what grounds, then, can we refuse to co-operate with non-Party people? As to all those who are willing to, or in all probability can, co-operate with us, we have not only the duty to co-operate with them but absolutely no right to exclude them. But, failing to realise this, some of our members despise or even exclude those who are willing to co-operate with us. There is no ground whatsoever for doing so. Have Marx, Engels, Lenin and Stalin given us any ground for that? No. On the contrary, they have always earnestly enjoined us to link ourselves closely with the masses and not isolate ourselves from them. Has the Central Committee of the Communist Party given us any ground? No. There is not a single one among all its decisions that says that we can isolate ourselves from the masses and stand alone. On the contrary, the Central Committee has always told us to link ourselves closely with the masses and not to isolate ourselves from them. Thus any practice that isolates us from the masses has no sanction at all, and it is simply the mischief done by the sectarian ideas of some comrades' own invention. As the error of sectarianism is still very serious in a section of our Party members and forms a hindrance to the implementation of the Party line, we should start a great educational campaign within the Party to deal with it. First of all, we should make our cadres thoroughly understand how serious the problem is and how utterly impossible it is to overthrow our enemy and attain the goal of revolution, unless the Communists are united with the non-Party cadres and people.

All sectarian ideas are imbued with subjectivism and are incompatible with the practical needs of the revolution, hence the struggle against subjectivism and the struggle against sectarianism should go on simultaneously.

There is no time to deal with the Party "eight-legged essay" today, and I shall reserve it for another occasion. The Party "eight-legged essay" is a sewer in which all that is evil and vile finds a home, a form of expression for subjectivism and sectarianism. It does people harm and damages the revolution, and we must thoroughly rid ourselves of it.

To oppose subjectivism we must propagate materialism and dialectics. There are, however, many comrades in our Party who still do not care to propagate either. Some even listen to others' propaganda on subjectivism with equanimity and indifference. They think they believe in Marxism, but they make no effort to propagate materialism and never give a moment's thought to or express any opinion on the subjective stuff that comes to their ears or eyes. This is not the attitude of a Communist. In consequence, the virus of subjectivism has infected many of our comrades, leading to inertia and apathy. We must therefore start an enlightenment campaign in the Party to liberate the minds of many comrades from the bondage of subjectivism and doctrinairism and call upon our comrades to boycott subjectivism, sectarianism and the Party "eight-legged essay". Such things are very much like Japanese goods, and only our enemy wishes us to preserve these foul things and continue to be befouled by them; we ought, therefore, to advocate boycotting them just like boycotting Japanese goods.[7] Whatever is tainted with subjectivism, sectarianism and the Party "eight-legged essay" should be boycotted so that it will lose its market, and its purveyors must not be allowed to take advantage of the Party's low theoretical level and sell their stock. For this purpose, our comrades must be trained to have a good nose; they must take a sniff at a thing to distinguish the good from the bad before they decide to accept or reject it. Communists should never fail to ask "why?" about anything; they should always use their brains and think hard how far it is real and what, if any, is the reason for it, and should never follow blindly or advocate slavish obedience.

Finally, in opposing subjectivism, sectarianism and the Party "eight-legged essay", we must bear in mind two principles: first, "learn from past experience in order to avoid future mistakes"; and secondly, "treat the illness in order to save the man". We must expose without personal considerations all past errors, analyse and criticise them scientifically so that we will be more careful and do better work in future. This is the meaning of the principle: "learn from past experience in order to avoid future mistakes". But in exposing errors and criticising defects, our whole purpose is the same as the doctor's in treating a case; namely, to cure the patient but not to kill him. A person suffering from appendicitis will recover if his appendix is removed by the surgeon. Any person who has committed errors is welcome to treatment until he is cured and becomes a good comrade, so long as he does not conceal his malady for fear of taking medicine or persist in his errors until he becomes incorrigible, but honestly and sincerely wishes to be cured and made better. You cannot cure him by subjecting him to hearty abuse or giving him a sound thrashing. In treating a case of ideological or political illness, we should never resort to violence, but should adopt the attitude of "treating the illness in order to save the man", which alone is the correct and effective method.

I have availed myself of this occasion, the opening of the Party School, to speak at great length, and I hope our comrades will think over what I have said.

February 1, 1942

OPPOSE THE PARTY "EIGHT-LEGGED ESSAY"

This is a speech delivered at a cadres' meeting in Yenan.

Comrade K'ai-feng has just stated the purpose of today's meeting. Now I want to talk about how subjectivism and sectarianism use the Party "eight-legged essay"[1] as an instrument of propaganda or a form of expression. We oppose subjectivism and sectarianism, but if the Party "eight-legged essay" is not eliminated, the two will still have a hole to hide themselves in. If we also abolish the Party "eight-legged essay", we shall checkmate both subjectivism and sectarianism and, showing these two monsters in their true colours, we can easily annihilate them—just as "everyone calls 'Kill it!' when a rat is seen to run across the street".

It would not be a serious matter if a person were to write Party "eight-legged essays" merely for his own perusal. If he gives them to another person to read, then the number of people concerned is doubled and the harm is great enough. If he further has them posted on the wall, or mimeographed, or published in newspapers, or printed in the form of a book, then the problem becomes very serious indeed, because many people will come under their influence. Writers of Party "eight-legged essays", however, always wish to have a large audience. Thus it becomes imperative to expose and abolish the Party "eight-legged essay".

The Party "eight-legged essay" is a brand of foreign "eight-legged essay". The latter was combated by Lu Hsun a long time ago. Why then do we now call it the Party "eight-legged essay"? Because, besides the exotic flavour, it has also the smell of native soil. Perhaps it too can be counted as some kind of creative work! Who says that our people have no creative work at all? Here is one! (*Uproarious laughter.*)

The Party "eight-legged essay" has a long history in our Party and, especially during the Agrarian Revolution, it became sometimes even quite rampant.

46

Viewed historically, the Party "eight-legged essay" is a reaction to the May 4 Movement.

During the May 4 Movement, modern-minded people opposed the classical diction in favour of the vernacular, and the traditional dogmas in favour of science and democracy; in all this they were quite right. At that time, the movement was lively, progressive and revolutionary. The ruling class of that time indoctrinated students with Confucian teachings and compelled the people to believe reverently in the whole Confucian caboodle as if it were religious dogma, and all writers wrote in the classical style. In short, at that time the things written and taught by the ruling class and its toadies were in the nature of the "eight-legged essay", of dogma, whether in form or in content. These were the old "eight-legged essay" and old dogma. In exposing to the people the ugliness of the old "eight-legged essay" and dogma and calling on them to oppose both, the May 4 Movement made a great achievement. Another of its great achievements which is linked to this is the opposition to imperialism, but the struggle against the old "eight-legged essay" and dogma remains one of its great achievements. Later on, however, the foreign "eight-legged essay" and foreign dogma came into being. Having departed from Marxism, certain people in our Party developed the foreign "eight-legged essay" and foreign dogma into subjectivism, sectarianism and the Party "eight-legged essay". These are the new "eight-legged essay" and new dogma. They are so deeply ingrained in the minds of many comrades that even today it calls for great efforts on our part to carry out the work of reform. Thus we see that the lively, progressive and revolutionary May 4 Movement which fought against the old feudal "eight-legged essay" and dogma was later turned by some people into its very opposite, and the new "eight-legged essay" and dogma emerged. These things are not lively but dead and stiff, not progressive but retrogressive, and not revolutionary but an obstacle to the revolution. That is to say, the foreign "eight-legged essay" or the Party "eight-legged essay" is a reaction to the very nature of the May 4 Movement. The May 4 Movement, however, had its own weaknesses. Many of the leaders of that time still lacked the critical spirit of Marxism and the method they used was generally that of the bourgeoisie, *i.e.* the formalistic method. They were quite right in opposing the old "eight-legged essay" and dogma and in advocating science and democracy. But with regard to the existing conditions of that time, to history and to things foreign, they lacked the critical spirit of historical materialism and regarded what was called bad as absolutely, totally bad and what was called good as absolutely, totally good. This formalistic approach to problems affected the subsequent development of the movement. In the course of its development, the May 4 Movement branched out in two directions. One section of people inherited the scientific and democratic spirit of the May 4 Movement and remoulded it on the Marxist basis; this is what the Communists and some non-Party Marxists have done. Another section took the road of the bourgeoisie, and this marked the development of formalism towards the Right. But the Communist Party was not all of a piece; a section of it, failing to hold firm to Marxism, went astray, and committed the mistake of formalism, *i.e.* of subjectivism, sectarianism and the Party "eight-legged essay", which marked the development of formalism towards the "Left". From this it can be seen that the Party "eight-legged essay" is on the one hand a reaction to the positive elements of the May 4 Movement and on the other a legacy, continuation or development of its negative elements, and is not something accidental. It is good for us to realise this point. If it was revolutionary and necessary to fight against the old "eight-legged essay" and old doctrinairism during the period of the May 4 Movement, so it is for us at present in the light of Marxism to criticise the new "eight-legged essay" and new doctrinairism. If there had been no fight against the old "eight-legged essay" and doctrinairism at that time, the minds of the Chinese people would not have been freed from their bondage and China would have no hope of freedom and independence. The May 4 Movement marked merely the beginning of this undertaking, and the complete deliverance of the whole people from the domination of the old "eight-legged essay" and doctrinairism still requires great efforts on our part and remains for us a tremendous piece of work on the road of revolutionary remoulding. If today we do not also oppose the new "eight-legged essay" and new doctrinairism, the minds of the Chinese people would be in the bondage of another kind of formalism. If we do not get rid of the poison of the Party "eight-legged essay" and the mistake of doctrinairism found among a section (only a section, of course) of comrades in our Party, then the lively revolutionary spirit cannot be aroused, the wrong attitude towards Marxism which has hardened into a habit cannot be rectified, true Marxism cannot be widely disseminated and developed and, furthermore, a vigorous struggle cannot be conducted against the influence of the old "eight-legged essay" and dogma among the whole people or against that of the foreign "eight-legged essay" and foreign dogma among many people, nor can the goal of destroying and abolishing all these things be attained.

Subjectivism, sectarianism and the Party "eight-legged essay"—all three are anti-Marxist and are needed not by the proletariat but by the exploiting classes. They reflect petty-bourgeois ideology in our Party. As China is a country with a very large petty bourgeoisie, our Party is surrounded by this enormous class, and it is natural that a very great number of our members of this class origin join the Party without shedding their petty-bourgeois tails, long or short. The fanaticism and one-sidedness of petty-bourgeois revolutionaries, if not checked and rectified, are liable to engender subjectivism and sectarianism, one of whose forms of expression is the foreign or Party "eight-legged essay".

It is not easy to liquidate these things and sweep them clean. We must do it properly; in other words, we must use persuasive reasoning. If our reasoning is persuasive and to the point, it will be effective. In reasoning we must begin by administering a shock and shouting at the patient, "You are ill!" so that he is frightened into a sweat, and then we tell him gently that he needs treatment.

Let us now analyse the Party "eight-legged essay" and see where its evils lie. We might also present an "eight-legged thesis" in the manner of the "eight-legged essay" by way of administering poison as the antidote of poison, and call it "The Eight Serious Indictments".

The first indictment against the Party "eight-legged essay" is that it fills endless pages with empty talk. Some comrades love to write long articles, but such articles, void of matter,

are veritably like the "foot-bandages of a slut, long as well as
smelly". Why should they write things so long and yet so
hollow? There can be only one explanation—they are determined not to let the masses read them. As their writings are
long and hollow, the masses will shake their heads at the sight
of them, let alone read them through. Thus the only thing for
these comrades to do is to bluff naïve people, thereby spreading
a bad influence and fostering bad habits. The war against
aggression which the Soviet Union has been fighting since
June 22 last year is simply gigantic, yet Stalin's speech on
July 3 was only the length of an editorial in our *Liberation
Daily*. Had any of our gentlemen written that speech, it would
have run to the horrible length of at least scores of thousands
of words. We are now in a period of war and should study
how to write short and pithy articles. Although there is yet no
fighting here in Yenan, our troops at the front are daily
engaged in battles, and people in the rear are all saying that
they have lots of work to do. If the articles are too long, who
will read them? Some comrades at the front also like to write
long reports. They take pains to write them and send them
here for us to read. Yet who has the courage to read them? If
long and hollow writings are not good, then how about short
and hollow ones? Not good either. We must ban all empty
verbiage. But our first and foremost task is to throw immediately into the dustbin the slut's long and smelly foot-bandages.
Some might ask, "Isn't *Das Kapital* very long? What are we
to do with it?" That is very simple: go on reading it. A
proverb has it, "Sing different songs on different mountains";
another runs, "Regulate the appetite according to the dishes,
cut the dress according to the figure". Whatever we do must
be done according to actual conditions, and writing articles
and making speeches are no exceptions. What we oppose is
the long-winded "eight-legged essay" void of matter, but we
do not mean that all good writings should be short. Of course
we need short articles in war-time, but above all we need
articles that have substance. Articles devoid of substance are
the least justifiable and the most objectionable. The same
applies to speeches; we must stop all empty, long-winded
tirades.

The second indictment against the Party "eight-legged

essay" is that it is pretentious with a view to bluffing people. Since some Party "eight-legged essays" are not only long and hollow but also deliberately pretentious in order to bluff people, they contain the worst kind of poison. To fill endless pages with empty talk may still be called childish, but to be pretentious with a view to bluffing people is something more than that—it is downright knavish. Lu Hsun criticised people who sinned in this respect, saying: "Making insults and threats is emphatically not fighting."[2] What is scientific can bear criticism at any time, for science is truth and stands in no fear of refutation. But subjective and sectarian stuff expressed in articles and speeches in the style of the Party "eight-legged essay" is mortally afraid of being refuted; it is very cowardly and therefore resorts to pretentiousness to bluff people, as if it could bluff people into silence and then return home in triumph. Such pretentiousness will not help bring truth to light but will be an obstacle to its discovery. Whatever is true never poses to bluff people; it talks and acts simply and honestly. Two terms used to appear in the articles and speeches of some comrades; one was "ruthless struggle" and the other "merciless blows". These measures are entirely necessary in coping with the enemy and the enemy ideology, but it is wrong to apply them to our own comrades. It often happens that enemies and enemy ideologies infiltrate into the Party, as described in Item 4 of the Conclusion of the *History of the Communist Party of the Soviet Union, Short Course*. Against our enemies, we must beyond doubt adopt the measures of waging ruthless struggle and dealing merciless blows because they are applying the same measures against the Party, and any leniency on our part will make us fall into the very traps laid by these villains. But we should not employ the same measures against comrades who have occasionally committed a mistake; in their case we should apply the method of criticism and self-criticism, *i.e.* the method described in Item 5 of the Conclusion of the same book. The reason why even in such cases some comrades used to resort to "ruthless struggle" and "merciless blows" was that, on the one hand, they failed to define their own objective and, on the other, they were pretentious in order to bluff people. The method of pretentiousness and bluff will never do, no matter whom one is dealing with. For against

our enemy such a tactic of bluff is utterly ineffective, while
to our own comrades it is simply harmful. The exploiting
classes and the *lumpen*-proletariat usually resort to it, but the
proletariat does not need it. For the proletariat, there is only
one weapon that is the sharpest and the most effective, namely,
the serious and militant scientific attitude. A Communist lives
not upon bluff but upon the truth of Marxism-Leninism, upon
the spirit of seeking truth from facts and upon science. As to
the idea of attaining fame and position by pretentiousness, it is,
needless to say, simply contemptible. In short, when any
organisation makes decisions and issues instructions, or when
any comrade writes articles and makes speeches, only the truth
of Marxism-Leninism and usefulness are the stand-by. Only
by means of this stand-by can we achieve victory in the
revolution; all others are futile.

The third indictment against the Party "eight-legged essay"
is that it shoots at random and disregards the audience. A few
years ago, the following slogan was seen on the city wall of
Yenan: "Working men and farmers unite to win victory in the
War of Resistance." The idea of the slogan was quite good,
but the character "工" [*Kung*, meaning working], with its
second stroke changed from a perpendicular line into a zigzag,
was written as "工". How about the character "人" [*Jen*,
meaning men]? It had three stripes on its right leg and
became "人". That comrade who wrote them was no doubt
a disciple of ancient writers and scholars, but how odd that he
should have written such characters on the wall of Yenan at
a time of the War of Resistance! Perhaps he had vowed not
to allow the common people to read the slogan, for it would be
difficult to explain it otherwise. Communists who really want
to do propaganda work must consider their audience and think
over the question of who are to read their articles and hand-
writing, or to listen to their speeches and talks; otherwise it is
as good as making up their minds not to be read or listened
to by anyone. Many people often take it for granted that what
they write and say is easy to understand, but actually this is not
true at all. Since their writings and speeches are Party "eight-
legged essays", how can people understand them? The saying
"to play the harp to a cow" implies a gibe at the audience.
If we replace this connotation with the idea of respect for the

audience, then the gibe would be turned against the player. Why should he strum away without considering his audience? The Party "eight-legged essay" is even worse—it is simply like a raven cawing insistently to the masses of the people! When one shoots an arrow, one must look at the target; when one plays the harp, one must consider the audience. Can one then write articles or make speeches without taking the readers or audience into account? Suppose I make friends with some-one, no matter whom. Can I become his bosom friend if we do not know each other's mind and what is on it? It will never do for those engaged in agitation work simply to rattle on without investigating, studying and analysing what constitutes their audience.

The fourth indictment against the Party "eight-legged essay" is that its dry, savourless style suggests the *piehsan*.[3] Like our Party "eight-legged essay" such starvelings, called in Shanghai "little *piehsan*", are very wizened and ugly-looking. If an article or a speech merely repeats a few catchwords in the manner of a schoolboy's composition without a trace of spirited and vigorous language, isn't it rather like a *piehsan* who is insipid in speech and repulsive in appearance? In the case of a person who entered primary school at seven, went to middle school in his teens and graduated from college in his twenties, we cannot blame him for the poverty and monotony of his language because he has never come into contact with the masses of the people. But if we revolutionaries who work for the masses do not learn the language of the masses, we cannot work well. Now even many comrades engaged in agitational work do not learn that language. Consequently their agitation is extremely insipid and their articles can find few readers and their speeches few listeners. Why should we bother to learn language and, what is more, study it intensely? Because one cannot learn a language unless one studies hard. First, we must learn language from the people. The people's vocabulary is rich, lively and expressive of real life. Since many of us have not mastered language, our speeches and articles contain few sentences that are lively, effective and powerful, but are like the *peihsan*, a mere bundle of rigid muscles, disagreeably emaciated and not like a man enjoying good health. Secondly, we must absorb what we need from foreign languages. We

are not to adopt foreign expressions mechanically or to use
them indiscriminately, but to absorb from foreign languages
all that is fine and suits our needs. As it is, the Chinese
vocabulary is insufficient, and we have already incorporated
many foreign expressions into our current vocabulary. For
example, we are now at a meeting of *Kanpu* [cadres], and the
term *Kanpu* is derived from a foreign expression. We have yet
to absorb many more foreign things that are fresh, not only
the progressive ideas but also the new expressions. Thirdly,
we must also learn to adopt what is still alive in the language
of the ancients. Because we have not exerted ourselves to learn
language, we have not made full and reasonable use of much
that is still alive in the ancient language. It goes without saying
that we are resolutely opposed to the use of expressions or
classical allusions that are already dead, but what is good and
useful should be taken over. At present, since those who are
too deeply poisoned by the Party "eight-legged essay" refuse
to make any painstaking study of what is useful in popular,
foreign and ancient languages, the masses do not welcome their
uninspiring agitation and neither do we need such worthless
and incompetent agitators. Who are the agitators? Not only
the teachers, the journalists and the writers, but also our cadres
working in all fields. Take the military commanders, for
example. Though they make no public statements, they talk
to the soldiers and make contact with the people—isn't that
a form of agitation? Whenever a person speaks to others, he
does agitational work. And unless he is dumb, he always has
a few words to say. Thus it is imperative that our comrades
should study language.

The fifth indictment against the Party "eight-legged essay"
is that it arranges items into A, B, C, D ... as if setting up a
Chinese drug-store. Go and take a look at any Chinese drug-
store; there you see a cabinet with innumerable drawers, each
bearing the name of the drug: toncal, foxglove, rhubarb,
saltpetre—indeed everything that should be there. This method
has been picked up by our comrades. In their articles and
speeches, their books and reports, they first use the Chinese
capitalised numerals, then the Chinese small numerals, then
the characters of the ten heavenly stems, then the twelve
horary characters, and then A, B, C, D, a, b, c, d, the Arabic

numerals, and what not. How lucky that the ancients and foreigners have made all these symbols for us so that we can open a drug-store with great ease! An article bristling with such numerals and symbols neither formulates problems, nor analyses them, nor solves them; it is neither for nor against anything; for all its verbiage, it has no real content and remains a drug-store. I am not saying that characters like those denoting the ten heavenly stems, etc., are not to be used; all I say is that the approach is wrong. The method imitated from the Chinese drug-store, with which many of our comrades are now infatuated, is the most rudimentary, infantile and philistine of all methods. It is the method of formalism which classifies things according to their external features instead of their internal relations. If, merely according to the external features of things, a person arranges a conglomeration of concepts not internally related to each other into an article, a speech or a report, he is indulging in mental gymnastics and will induce other people to do the same and make them contented with a superficial arrangement of items in the order of the heavenly stems, etc., instead of using their heads to ponder problems and the essence of things. What is a problem? It is the contradiction of things. Where there is an unsolved contradiction, there is a problem. Once a controversy arises on a problem, you must be in favour of one side and oppose the other; and you must formulate the problem. To formulate the problem, you must first make a general study of the two main aspects of the problem or contradiction so that you may understand the nature of the contradiction: this is the process of discovering the problem. Through general investigation and study the problem can be discovered and formulated, but it cannot yet be solved. To solve it you must further make a systematic and minute investigation and study: this is the process of analysis. Even in formulating a problem an analysis has to be made, otherwise, faced with a chaotic mess of phenomena, you will not know where the problem or contradiction lies. The analysis in question, however, refers to the process of a systematic, minute analysis. It often happens that, although the problem has been formulated, it cannot be solved; this is because we have not brought to light the internal relations of things or completed the process of such a systematic, minute analysis, and are consequently unable to see clearly the features of the problem, to make a synthesis and to solve the problem properly. An article or a speech, if it is important and can serve as a sort of guidance, should first set forth a certain problem and analyse it, and then present a synthesis, point out the nature of the problem and offer a solution; in this case no formalist methods are of any use. Since such infantile, rudimentary, philistine and thoughtless formalist methods are very fashionable in our Party, we must expose them so that everybody will learn to use the Marxist methods to observe, formulate, analyse and solve problems, that we can do better work and attain victory of the revolution.

The sixth indictment against the Party "eight-legged essay" is that its irresponsibility does harm to people everywhere. All the offences indicted above are due partly to infantilism and partly to deficiency in the sense of responsibility. Take for instance the washing of our faces. We all wash our faces every morning, and many of us even do it more than once a day and look carefully into the mirror after washing to make some "investigation and study" (*Uproarious laughter*), in case we have not done justice to our faces. Just think, what a sense of responsibility! If our articles are written and speeches made with the same sense of responsibility, they would leave not much to be desired. If your stuff is not good enough to see the light, then tuck it away. Always bear in mind that it may influence the thoughts and actions of others! If a man has not washed his face for several days, that of course would be quite bad; if he has washed it but has left a smudge or two on it, that of course would not be good form; but in neither case is there any serious danger. The case is entirely different in writing articles or making speeches, for they are intended exclusively to influence people and, in taking them lightly, our comrades show themselves really lacking in a sense of proportion. Many people write articles and make speeches without preliminary study or preparation and, having finished writing them, they do not even bother to go over them a few times, in the same way as they would look into the mirror after washing their faces, but carelessly send them to the press. The result is often like this: "A thousand words from the pen in a stream, but ten thousand *li* away from the theme"; these writers seem to be geniuses, but really do harm to people everywhere. This bad habit arising from a deficient sense of responsibility must be removed.

The seventh indictment against the Party "eight-legged essay" is that if the whole Party is poisoned by it the revolution will be endangered. The eighth indictment is that the dissemination of this poison will cause harm to the nation. These two indictments are self-evident and require no explanation. In other words, if the Party "eight-legged essay" is not rectified but is allowed to develop, the consequences will be so serious that the worst will happen. The poison of subjectivism and sectarianism hidden in the Party "eight-legged essay", if allowed to spread, will do harm to both the Party and the country.

The aforesaid eight counts form our declaration of war on the Party "eight-legged essay".

As a form, the Party "eight-legged essay" is not only unsuitable for expressing the revolutionary spirit but is apt to stifle it. To develop the revolutionary spirit we must throw away the Party "eight-legged essay" and adopt the lively and vigorous Marxist-Leninist style in writing. This style has long been in existence, but it is not yet enriched and popularised. Once we have destroyed the foreign "eight-legged essay" and the Party "eight-legged essay", this new style will be enriched and popularised and the Party's revolutionary undertaking will be pushed forward.

The Party "eight-legged essay" is not, however, confined to articles and speeches; it is also found in the agenda of meetings: "1. Opening announcements; 2. Reports; 3. Discussions; 4. Concluding remarks; 5. Adjournment". Is it not also in the style of the Party "eight-legged essay" to repeat this procedure rigidly over and over again at every meeting, large or small, here and everywhere? Reports presented at meetings almost invariably contain the same points: "1. the international situation; 2. the national situation; 3. the situation in the border region; and 4. the situation in our department", and the meetings often last from morning till night, at which those who have nothing to say also take the floor as if they owed it to others to do so. In short, there is a complete disregard of the actual conditions as well as a strict adherence to the rigid old forms and practices. Shouldn't we correct all these things?

Many people nowadays advocate transformation along national, scientific and popular lines; this is very good. But what we mean by "transformation" is a change from top to bottom, from the outside to the inside, whereas some people advocating "transformation" have not even changed *a bit*. I would therefore advise these comrades to change *a bit* before they proceed to "transform" things; otherwise they are still in the coils of doctrinairism and the Party "eight-legged essay" —this is to have sharp eyes but clumsy hands, to have great ambition but little talent, and this will prove futile. Great care should be taken, for instance, by those who talk about transformation along popular lines but actually do things as their small groups see fit, for some day they may meet a member of the populace and be told, "Gentlemen, let me see your 'transformation'!" Then they will be in a fix. Those who do not just prate about transformation along popular lines but really hope to carry it out must honestly learn from the common people, or else they will never be able to "transform" things. If those who daily shout about transformation along popular lines cannot even say three sentences in the language of the common people, then obviously they have never made up their minds to learn from the common people and what they really mean is transformation along the lines of a small group.

Distributed at today's meeting is a pamphlet entitled *A Guide to Propaganda* containing four articles which I advise our comrades to read over and over again.

The first article, selected from the *History of the Communist Party of the Soviet Union, Short Course*, deals with the way Lenin carried on agitation. It describes how Lenin wrote leaflets:

"Under Lenin's guidance, the St. Petersburg League of Struggle for the Emancipation of the Working Class was the first body in Russia that began to link Socialism with the working-class movement. When a strike broke out in some factory, the League of Struggle, which through the members of its circles was kept well posted on the state of affairs in the factories, immediately responded by issuing leaflets and Socialist proclamations. These leaflets exposed the oppression of the workers by the manufacturers, explained how the workers should fight for their interests, and set forth the workers' demands. The leaflets told the plain truth about the ulcers of capitalism, the poverty of the workers, their intolerably hard working day of 12 to 14 hours, and their utter lack of rights. They also put forward appropriate political demands."

You see, one must be "well posted on the state of affairs", and tell "the plain truth". Again:

"With the collaboration of the worker Babushkin, Lenin at the end of 1894 wrote the first agitational leaflet of this kind and an appeal to the workers of the Semyannikov Works in St. Petersburg who were on strike."

To write a leaflet, one must consult with comrades who are well posted on the state of affairs. On the basis of such investigation and study, Lenin wrote his articles and did all his work.

"Every leaflet greatly helped to stiffen the spirit of the workers. They saw that the Socialists were helping and defending them."

Don't we agree with Lenin? If we do, we should work in the spirit of Lenin. That is, we must do as Lenin did, and not fill endless pages with empty verbiage, or shoot at random, or become cocksure braggarts.

The second article is selected from Dimitrov's *Report to the Seventh World Congress of the Communist International*. What did Dimitrov say? He said:

"We must learn to talk to the masses, not in the language of book formulas, but in the language of fighters for the cause of the masses, whose every word, whose every idea reflects the innermost thoughts and sentiments of millions."

And again:

"Furthermore, it must be borne in mind that *the masses cannot assimilate our decisions unless we learn to speak the language which the masses understand*. We do not always know how to speak simply, concretely, in images which are familiar and intelligible to the masses. We are still unable to refrain from abstract formulas which we have learned by rote. As a matter of fact, if you look through our leaflets, newspapers, resolutions and theses, you will find that they are often written in a language and style so heavy that they are difficult for even our Party's functionaries to understand, let alone the rank-and-file workers."

Well, didn't Dimitrov put his finger on our weak spot? True, the Party "eight-legged essay" exists in foreign countries as well as in China, and is apparently a common disease. (*Laughter.*) But at any rate we must cure ourselves of it quickly according to Comrade Dimitrov's advice.

Every one of us must make this a law, a Bolshevik law, an elementary rule:

"When writing or speaking always have in mind the rank-and-file worker who must understand you, must believe in your appeal and be ready to follow you. You must have in mind those for whom you write, to whom you speak."

This is the prescription made out for us by the Communist International, a prescription that must be followed. Let this be a *law* for us!

The third article, selected from the *Complete Works of Lu Hsun*, is the author's reply to the *Great Dipper* magazine[4] on how to write. What did Lu Hsun say? He laid down altogether eight rules of writing, some of which I should like to mention here.

Rule 1: "Pay close attention to all kinds of things; observe more, and do not write if you have seen only a little."

He said that we should "pay close attention to all kinds of things", not just one thing or half of it. He asked us to "observe more", not just cast casual glances. How about us? Are we not doing exactly the opposite in writing about the little we have seen?

Rule 2: "Do not force yourself to write when you have nothing to write about."

How about us? Do we not often force ourselves to write a great deal when we have evidently nothing to say? It is sheer irresponsibility to pick up the pen and force oneself to write without any preliminary investigation or study.

Rule 4: "When you have finished writing, read what you have written at least twice, and do your best to strike out ruthlessly redundant words, sentences and paragraphs. Rather condense the material for a novel into a sketch than spin out the material for a sketch into a novel."

Confucius advised, "Think twice,"[5] and Han Yu also said, "A deed is accomplished through thought";[6] both were referring to matters in ancient times. Today matters have become very complicated and sometimes it is not enough even to think three or four times. Lu Hsun said, "Read what you have written at least twice," but how many times "at most"? That he didn't say; in my opinion, it does no harm to go over an important article more than ten times and revise it carefully before it is published. Articles are the reflection of objective events and things which, with their intricacy and complexity, must be studied over and over again before they can be exactly and properly reflected; to be crude and careless in this respect is simply to be ignorant of the ABC of writing.

Rule 6: "Do not crudely coin epithets or the like that are intelligible to none but yourself."

We have "crudely coined" too many expressions, all of which are "intelligible to none" but ourselves. Sometimes a sentence of forty or fifty words is packed with "epithets or the like that are intelligible to none" but ourselves. Many who are never tired of glibly professing themselves followers of Lu Hsun are exactly the people who turn their backs on his teachings.

The last article is a comment on how to carry on agitation in keeping with national usage, given by the Chinese Communist Party's Central Committee at its plenary session (the sixth since the Sixth National Congress). At this session held in 1938 we said that any "talk about Marxism apart from China's characteristics" is "only Marxism in the abstract, Marxism in the void". That is to say, we must oppose all empty talk on Marxism, and any Communist who lives in China must study Marxism in connection with the actual conditions of the Chinese revolution.

"The foreign 'eight-legged essay' must be banned, empty and abstract talk must be stopped, and doctrinairism must be laid to rest to make room for the fresh and lively things of Chinese style and Chinese flavour which the common folk of China love to see and hear. To separate the content of internationalism from national forms is the practice of those who understand nothing of internationalism; we on the other hand want to link up the two closely. In this matter there are within our ranks serious mistakes which should be conscientiously corrected."

In that article we called for banning the foreign "eight-legged essay", but some comrades have actually been promoting it. In that article we demanded that empty and abstract talk must be stopped, but some comrades have been obstinately keeping on with it. In that article we called for laying doctrinairism to rest, but some comrades have dragged it out of bed. In short, this report endorsed by the plenary session of the Central Committee was dismissed as merely idle words by many people who seemed as if wilfully opposed to it.

Now the Central Committee has decided that we must cast off once for all the Party "eight-legged essay", doctrinairism and the like, and that is why I have talked at such length. I hope that comrades will think over and analyse what I have said and each make an analysis of his own particular case. Everybody should think things out about himself, talk the results over with his close friends and the comrades around him, and overcome effectively his own defects.

February 8, 1942

TALKS AT THE YENAN FORUM ON ART AND LITERATURE

INTRODUCTION

Comrades! You have been invited to this forum today to exchange views and ascertain the proper relationship between our work in the artistic and literary fields and our revolutionary work in general, to determine what is the proper path of development of revolutionary art and literature and how they can give better help to other revolutionary activities, so that we can overthrow the enemy of our nation and accomplish the task of national liberation.

In our struggle for the liberation of the Chinese people there are various fronts, of which two may be mentioned: the civilians' front and the soldiers' front, *i.e.* the cultural front and the military front. In order to defeat the enemy we must rely primarily on an army with guns in its soldiers' hands. But this is not enough; we also need a cultural army which is absolutely indispensable for uniting ourselves and defeating the enemy. Since the May 4 Movement of 1919 this cultural army has taken shape in China and has helped the Chinese revolution in gradually reducing the domain and weakening the influence of China's feudal culture and her comprador culture which is adapted to imperialist aggression. By now the Chinese reactionaries can only propose what they call "quantity versus quality" as a means of opposing the new culture; in other words, the reactionaries who can afford to blow the expense are straining to turn out an immense quantity of stuff, though they are unable to produce anything good. On the cultural front, art and literature have formed an important and victorious sector since the May 4 Movement. The movement of revolutionary art and literature made much progress during the ten years' civil war. Although this movement and the revolutionary war headed in the same general direction, yet as the two brother armies participating in them were cut off from each other by the reactionaries, they lacked co-ordination in their practical activities. It is a very good thing that since the outbreak of the War of Resistance more and more revolutionary artists and writers have come to Yenan and other anti-Japanese base areas. But their arrival at these base areas is not the same as their complete merging with the people there. If the revolutionary work is to be pushed forward, a complete merging must be effected. The purpose of our meeting today is precisely to fit art and literature properly into the whole revolutionary machine as one of its component parts, to make them a powerful weapon for uniting and educating the people and for attacking and annihilating the enemy, and to help the people to fight the enemy with one heart and one mind. What are the problems to be solved in order to achieve this objective? I think they are the problems of the standpoint, the attitude and the audience of the artists and writers and of how they should work and how they should study.

Standpoint: Our standpoint is that of the proletariat and the broad masses of the people. For members of the Communist Party this means that they must adopt the standpoint of the Party and adhere to Party spirit and Party policies. Are there any of our artists and writers who still lack a correct or clear understanding on this point? I think there are. Quite a number of our comrades have often departed from the correct standpoint.

Attitude: Our specific attitudes towards specific things arise from our standpoint. For example: Should we praise or should we expose? This is a question of attitude. Which of these two attitudes should we adopt? I should say both and it all depends on whom you are dealing with. There are three kinds of people: the enemy, the allies in the united front and our own people, namely, the masses and their vanguard. Three different attitudes must be adopted towards these three kinds of people. With regard to our enemies, i.e. the Japanese imperialists and all other enemies of the people, the task of revolutionary artists and writers is to expose their cruelty and chicanery, point out the tendency of their inevitable defeat and encourage the anti-Japanese army and people to fight them with one heart and one mind and overthrow them resolutely. In our attitude towards our various allies in the united front, we ought to promote unity as well as criticism, and there should be different kinds of unity and different kinds of criticism. We support their resistance to Japan and commend them for their achievements. But we ought to criticise them if they do not put up an active resistance to Japan. We must resolutely combat anyone if he opposes communism and the people and moves farther down the path of reaction with every passing day. As to the masses of the people, their toil and struggle, their army and their party, we should of course praise them. The people also have their shortcomings. Many among the proletariat still retain petty-bourgeois ideas, while both the peasantry and the urban petty bourgeoisie entertain backward ideas—these are the burdens handicapping them in their struggles. We should spend a long time and be patient in educating them and helping them to remove the burdens from their backs and to fight against their own shortcomings and errors so that they can take big strides forward. In the course of their struggles they have remoulded or are remoulding themselves, and our art and literature should depict this process of remoulding. We should not take a one-sided view and mistakenly ridicule them or even be hostile towards them unless they persist in their errors. What we produce should enable them to unite, to advance and to stride forward with one heart and one mind, discarding what is backward and promoting what is revolutionary; it certainly should not do the opposite.

Audience, *i.e.* for whom are the artistic and literary works produced? In the Shensi-Kansu-Ningsia border region and the anti-Japanese base areas in North and Central China, the problem is different from that in the Kuomintang-controlled areas and particularly from that in Shanghai before the War of Resistance. In Shanghai at that time a section of the students, office workers and shop assistants formed the bulk of the audience for revolutionary art and literature. In the Kuomintang-controlled areas since the start of the War of Resistance, the scope has been widened to some extent, but basically these people remain the chief audience because the government there has kept the workers, peasants and soldiers away from revolutionary art and literature. In our base areas the situation is entirely different. Here the audience for art and literature is composed of workers, peasants, soldiers and revolutionary cadres. There are students too, but they are different from the students of the old type in that they are either ex-cadres or would-be cadres. Cadres of all kinds—soldiers in the army, workers in the factories and peasants in the villages—want to read books and newspapers if they are literate, and to see plays and pictures, sing songs and listen to music if they are not; they are the audience for our art and literature. Take the cadres only: they are not, as you imagine, small in number, but are actually much more numerous than the prospective readers of a new book published in the Kuomintang-controlled areas. There one edition of a book usually runs to only about two thousand copies and three editions total only six thousand, while here in our base areas the cadres who can read number more than ten thousand in Yenan alone. Moreover, many of them are well-steeled revolutionaries who have come from all parts of the country and will go to different places to work; thus the education of these people is a task of great importance. Our artists and writers should do good work on their behalf.

Since the audience for our art and literature is made up of workers, peasants, soldiers and their cadres, the problem arises of how to understand these people and to know them well. A great deal of work has to be done in order to understand them and to know them well, to understand and to know well all kinds of things and people in the Party and government organisations, in the villages and factories and in the Eighth Route and New Fourth Armies. Our artists and writers should work in their own field, which is art and literature, but their duty first and foremost is to understand and know the people well. How did they stand in this regard in the past? I would say that they failed to know the people well and failed to understand them, and were like heroes with no scope for displaying their heroism. What did they fail to know well? They failed to know the people well. They did not know well either what they were describing or their audience; they were even perfect strangers to both. They did not know well the workers, peasants, soldiers and their cadres. What did they fail to understand? They failed to understand language, i.e. they lacked an adequate knowledge of the rich and lively language of the masses of the people. (Many artists and writers, withdrawing themselves from the people into a void, are of course unfamiliar with the people's language, and thus their works are not only written in a language without savour or sap but often contain awkward expressions of their own coinage which are opposed to popular usage.) Many comrades love to talk about "transformation along the popular line", but what does that mean? It means that the ideas and feelings of our artists and writers should be fused with those of the broad masses of workers, peasants and soldiers. In order to do so one should conscientiously learn the language of the masses. If one finds much of the language of the masses unintelligible, how can one talk about artistic and literary creation? When I say heroes with no scope for displaying their heroism, I mean that the masses do not appreciate your high-sounding talk. The more you put on airs as veterans, as "heroes", and the harder you try to sell your wares, the more the people refuse to be impressed. If you want the masses to understand you and want to become one with them, you must be determined to undergo a long and even painful process of remoulding. In this connection I might mention the transformation of my own feelings. I began as a student and acquired at school the habits of a student; in the presence of a crowd of students who could neither fetch nor carry for themselves, I used to feel it undignified to do any manual labour, such as shouldering my own luggage. At that time it seemed to me that the intellectuals were the only clean persons in the world, and the workers and peasants seemed rather dirty beside them. I could put on the clothes of other intellectuals because I thought they were clean, but I would not put on clothes belonging to a worker or peasant because I felt they were dirty. Having become a revolutionary I found myself in the same ranks as the workers, peasants and soldiers of the revolutionary army, and gradually I became familiar with them and they with me too. It was then and only then that a fundamental change occurred in the bourgeois and petty-bourgeois feelings implanted in me by the bourgeois schools. I came to feel that it was those unremoulded intellectuals who were unclean as, compared with the workers and peasants, while the workers and peasants are after all the cleanest persons, cleaner than both the bourgeois and the petty-bourgeois intellectuals, even though their hands are soiled and their feet smeared with cow dung. This is what is meant by having one's feelings transformed, changed from those of one class into those of another. If our artists and writers from the intelligentsia want their works to be welcomed by the masses, they must transform and remould their thoughts and feelings. Without such transformation and remoulding they can do nothing well and will be ill-adapted to any kind of work.

The last problem is that of study; I mean the study of Marxism-Leninism and of society. One who considers himself a Marxist revolutionary writer, especially a Communist writer, must have a knowledge of Marxism-Leninism. But some comrades still lack a grasp of the basic concepts of Marxism. For example, one of its basic concepts is that existence determines consciousness, i.e. the objective reality of the class struggle and national struggle determines our thoughts and feelings. Some of our comrades, however, reverse the proper order of things and maintain that everything ought to start from "love". Now as for "love", in a class society there can be only class love; but these comrades are seeking a love that transcends the classes, love in the abstract as well as freedom in the abstract, truth in the abstract, human nature in the abstract, etc. This shows that these comrades have been deeply influenced by the bourgeoisie. They must thoroughly liquidate this influence and study Marxism-Leninism with an open mind. True, artists and writers should learn to create artistic and literary works, but Marxism-Leninism is the science that all revolutionaries should study, and artists and writers cannot be exceptions. Artists and writers should study society; i.e. study the various classes in society, their mutual relations and respective conditions and their physiognomy and psychology. Only when these things are clearly grasped will our art and literature be rich in content and correct in orientation.

Today I raise these problems by way of preamble and hope you all will give your opinions on these and other related issues.

May 2, 1942

CONCLUSION

Comrades! We have met three times during this month. In the pursuit of truth, heated debates have taken place and scores of Party and non-Party comrades have spoken, laying bare the issues and making them concrete. I think this is very profitable to the whole artistic and literary movement.

In discussing any problem we should start from actual facts and not from definitions. We shall be following the wrong method if we first look up definitions of art and literature in the textbooks and then use them as criteria in determining the direction of the present artistic and literary movement or in judging the views and controversies that arise today. We are Marxists and Marxism teaches that in our approach to a problem we should start not from abstract definitions but from objective facts and, by analysing these facts, determine the way we shall go, our policies and methods. We should do the same in our present discussion of art and literature.

What are the facts at the present time? The facts are: the War of Resistance that China has been waging for five years; the world-wide anti-fascist war; the vacillation of China's big landlords and big bourgeoisie in waging the War of Resistance as well as their high-handed policy towards the people; the movement of revolutionary art and literature since May 4, 1919—its great contributions to the revolution in the last twenty-three years and its many shortcomings; the anti-Japanese democratic base areas of the Eighth Route and New Fourth Armies, and the alignment there of large numbers of artists and writers with the two armies and with the workers and peasants; the difference in circumstances and tasks between the artists and writers in our base areas and those in the Kuomintang-controlled areas; and the controversies which have arisen over art and literature in Yenan and other anti-Japanese base areas. These are the undeniable actualities and we have to examine our problems in the light of them.

What then is the crux of our problems? I think our problems are basically those of working for the masses and of how to work for them. If these two problems are not solved, or solved inadequately, our artists and writers will be ill-adapted to their circumstances and unfit for their tasks, and will come up against a series of problems from within and without. My conclusion will centre round these two problems, while touching upon some other problems related to them.

I

The first problem is: For whom are our art and literature intended?

This problem has, as a matter of fact, been solved long ago by Marxists, and especially by Lenin. As far back as 1905 Lenin emphatically pointed out that our art and literature should "serve the millions upon millions of working people".[1]

It might seem that this problem has been solved by our comrades working in art and literature in the anti-Japanese base areas and needs no further discussion. But actually this is not the case. Many comrades have by no means arrived at a clear-cut solution of this problem. Consequently their sentiments, their works, their actions and their ideas concerning the guiding principles of art and literature have been more or less at variance with the needs of the masses and the demands of actual struggles. Among the large number of men of culture, of artists, writers and workers in art and literature in general who, together with the Communist Party and the Eighth Route and New Fourth Armies, have participated in the great struggle for liberation, there may of course be some opportunists who will stay only a while, but the greatest majority are energetically working for the common cause. Thanks to the efforts of these comrades, the achievements in our literature, theatre, music and fine arts have been considerable. Many of these artists and writers have begun their work since the Anti-Japanese War, while others took up revolutionary work even long before the war, undergoing numerous hardships and influencing the broad masses of the people by their actions and their works. Why, then, should I say that even some of these comrades have not clearly solved the problem—for whom are art and literature intended? Is it possible that some of them still maintain that revolutionary art and literature are intended not for the broad masses of the people but for the exploiters and oppressors?

Quite true, there exist art and literature intended for the

exploiters and oppressors. The art and literature for the landlord class are feudal art and literature. Such are the art and literature of the ruling classes of China's feudal epoch. Even today such art and literature still retain a considerable influence in China. The art and literature for the bourgeoisie are bourgeois art and literature. People like Liang Shih-ch'iu,[2] whom Lu Hsun severely criticised, may talk about art and literature as transcending the classes, but in fact they all uphold bourgeois art and literature and oppose proletarian art and literature. The art and literature for imperialism, as represented by Chou Tso-jen, Chang Tzu-p'ing[3] and their like, is called collaborationist art and literature. So far as we are concerned, art and literature are not intended for any of the above-mentioned persons, but for the people. We have said that China's new culture at the present stage is an anti-feudal, anti-imperialist culture of the broad masses of the people under the leadership of the proletariat. Everything that truly belongs to the broad masses of the people must now of necessity be under the leadership of the proletariat. (Nothing under the leadership of the bourgeoisie can possibly belong to the broad masses of the people.) Naturally the same applies to the new art and literature in the new culture. We should take over the rich legacy and succeed to the fine tradition of Chinese and foreign art and literature of the past, but we must do this with our eyes upon the broad masses of the people. We do not refuse to make use of the artistic and literary forms of the past, but in our hands these old forms, remoulded and filled with new content, also become things which are revolutionary and serve the people.

Who, then, are the broad masses of the people? The broadest masses of the people who constitute more than 90 per cent of the total population are the workers, peasants, soldiers and the urban petty bourgeoisie. So our art and literature are first of all for the workers who form the class which leads the revolution. Secondly, they are for the peasants who form the most numerous and steadfast allies in the revolution. Thirdly, they are for the armed workers and peasants, i.e. the Eighth Route and New Fourth Armies and other people's armed forces, which are the main forces of the revolutionary war. Fourthly, they are for the working masses of the urban petty bourgeoisie together with its intelligentsia, who are also allies in the revolution and are capable of lasting co-operation with us. These four kinds of people form the overwhelming majority of the Chinese nation and consequently are the broadest masses of the people.

Our art and literature should be intended for the four kinds of people mentioned above. To serve these four kinds of people we must take the stand of the proletariat instead of that of the petty bourgeoisie. It is impossible today for writers who persist in their individualist petty-bourgeois stand to serve faithfully the masses of revolutionary workers, peasants and soldiers, because they are interested mainly in the small number of intellectuals of the petty bourgeoisie. Here is precisely the reason why some of our comrades are unable to solve correctly the problem of for whom are our art and literature intended. I am not referring to their theory. In theory or in words, none in our ranks would consider the masses of workers, peasants and soldiers less important than the petty-bourgeois intellectuals. I am speaking of their deeds and actions. In deed and action, do they regard the petty-bourgeois intellectuals as more important than the workers, peasants and soldiers? I think they do. Many comrades are concerned with studying the petty-bourgeois intellectuals, analysing their psychology, giving emphatic expression to their life and excusing or defending their shortcomings, rather than with leading these people, together with themselves, to get closer to the masses of workers, peasants and soldiers, to participate in their actual struggles or to give expression to their life and educate them. Many comrades, because they are petty bourgeois in origin and intellectuals themselves, seek friends only in the ranks of the intellectuals and concentrate their attention on studying and describing them. This would be quite proper if they made such a study and description from a proletarian standpoint. But they do not do so, or do not fully do so. They take the stand of the petty bourgeoisie and produce their works as a kind of self-expression of the petty bourgeoisie, as can be seen in quite a number of our artistic and literary works. Quite often they express heart-felt sympathy for the intellectuals of petty-bourgeois origin, they sympathise with or even praise their shortcomings. As to the masses of workers, peasants and soldiers, they seldom come into contact with them, do not understand or study them, do not have bosom friends among them and are not adept at describing them and, when they do describe them, the result is merely petty-bourgeois intellectuals in the clothing of working people. In certain respects they also love the workers, peasants and soldiers and the cadres springing from them; but there are times when they do not love them, and there are some respects in which they do not love them— they do not appreciate their emotions, their manners, their budding art and literature (such as wall newspapers, murals, folk songs, folk tales, etc.). To be sure, sometimes they like these things too, but this is because of their novelty for the sake of embellishing their own works, or even for the backward qualities embodied in them. At other times they openly despise these things and prefer what belongs to the petty-bourgeois intellectuals or even the bourgeoisie. These comrades still stand on the side of the petty-bourgeois intellectuals, or, to put it more elegantly, their innermost soul is still a kingdom of the petty-bourgeois intelligentsia. Thus they have not yet solved or unequivocally solved the problem, "For whom are art and literature intended?" And this refers not only to the new-comers to Yenan; even among those who have been to the front and worked for a few years in our base areas and in the Eighth Route and New Fourth Armies, many have not solved this problem thoroughly. To solve this problem thoroughly, a long time is required, say, eight or ten years. But no matter how long it takes, we must solve it, and solve it unequivocally and thoroughly. Our artists and writers must accomplish this task and shift their stand—gradually shift it over to the side of the masses of workers, peasants and soldiers, to the side of the proletariat, in the course of going into their midst and into the heart of the actual struggle and in the course of studying Marxism and society. Only thus can we have art and literature that are truly for the workers, peasants and soldiers, and that are truly proletarian.

The problem of "for whom" is a fundamental one, one of principle. Hitherto the disputes, divergences, antagonism and discord among some of our comrades have not arisen on this fundamental issue of principle but on secondary issues or even issues devoid of principle. On this question of principle the contending sides have shown little divergence but have in almost perfect agreement tended to some extent to look down on the workers, peasants and soldiers and isolate themselves from the masses. I say "to some extent" because, generally speaking, these comrades differ from the Kuomintang in its disdain of the workers, peasants and soldiers and its isolation from the masses; but all the same the tendency is there. Unless this fundamental problem is solved, it will be difficult to solve many others. Take, for example, the sectarianism in artistic and literary circles which also involves a question of principle. It can be eradicated only by putting forward such slogans as "Serve the workers and peasants!" "Serve the Eighth Route and New Fourth Armies!" and "Go into the midst of the masses!" and by thoroughly carrying them out; otherwise the problem of sectarianism can never be solved. Lu Hsun once said:

> "The necessary conditions for the united front is a common aim. . . . The discord in our front shows that we are not agreed on the aim, some working only for small groups and others working in fact for themselves. If we all place our aim in the broad masses of workers and peasants, our front will of course be united."[4]

The same problem cropped up in Shanghai in Lu Hsun's time just as it now crops up in Chungking. In such places it is hard to solve the problem thoroughly, because the rulers there oppress the revolutionary artists and writers and deprive them of the freedom to go into the midst of the masses of workers, peasants and soldiers. But here among us the situation is entirely different. Here we encourage revolutionary artists and writers to get actively into contact with the workers, peasants and soldiers, and give them full freedom to go into their midst to create genuinely revolutionary art and literature. The problem with us here is therefore nearing solution. Yet to be nearing the solution is not the same as to arrive at a complete and thorough solution, and it is precisely for this complete and thorough solution that we must, as we have said above, study Marxism and society. By Marxism we mean the living Marxism that can have practical bearing on the life and struggle of the masses, and not Marxism in words. When

Marxism in words is transformed into Marxism in practical life, there will be no more sectarianism. And not only will the problem of sectarianism be solved but many other problems as well.

II

The question of "whom to serve" having been solved, the question of "how to serve" comes up. To put it in the words of our comrades: Should we devote ourselves to elevation or to popularisation?

In the past some comrades rather or even very much despised and neglected popularisation and unduly stressed elevation. Elevation should be stressed, but it is wrong to stress it lopsidedly and solely and excessively. The afore-mentioned lack of clarity and thoroughness in the solution of the problem of "for whom", also manifests itself in this connection. As they are not clear about the question, naturally they fail to find any proper criterion for what they mean by "elevation" and "popularisation", let alone the proper relation between the two. Since our art and literature are basically intended for the workers, peasants and soldiers, popularisation means extending art and literature among these people while elevation means raising their level of artistic and literary appreciation. What should we popularise among them? The stuff that is needed and can be readily accepted by the feudal landlord class? Or that which is needed and can be readily accepted by the bourgeoisie? Or that which is needed and can be readily accepted by the petty-bourgeois intelligentsia? No, none of these will do. We must popularise what is needed and can be readily accepted by the workers, peasants and soldiers themselves. Consequently the duty of learning from the workers, peasants and soldiers precedes the task of educating them. This is even more true of elevation. There must be a basis to elevate from. When we lift up a bucket of water, for instance, aren't we lifting up something that lies on the ground and does not float in mid-air? What then is the basis from which the standard of our art and literature is to be raised? From the feudal basis? The bourgeois basis? The basis of the petty-bourgeois intelligentsia? No. It can only be raised from the basis of the masses of the workers, peasants and soldiers. This means not that we raise the workers, peasants and soldiers to the level of the feudal class, the bourgeoisie or the petty-bourgeois intelligentsia, but that we raise them up along their own line of advance, along the line of advance of the pro-letariat. Here again the task of learning from the workers, peasants and soldiers comes in. Only by starting from the workers, peasants and soldiers can we have a correct under-standing of elevation and popularisation and find the proper relation between the two.

What after all is the source of any kind of art and literature? An artistic or literary work is ideologically the product of the human brain reflecting the life of a given society. Revolutionary art and literature are the products of the brains of revolution-ary artists and writers reflecting the life of the people. In the life of the people itself lies a mine of raw material for art and literature, namely, things in their natural state, things crude, but also most lively, rich and fundamental; in this sense, they throw all art and literature into the shade and provide for them a unique and inexhaustible source. This is the only source, for there can be no other source. Some may ask: Is there not another source in the books, in the artistic and literary works of ancient times and foreign countries? As a matter of fact, artistic and literary works of the past are not the source but the flow; they are the products which the ancients and the foreign-ers created out of the artistic and literary raw material they lit upon in the people's life of their own times and places. We must take over all the fine artistic and literary legacy, critically assimilate from it whatever is beneficial to us and hold it up as an example when we try to work over the artistic and literary raw material derived from the people's life of our own time and place. It makes an enormous difference whether or not one has such examples to look up to, a difference which explains why some works are refined and others crude, some polished and others coarse, some superior and others inferior, some smoothly done and others laboriously executed. There-fore we must not refuse to take over the legacy from the ancients and the foreigners and learn from such examples, whether feudal or bourgeois. But succession to a legacy and learning from examples should never take the place of the creation of our own work, for nothing can take its place. In art and literature, the uncritical appropriation and imitation of the ancients and foreigners represent the most sterile and harmful artistic and literary doctrinairism. All revolutionary artists and writers of China, all artists and writers of high promise, must, for long periods of time, unreservedly and whole-heartedly go into the midst of the masses, the masses of workers, peasants and soldiers; they must go into fiery struggles, go to the only, the broadest, the richest source to observe, learn, study and analyse all men, all classes, all kinds of people, all the vivid patterns of life and struggle and all raw material of art and literature, before they can proceed to creation. Otherwise, for all your labour, you will have nothing to work on and will become the kind of "empty-headed artists or writers" against whom Lu Hsun, in his testament, so earnestly cautioned his son.[5]

Though man's social life constitutes the only source for art and literature, and is incomparably more vivid and richer than art and literature as such, the people are not satisfied with the former alone and demand the latter. Why? Because, although both are beautiful, life as reflected in artistic and literary works can and ought to be on a higher level and of a greater power and better focused, more typical, nearer the ideal, and therefore more universal than actual everyday life. Revolutionary art and literature should create all kinds of characters on the basis of actual life and help the masses to push history forward. For example, on the one hand there are people suffering from hunger, cold and oppression and on the other hand there are men exploiting and oppressing men—a contrast that exists everywhere and seems quite commonplace to people; artists and writers, however, can create art and literature out of such daily occurrences by organising them, bringing them to a focal point and making the contradictions and struggles in them typical—create art and literature that can awaken and arouse the masses and impel them to unite and struggle to change their environment. If there were no such art and literature, this task could not be fulfilled or at least not effectively and speedily fulfilled.

What are popularisation and elevation in art and literature? What is the relation between the two? Works of popularisation are simpler and plainer and therefore more readily accepted by the broad masses of the people of today. Works of a higher level are more polished and therefore more difficult to produce and less likely to win the ready acceptance of the broad masses of people of today. The problem facing the workers, peasants and soldiers today is this: engaged in a ruthless and sanguinary struggle against the enemy, they remain illiterate and uncultured as a result of the prolonged rule of the feudal and bourgeois classes and consequently they badly need a widespread campaign of enlightenment, and they eagerly wish to have culture, knowledge, art and literature which meet their immediate need and are readily acceptable to them so as to heighten their passion for struggle and their confidence in victory, to strengthen their solidarity, and thus to enable them to fight the enemy with one heart and one mind. In meeting their primary need, we are not to "add flowers to a piece of brocade" but "offer fuel to a person in snowy weather". Under the present conditions, therefore, popularisation is the more pressing task. It is wrong to despise and neglect this task.

But popularisation and elevation cannot be sharply separated. Not only is it possible to popularise even now a number of works to a higher level, but the cultural level of the broad masses is also steadily rising. If popularisation remains always on the same level—for one, two or three months, for one, two or three years, dealing out always the same stuff like "Little Cowherd",[6] or the characters of "man, hand, mouth, knife, cow, goat",[7] then will not the educator and the educated remain much of a muchness? What is such popularisation good for? The people need popularisation, but along with it they need elevation too, elevation month by month and year by year. Popularisation is popularisation for the people, and elevation is elevation of the people. Such elevation does not take place in mid-air, nor behind closed doors, but on the basis of popularisation. It is at once determined by popularisation and gives direction to it. In China, the revolution and revolutionary culture are uneven in their development and they broaden out only gradually; thus in one place the work of popularisation may have been carried out, and also elevation on the basis of popularisation, while in other places the work of popularisation may not yet have begun. Therefore the helpful experiences of elevation on the basis of popularisation in one place may be applied in another, so as to serve as guidance to the work of popularisation and elevation there and save a good deal of labour. Internationally, the helpful experiences of foreign countries, especially the experiences of the Soviet Union, can serve as our guide. Thus our elevation is on the basis of popularisation while our popularisation is under the guidance of elevation. This being the case, the work of popularisation in our sense not only constitutes no obstacle to elevation but affords a basis for our work of elevation on a limited scale at present, as well as preparing the necessary conditions for our far more extensive work of elevation in the future.

Besides the elevation that directly meets the need of the masses there is the elevation that meets their need indirectly, namely, the elevation needed by the cadres. Being advanced members of the masses, the cadres are generally better educated than the masses, and art and literature of a higher level are entirely necessary to them; and it would be a mistake to ignore this. Anything done for the cadres is also entirely done for the masses, because it is only through the cadres that we can give education and guidance to the masses. If we depart from this objective, if what we give to the cadres cannot help them to educate and guide the masses, then our work of elevation will be like aimless shooting, *i.e.* deviating from our fundamental principle of serving the broad masses of the people.

To sum up: through the creative labour of revolutionary artists and writers the raw material of art and literature in the life of the people becomes art and literature in an ideological form in service of the masses of the people. Hence there are, on the one hand, the more advanced art and literature which are developed upon the basis of elementary art and literature and needed by the elevated section of the masses, or primarily by the cadres; and on the other hand, elementary art and literature which are produced under the guidance of the more advanced art and literature and often meet the urgent need of the broadest masses of today. Whether advanced or elementary, our art and literature are intended for the masses of the people, primarily for the workers, peasants and soldiers, created for them and to be used by them.

Since we have solved the problem of the relation between popularisation and elevation, the problem of the relation between experts and popularisers can also be settled. Our experts should serve not only the cadres but chiefly the masses. Our experts in literature should pay attention to the wall newspapers of the masses and the reportage literature in the army and the villages. Our experts in drama should pay attention to the small troupes in the army and the villages. Our experts in music should pay attention to the songs of the masses. Our experts in the fine arts should pay attention to the fine arts of the masses. All these comrades should keep in close touch with the popularisers of art and literature among the masses, help and guide the popularisers as well as learn from them, and through them draw nourishment from the masses to develop and enrich themselves and to prevent their specialities from becoming empty, lifeless castles in the air detached from the masses and from reality. Experts should be respected; they are very valuable to our cause. But we should also remind them that no revolutionary artist or writer can produce any work of significance unless he has contact with the masses, gives expression to their thoughts and feelings, and becomes their loyal spokesman. Only by speaking for the masses can he educate them and only by becoming their pupil can he become their teacher. If he regards himself as the master of the masses or as an aristocrat who lords it over the "low people", then no matter how great his talent, he will not be needed by the people and his work will have no future.

Is this attitude of ours one of utilitarianism? Materialists are not opposed to utilitarianism in general, but to the utilitarianism of the feudal, bourgeois and petty-bourgeois classes, to those hypocrites who attack utilitarianism in words but embrace the most selfish and shortsighted utilitarianism in deeds. There is no transcendental utilitarianism in this world, and in a class society utilitarianism is either of this or of that particular class. Being proletarian, revolutionary utilitarians, we take as our point of departure the uniting of the present and future interests of the broadest masses who constitute over 90 per cent of the population; therefore we are revolutionary utilitarians who envisage the interests of the broadest scope and the longest range, not narrow utilitarians who look after only what is partial and immediate. If, for instance, you reproach the masses for their utilitarianism, and yet for the benefit of an individual or a clique you insist upon placing on the market and advertising among the masses a certain work which wins the favour of only a few but proves useless or even harmful to most people, then you are not only insulting the masses but revealing your own lack of self-knowledge. A thing is good only when it brings real benefit to the masses of the people. Granted that your work is as good as "The Spring Snow"; but for the time being it caters only for a few, and the masses are still enjoying the "Pa Emigrants in the Poor Quarters";[8] if you simply denounce the masses instead of elevating them, you will get nowhere for all your denunciations. The problem now is how to unite "The Spring Snow" with the "Pa Emigrants in the Poor Quarters", to unite elevation with popularisation. If the two are not united, then any artistic work of the highest quality produced by an expert will only have the smallest use and, if one calls that "lofty and pure", one is simply flattering oneself and the masses will not endorse one's opinion.

Having solved the problem concerning the fundamental principle of serving the workers, peasants and soldiers and of the way to serve them, we have also solved such problems as whether to depict the bright or the dark side of life and how to achieve unity among our artists and writers. If this is the fundamental principle we all agree upon, then it must be adhered to by our artists and writers, our schools of art and literature, our artistic and literary publications and organisations, and all our artistic and literary activities. It is wrong to deviate from this principle, and anything at variance with it must be duly corrected.

III

Since our art and literature are intended for the broad masses of the people, we can proceed to discuss a problem of inner-Party relations, *i.e.* the relation between the Party's artistic and literary activity and the Party's activity as a whole, and a problem of the Party's external relations, *i.e.* the relation between Party artistic and literary activity and non-Party artistic and literary activity—the problem of the united front in art and literature.

Let us take up the first problem. In the world today all culture, all art and literature belong to definite classes and follow definite political lines. There is in reality no such thing as art for art's sake, art which stands above classes or art which runs parallel to or remains independent of politics. Proletarian art and literature are part of the entire cause of the proletarian revolution, in the words of Lenin, "cogs and screws in the whole machine".[9] Therefore the Party's artistic and literary activity occupies a definite and assigned position in the Party's total revolutionary work and is subordinated to the prescribed revolutionary task of the Party in a given revolutionary period. Any opposition to this assignment will certainly lead to dualism or pluralism, and in essence amounts to Trotsky's formula: "politics—Marxist; art—bourgeois". We are not in favour of erroneously over-emphasising the importance of art and literature, but neither are we in favour of underestimating it. Art and literature are subordinate to politics, but they in turn also exert a great influence on politics. Revolutionary art and literature are part of the entire cause of the revolution, they are its cogs and screws; though in comparison with certain other parts they may be less important and less urgent and occupy only a secondary position, yet they are, as cogs and screws, indispensable to the whole machine, and form an indispensable part of the entire cause of the revolution. If we had no art and literature even in the broadest and most general sense, then the revolutionary movement could not be carried on to victory. It would be wrong not to realise this. Furthermore, in saying that art and literature are subordinate to politics, we mean here class politics and mass politics, not the politics of a few so-called statesmen. Politics, whether revolutionary or counter-revolutionary, represents the struggle of one class against another, not the activity of a few individuals. Revolutionary struggles on the ideological and artistic fronts must be subordinate to the political struggle because only through politics can the needs of the class and the masses be expressed in concentrated form. The revolutionary statesmen or political experts who have mastered the science or art of revolutionary politics are merely leaders of millions of statesmen, namely, the masses, with the task of collecting the ideas of these mass-statesmen, submitting these ideas to a refining process and then passing the refined products back to the masses for them to accept and put into practice; they are therefore not the kind of aristocratic "statesmen" who draw up plans all by themselves with the conceit that they have a monopoly of wisdom—herein lies the difference in principle between the statesmen of the proletariat and those of the decadent bourgeoisie. It is precisely for this reason that the political character of our art and literature becomes entirely at one with its truthfulness. It would be wrong to fail to recognise this point and vulgarise the politics and statesmanship of the proletariat.

Let us take up next the question of the united front in art and literature. Since art and literature are subordinate to politics and since China's first and foremost political problem today is resistance to Japan, Party artists and writers must first of all unite on this issue with all non-Party artists and writers (from Party sympathisers, petty-bourgeois artists and writers to all bourgeois and landlord-class artists and writers who are in favour of resisting Japan). We should also unite with them on the issue of democracy; on this issue, however, not all the anti-Japanese artists and writers agree, so the range of unity will be more limited. Then again, we must unite with them on the special issue in artistic and literary circles— that of method and style in art and literature, but as we are for socialist realism and a section of artists and writers is against it, the range of unity may be further limited. Unity can be achieved on one issue while struggle and criticism take place on another. All the issues are at once separate and connected; thus on the issues which call for unity, such as resistance to Japan, there are at the same time struggle and criticism. In a united front, all unity and no struggle on the one hand, and all struggle and no unity on the other—to put into practice, as some of our comrades did in the past, Right capitulationism, tailism, or "Left" exclusivism and sectarianism—are both wrong policies. This applies to politics as well as to art.

Petty-bourgeois artists and writers in China constitute an important force in the united front of art and literature. Although there are many shortcomings in their ideology and in their works, they are comparatively inclined towards the revolution and comparatively close to the working people.

Therefore it is an especially important task to help them to overcome their shortcomings and win them over to the front of serving the working people.

IV

One of the principal methods of struggle in the artistic and literary sphere is art and literary criticism. It should be developed and, as many comrades have rightly pointed out, our work in this respect was quite inadequate in the past. Art and literary criticism presents a complex problem which requires much study of a special kind. Here I shall stress only the basic problem of criteria in criticism. I shall also comment briefly on certain other problems and incorrect views brought up by some comrades.

There are two criteria in art and literary criticism: political and artistic. According to the political criterion, all works are good that facilitate unity and resistance to Japan, that encourage the masses to be of one heart and one mind and that oppose retrogression and promote progress; on the other hand, all works are bad that undermine unity and resistance to Japan, that sow dissension and discord among the masses and that oppose progress and drag the people back. And how can we tell the good from the bad here—by the motive (subjective intention) or by the effect (social practice)? Idealists stress motive and ignore effect, while mechanical materialists stress effect and ignore motive; in contradistinction from either, we dialectical materialists insist on the unity of motive and effect. The motive of serving the masses is inseparable from the effect of winning their approval, and we must unite the two. The motive of serving the individual or a small clique is not good, nor is the motive of serving the masses good if it does not lead to a result that is welcomed by the masses and confers benefit on them. In examining the subjective intention of an artist, *i.e.* whether his motive is correct and good, we do not look at his declaration but at the effect his activities (mainly his works) produce on society and the masses. Social practice and its effect are the criteria for examining the subjective intention or the motive. We reject sectarianism in our art and literary criticism and, under the general principle of unity and resistance to Japan, we must tolerate all artistic and literary works expressing every kind of political attitude. But at the same time we must firmly uphold our principles in our criticism, and adhere to our standpoint and severely criticise and repudiate all artistic and literary works containing views against the nation, the sciences, the people and communism, because such works, in motive as well as in effect, are detrimental to unity and the resistance to Japan. According to the artistic criterion, all works are good or comparatively good that are relatively high in artistic quality; and bad or comparatively bad that are relatively low in artistic quality. Of course, this distinction also depends on social effect. As there is hardly an artist who does not consider his own work excellent, our criticism ought to permit the free competition of all varieties of artistic works; but it is entirely necessary for us to pass correct judgments on them according to the criteria of the science of art, so that we can gradually raise the art of a lower level to a higher level, and to change the art which does not meet the requirements of the struggle of the broad masses into art that does meet them.

There is thus the political criterion as well as the artistic criterion. How are the two related? Politics is not the equivalent of art, nor is a general world outlook equivalent to the method of artistic creation and criticism. We believe there is neither an abstract and absolutely unchangeable political criterion, nor an abstract and absolutely unchangeable artistic criterion, for every class in a class society has its own political and artistic criteria. But all classes in all class societies place the political criterion first and the artistic criterion second. The bourgeoisie always rejects proletarian artistic and literary works, no matter how great their artistic achievement. As for the proletariat, they must treat the art and literature of the past according to their attitude towards the people and whether they are progressive in the light of history. Some things which are basically reactionary from the political point of view may yet be artistically good. But the more artistic such a work may be, the greater harm will it do to the people, and the more reason for us to reject it. The contradiction between reactionary political content and artistic form is a common characteristic of the art and literature of all exploiting classes in their decline.

What we demand is unity of politics and art, of content and form, and of the revolutionary political content and the highest possible degree of perfection in artistic form. Works of art, however politically progressive, are powerless if they lack artistic quality. Therefore we are equally opposed to works with wrong political approaches and to the tendency towards so-called "poster and slogan style" which is correct only in political approach but lacks artistic power. We must carry on a two-front struggle in art and literature.

Both tendencies can be found in the ideologies of many of our comrades. Those comrades who tend to neglect artistic quality should pay attention to its improvement. But as I see it, the political side is more of a problem at present. Some comrades lack elementary political knowledge and consequently all kinds of muddled ideas arise. Let me give a few instances found in Yenan.

"The theory of human nature." Is there such a thing as human nature? Of course there is. But there is only human nature in the concrete, no human nature in the abstract. In a class society there is only human nature that bears the stamp of a class, but no human nature transcending classes. We uphold the human nature of the proletariat and of the great masses of the people, while the landlord and bourgeois classes uphold the nature of their own classes as if—though they do not say so outright—it were the only kind of human nature. The human nature boosted by certain petty-bourgeois intellectuals is also divorced from or opposed to that of the great masses of the people; what they call human nature is in substance nothing but bourgeois individualism, and consequently in their eyes proletarian human nature is contrary to their human nature. This is the "theory of human nature" advocated by some people in Yenan as the so-called basis of their theory of art and literature, which is utterly mistaken.

"The fundamental point of departure for art and literature is love, the love of mankind." Now love may serve as a point of departure, but there is still a more basic one. Love is a concept, a product of objective practice. Fundamentally, we do not start from a concept but from objective practice. Our artists and writers who come from the intelligentsia love the proletariat because social life has made them feel that they share the same fate with the proletariat. We hate Japanese imperialism because the Japanese imperialists oppress us. There is no love or hatred in the world that has not its cause. As to the so-called "love of mankind", there has been no such all-embracing love since humanity was divided into classes. All the ruling classes in the past liked to advocate it, and many so-called sages and wise men also did the same, but nobody has ever really practised it, for it is impracticable in a class society. Genuine love of mankind will be born only when class distinctions have been eliminated throughout the world. The classes have caused the division of society into many opposites and as soon as they are eliminated there will be love of all mankind, but not now. We cannot love our enemies, we cannot love social evils, and our aim is to exterminate them. How can our artists and writers fail to understand such a common sense matter?

"Art and literature have always described the bright as well as the dark side of things impartially, on a fifty-fifty basis." This statement contains a number of muddled ideas. Art and literature have not always done so. Many petty-bourgeois writers have never found the bright side and their works are devoted to exposing the dark side, the so-called "literature of exposure"; there are even works which specialise in propagating pessimism and misanthropy. On the other hand, Soviet literature during the period of socialist reconstruction portrays mainly the bright side. It also describes shortcomings in work and villainous characters, but such descriptions serve only to bring out the brightness of the whole picture, and not on a "compensating basis". Bourgeois writers of reactionary periods portray the revolutionary masses as ruffians and describe the bourgeois as saints, thus reversing the so-called bright and dark sides. Only truly revolutionary artists and writers can correctly solve the problem whether to praise or to expose. All dark forces which endanger the masses of the people must be exposed while all revolutionary struggles of the masses must be praised—this is the basic task of all revolutionary artists and writers.

"The task of art and literature has always been to expose." This sort of argument, like the one mentioned above, arises from the lack of knowledge of the science of history. We have already shown that the task of art and literature does not consist solely in exposure. For the revolutionary artists and writers the objects to be exposed can never be the masses of the people, but only the aggressors, exploiters and oppressors and their evil aftermath brought to the people. The people have their shortcomings too, but these are to be overcome by means of criticism and self-criticism within the ranks of the people themselves, and to carry on such criticism and self-criticism is also one of the most important tasks of art and literature. However, we should not call that "exposing the people". As for the people, our problem is basically one of how to educate them and raise their level. Only counter-revolutionary artists and writers describe the people as "born fools" and the revolutionary masses as "tyrannical mobs".

"This is still a period of the essay, and the style should still be that of Lu Hsun." Living under the rule of the dark forces, deprived of freedom of speech, Lu Hsun had to fight by means of burning satire and freezing irony cast in essay form, and in this he was entirely correct. We too must hold up to sharp ridicule the fascists, the Chinese reactionaries and everything endangering the people; but in our border region of Shensi-Kansu-Ningsia and the anti-Japanese base areas in the enemy's rear, where revolutionary artists and writers are given full freedom and democracy and only counter-revolutionaries are deprived of them, essays must not be written simply in the same style as Lu Hsun's. Here we can shout at the top of our voice, and need not resort to obscure and veiled expressions which would tax the understanding of the broad masses of the people. In dealing with the people themselves and not the enemies of the people, Lu Hsun even in his "essay period" did not mock or attack the revolutionary masses and the revolutionary parties, and his style was also entirely different from that employed in his essays on the enemy. We have already said that we must criticise the shortcomings of the people, but be sure that we criticise from the standpoint of the people and out of a whole-hearted eagerness to defend and educate them. If we treat our comrades like enemies, then we are taking the standpoint of the enemy. Are we then to give up satire altogether? No. Satire is always necessary. But there are all kinds of satire; the kind for our enemies, the kind for our allies and the kind for our own ranks—each of them assumes a different attitude. We are not opposed to satire as a whole, but we must not abuse it.

"I am not given to praise and eulogy; works which extol the bright side of things are not necessarily great, nor are works which depict the dark side necessarily poor." If you are a bourgeois artist or writer, you will extol not the proletariat but the bourgeoisie, and if you are a proletarian artist or writer, you will extol not the bourgeoisie but the proletariat and the working people: you must do one or the other. Those works which extol the bright side of the bourgeoisie are not necessarily great while those which depict its dark side are not necessarily poor, and those works which extol the bright side of the proletariat are not necessarily poor, while those works which depict the so-called "dark side" of the proletariat are certainly poor—are these not facts recorded in the history of art and literature? Why should we not extol the people, the creator of the history of the human world? Why should we not extol the proletariat, the Communist Party, the New Democracy and socialism? Of course, there are persons who have no enthusiasm for the people's cause and stand aloof, looking with cold indifference on the struggle and the victory of the proletariat and its vanguard; and they only take pleasure in singing endless praises of themselves, plus perhaps a few persons in their own coterie. Such petty-bourgeois individualists are naturally unwilling to praise the meritorious deeds of the revolutionary masses or to heighten their courage in struggle and confidence in victory. Such people are the black sheep in the revolutionary ranks and the revolutionary masses have indeed no use for such "singers".

"It is not a matter of standpoint; the standpoint is correct, the intention good, and the ideas are all right, but the expression is faulty and produces a bad effect." I have already spoken about the dialectical materialist view of motive and effect, and now I want to ask: Is the question of effect not one of standpoint? A person who, in doing a job, minds only the motive and pays no regard to the effect, is very much like a doctor who hands out prescriptions and does not care how many patients may die of them. Suppose, again, a political party keeps on making pronouncements while paying not the least attention to carrying them out. We may well ask, is such a standpoint correct? Are such intentions good? Of course, a person is liable to mistakes in estimating the result of an action before it is taken; but are his intentions really good if he adheres to the same old rut even when facts prove that it leads to bad results? In judging a party or a doctor, we must look at the practice and the effect, and the same applies in judging an artist or a writer. One who has a truly good intention must take the effect into consideration by summing up experiences and studying methods or, in the case of creative work, the means of expression. One who has a truly good intention must criticise with the utmost candour his own shortcomings and mistakes in work, and make up his mind to correct them. That is why the Communists have adopted the method of self-criticism. Only such a standpoint is the correct one. At the same time it is only through such a process of practice carried out conscientiously and responsibly that we can gradually understand what the correct point of view is and have a firm grasp of it. If we refuse to do this in practice, then we are really ignorant of the correct point of view, despite our conceited assertion to the contrary.

"To call on us to study Marxism may again lead us to take the repetition of dialectical materialist formulas for literary creation, and this will stifle our creative impulse." We study Marxism in order to apply the dialectical materialist and historical materialist viewpoint in our observation of the world, society and art and literature, and not in order to write philosophical discourses in our works of art and literature. Marxism embraces realism in artistic and literary creation but cannot replace it, just as it embraces atomics and electronics in physics but cannot replace them. Empty, cut-and-dried dogmas and formulas will certainly destroy our creative impulse; moreover, they first of all destroy Marxism. Dogmatic "Marxism" is not Marxist but anti-Marxist. But will Marxism not destroy any creative impulse? It will; it will certainly destroy the creative impulse that is feudal, bourgeois, petty-bourgeois, liberal, individualistic, nihilistic, art-for-art's-sake, aristocratic, decadent or pessimistic, and any creative impulse that is not of the people and of the proletariat. As far as the artists and writers of the proletariat are concerned, ought not these kinds of impulse to be done away with? I think they ought; they should be utterly destroyed, and while they are being destroyed, new things can be built up.

V

What does the existence of the above-mentioned problems in Yenan artistic and literary circles signify? It signifies the fact that in artistic and literary circles there still remain incorrect styles in work to a serious extent, that among our comrades there still remain such defects as idealism, doctrinairism, utopianism, empty talk, contempt of practice and aloofness from the masses, and that we need a thorough-going and serious campaign for their rectification.

Many of our comrades are still not very clear about the difference between the proletariat and the petty bourgeoisie. Many Party members have joined the Party only organisationally while ideologically they have not yet joined it entirely, or have not joined it at all. Those who have not ideologically joined the Party still carry about in their heads many filthy things of the exploiting classes and have not the slightest idea what proletarian ideology, or communism, or the Party is. They say to themselves: "Proletarian ideology! Isn't it just the usual stuff?" They have no idea that to acquire this stuff is by no means easy; some people, for instance, have never in their lives had the slightest trace of a Communist about them, and cannot but end up by leaving the Party. Therefore, though the greater part of our Party members and our ranks are clean and honest, we must nevertheless make a conscientious overhauling organisationally and ideologically, so that we can lead the revolution to greater development and earlier victory. But organisational overhauling presupposes ideological overhauling, and we have to combat non-proletarian ideology with proletarian ideology. In artistic and literary circles in Yenan an ideological struggle has already begun, which is entirely necessary. Those intellectuals who are of petty-bourgeois origin always, through various ways and means, including artistic and literary means, stubbornly try to express themselves, spread their own opinions, and demand that people remould the Party and the world in their image. In these

circumstances it is our duty to shout to them: Comrades! Your
stuff won't do! The proletariat cannot compromise with you;
to yield to you is to yield to the big bourgeoisie and the big
landlord class and to run the risk of destroying our Party and
our country. Then whom should we take as the model? We
can only remould the Party and the world in the image of the
vanguard of the proletariat. We hope our comrades in artistic
and literary circles will realise the seriousness of this great
controversy and actively join in this struggle, so that every
comrade will become sound and healthy and our entire ranks
truly united and consolidated ideologically and organisationally.

As a result of ideological confusions, many comrades have
failed to distinguish clearly between our revolutionary base
areas and Kuomintang-controlled areas and have consequently
made many mistakes. A number of comrades have come from
the garrets of Shanghai[10] and, in coming from the garrets to
the revolutionary base areas, they have passed not only from
one region to another but also from one historical epoch to
another. The former belong to semi-feudal, semi-colonial
society under the rule of the big landlords and big bourgeoisie,
while the latter are a revolutionary society of New Democracy
under the leadership of the proletariat. Arriving at our bases
means coming under a régime of the broad masses of the
people, a régime unprecedented in the thousands of years of
Chinese history. Here we find an entirely different set of people
around us and a different audience for our propaganda. The
past epoch is gone and gone for ever. We must therefore
unite unhesitatingly with the new masses. If among the new
masses you comrades find that, as I said before, you "failed to
know them well, and failed to understand them, and were like
heroes with no scope for displaying their heroism", then you
will meet with difficulties not only when you go to the villages
but right here in Yenan. Some comrades think that they would
rather go on writing for the readers in the "big rear",[11] as they
know the conditions there well and can thus produce works
"of national significance". This way of thinking is entirely
wrong. The "big rear" is also changing; the readers there
expect authors in the revolutionary base areas to tell them
about the new people and a new world, and not to bore them
with the same old stories. Therefore the more a work is intended

for the masses of the revolutionary bases, the more national significance will it have. A. Fadeyev's *The Nineteen*[12] only depicts a small guerrilla unit and does not cater for the tastes of the readers of the old world; yet it has produced a world-wide effect, at least, as all of you here know, a tremendous effect in China. China is going forward, not backward, and what leads her forward is the revolutionary base areas, not any backward, retrogressive region. This is the fundamental fact that comrades must first of all clearly recognise in the course of the campaign to rectify the style in work.

Since we must adapt ourselves to the new epoch of the masses, we must thoroughly solve the question of the relationship between the individual and the masses. Lu Hsun's couplet should be our motto: "With frowning brows I coldly defy the thousands pointing their accusing fingers at me; with bowed head I meekly submit as an ox for the child to ride on."[13] The "thousands" here refer to the enemy, and we will never succumb to him no matter how fierce he may be. The "child" here refers to the proletariat and the broad masses of the people. All Communists, revolutionaries, revolutionary artists and writers, should follow the example of Lu Hsun and be the "ox" for the proletariat and the broad masses of the people, bending their shoulders to the task unto death. The intellectuals must go through a process of getting acquainted with the masses before they can unite with them and work for them. Although this process can be and is bound to be fraught with suffering and conflict, once you have made up your mind you will be equal to the task.

What I have talked about today covers only some of the fundamental problems of the direction of our movement of art and literature, and many other specific problems await further study. I believe that you comrades are determined to go in this direction. I believe that, in the course of the campaign to rectify the style in work and in the long period of study and work in future, you will be able to remould yourselves and change the character of your work, to create many excellent works which will be well received by the broad masses of the people, and to push forward the movement of art and literature of our revolutionary base areas and of the whole country to a glorious new stage.   *May 23, 1942*

AN EXTREMELY IMPORTANT POLICY

This is an editorial written for the *Liberation Daily*, published in Yenan.

Ever since the Central Committee of the Party set forth the policy of "picked troops and simplified administration", Party organisations in many anti-Japanese base areas have been making plans and carrying out the task as directed by the Central Committee. In the Shansi-Hopeh-Shantung-Honan border region, the comrades in charge are giving this task their closest attention and have furnished an example of picked troops and simplified administration. Comrades in some base areas, however, have not made any serious effort to carry the policy out because they do not understand it sufficiently. They have not yet understood its relation to the current situation or to the other policies of the Party, and have not yet taken it as a policy of the utmost importance. The *Liberation Daily* has repeatedly discussed this matter, and now wishes to offer a further elucidation.

All policies of the Party aim at defeating the Japanese invaders. After five years of resistance we are now truly facing the final stage of our fight for victory. This stage differs not merely from the first and second years of the Resistance, but also from the third and fourth. For a feature in the fifth and sixth years of the Resistance is that while victory is drawing near, the greatest difficulties are still in the way, namely, the "darkness before dawn". This feature is found not only in our base areas of the Eighth Route and the New Fourth Armies but also in all anti-fascist countries at the present stage and in the whole of China, but it is particularly salient in our areas. We are striving to defeat the Japanese invaders in the coming two years. These will be the years of the greatest difficulties and will widely differ from both the first and the second two years of the Resistance. The leadership of a revolutionary party and army must foresee this. Should they fail to do so, they would only drift with time and, strive as they might, they could not attain victory, and might even jeopardise the cause of the revolution. Although the situation, as it stands today

94

in the anti-Japanese base areas in the enemy's rear, has become several times more difficult than it used to be, it has not yet become difficult to the last degree. If we do not have a correct policy, we shall face the greatest difficulties. People in general are liable to be misled by past and present conditions into believing that the future will not be much different. They have not the ability to foresee that the ship may strike a reef, nor have they a clear head to steer her off it. What is the reef lying ahead of the ship of Resistance? It is a material difficulty, extremely grave in the final stage of the war. The Central Committee has pointed this out, warning us off the reef. Many of our comrades have already understood this, but some have not; this is the first obstacle we must remove. There must be unity in carrying on our War of Resistance and the attainment of unity involves many difficulties. These difficulties are political, which we faced before and may face again in the future. For five years, our Party has been overcoming them gradually with great effort; under the slogan of strengthening our unity, we must keep on doing it. But there is another difficulty, a material one. This difficulty will become more serious with the passing of time. As at present some comrades still take it easy and are not quite aware of its increasing seriousness, we must call their attention to it. All comrades in the anti-Japanese base areas must recognise that from now on material difficulties will increase, yet we must overcome them, and that one of our important ways and means to do so is "picked troops and simplified administration".

Why is the policy of "picked troops and simplified administration" an important one for overcoming material difficulties? Obviously, the present and especially the future war situation in the base areas do not permit us to hold on to our past viewpoint. Our enormous war machine is adapted to the past conditions. Conditions in the past made it possible as well as necessary for us to have such an organisation. But things are different now; as the base areas have shrunk and will perhaps continue to shrink for some time to come, we certainly cannot maintain the enormous war machine we used to do. At present, a contradiction has already been developing between our war machine and the war situation, and we must solve this contradiction. The enemy's objective is to intensify this contradiction

—witness his policy of triple atrocity.[1] If we go on maintaining our enormous machine, we shall fall into the enemy's trap. But if we reduce our organisation by having our troops picked and our administration simplified, our war machine will remain very powerful in spite of its decreased dimensions and, once we have adapted our war machine to the war situation after solving the contradiction inherent in the case of a big fish floundering in shallow water, we shall prove ourselves even stronger and shall not be defeated by the enemy but shall finally defeat him. Therefore we say that the policy of "picked troops and simplified administration" set forth by the Central Committee is a policy of the utmost importance.

But man's mind is liable to be under the bondage of existing conditions and habits, a bondage from which even revolutionaries sometimes cannot escape. We created the enormous machine with our own hands, little thinking that one day we should have to reduce it with the same hands and, when that day has come, we feel reluctant and hard put to it. The enemy is pressing upon us with his enormous machine; how can we reduce ours? We feel that once reduced, our troops will be too few to deal with the enemy. Such misgivings are due to an inability to transcend existing conditions and habits. We must change our clothes with the changes of season. Each year at the juncture between spring and summer, or summer and autumn, or autumn and winter, or winter and spring, we ought to change our clothes. But owing to the force of habit, people often neglect to do this at the juncture of seasonal change, and they fall ill. The present conditions in the base areas already require us to peel off our winter garments and put on summer clothing so that we can be agile in our movement when we come to grips with the enemy, but we are still puffed out from head to foot with cotton padding, top-heavy, quite unfit for fighting. You ask: how then can we cope with the enemy's enormous war machine? There is the example of the monkey coping with the Princess of the Iron Fan. Though the Princess was a very formidable monster, the monkey, by changing himself into a tiny insect, found his way into her entrails and quelled her.[2] Liu Tsung-yuan's description of "the donkey's trick in Kweichow"[3] also contains a valuable lesson. A huge monster of a donkey went to Kweichow, where a small tiger was terrified at the sight of him. But in the end the small tiger ate up the huge donkey. Our Eighth Route and New Fourth Armies are the monkey and the small tiger and are fully capable of coping with that monster or donkey of Japan. At present we have to effect a certain change, changing our body into a smaller but sturdier one, and we shall then become invincible.

September 7, 1942

THE TURNING-POINT IN WORLD WAR II

This is an editorial written for the *Liberation Daily*, published in Yenan.

The British and American press has compared the Battle of Stalingrad to the Battle of Verdun, and the phrase "the Red Verdun" is now current all over the world. The comparison is by no means appropriate. The present Battle of Stalingrad differs in nature from the Battle of Verdun in the First World War. Nevertheless there is one point of similarity, namely, even at such a moment many people are beguiled by the German offensive into thinking that Germany can still win the war. The First World War ended in the winter of 1918, and in 1916 the German forces launched several attacks on the French fortress of Verdun. The commander directing the campaign was the Crown Prince of Germany, and the forces thrown into the battle were the crack troops of the German army. The battle was of decisive significance. As the Germans made ferocious assaults in vain, the entire German-Austrian-Turkish-Bulgarian camp found itself in a fix; faced with increasing difficulties and deserted by its followers from that time onward, the camp disintegrated, crumbled and finally collapsed. But the situation was not grasped at the time by those in the British-American-French camp, who thought the German army was still very strong and were quite unaware of their own approaching victory. In the history of mankind all reactionary forces on the verge of extinction invariably exert themselves to give a dying kick at the revolutionary forces, and some of the revolutionaries are apt to be deluded for a while by the enemy's apparent strength which conceals his real weakness, and fail to grasp the essential fact that the enemy is nearing extinction while they themselves are approaching victory. The whole course of the rise of the fascist forces and their war of aggression carried on for some years is precisely an example of such a dying kick, and in this war the dying kick is especially manifested in the attack on Stalingrad. At this turning-point in history there are many people in the world anti-fascist front who, misled by the ferocious appearance of fascism, fail to detect its actual strength. From August 23 when the whole German force crossed the bend of the Don river and launched an all-out attack on Stalingrad, and a part of it broke on September 15 into the industrial district in the north-western section of the city, to October 9 when the Information Bureau of the U.S.S.R. announced that the Red Army had broken through the German line of encirclement in that district—altogether for forty-eight days raged a battle of bitterness unprecedented in the history of mankind. This battle was won by the Soviet people at last. During those forty-eight days the hearts of millions and millions of people beat in response to the news of defeat or victory from that city, now weighed down by dejection, now stirred with joy. The battle marks not only the turning-point in the Soviet-German war, or in this anti-fascist world war, but also the turning-point in the whole history of mankind. In these forty-eight days the people of the world watched Stalingrad with even greater concern than they had watched Moscow in October last year.

Until his victory on the western front, Hitler seems to have been rather cautious. He attacked Poland, Norway, Holland, Belgium, France and the Balkans, but each time he concentrated his forces on a single objective and dared not divert his attention elsewhere. Then, being dizzy with success on the western front, he attempted to defeat the Soviet Union in three months. In launching an all-out attack on this colossal and powerful socialist country on a wide front stretching from Murmansk in the north to the Crimea in the south, his forces were dispersed. The failure of his Moscow campaign in October last year marked the conclusion of the first stage of the Soviet-German war, and Hitler's first strategic plan came to nothing. The Red Army halted the German offensive last year and launched an all-out counter-offensive in the winter, ushering in the second stage of the Soviet-German war, with Hitler turning to retreat and defence. In this period, after dismissing his field commander-in-chief Brauchitsch and taking over the command himself, Hitler abandoned plans for an all-out offensive and combed all Europe for available forces for a final offensive on the southern front, an offensive which, though limited in scope, was considered fatal to the Soviet Union.

Because this offensive was final in character, and upon it hung
the fate of fascism, Hitler massed the greatest possible forces
and even called in a part of his aircraft and tanks operating
in North Africa. With the German attack on Kerch and
Sevastopol in May this year, the war entered upon its third
stage. Mobilising an army of over 1,500,000, supported by
the bulk of his air and tank forces, Hitler launched an attack
of unprecedented violence on Stalingrad and the Caucasus.
He endeavoured to take these two objectives by storm for the
twofold purpose of cutting off the Volga and seizing Baku,
and he would then attack Moscow to the north and open a
passage to the Persian Gulf to the south, while ordering the
Japanese fascists to mass their troops in Manchuria for an
attack on Siberia after the fall of Stalingrad. He was obsessed
by the crazy idea of winning victory for the fascist front by so
reducing Soviet strength as to free the German main force from
the Soviet theatre and transfer it to the Western Front to meet
the Anglo-American offensive as well as to seize the resources
in the Near East, effect a German-Japanese junction, and at
the same time to relieve Japan of possible attacks on its rear
so that its main force could be disengaged from the north and
marched westward against China and southward against
Britain and the United States. But how did things turn out
at this stage? Hitler was outwitted by the Soviet tactics that
sealed his doom. The Soviet Union laid its plans so that when
the enemy advanced deep into its territory he met with a
stubborn resistance. After five months of battle the Germans
have neither penetrated into the Caucasian oil-fields nor
seized Stalingrad, and Hitler is compelled to halt his troops
before high mountains and under the walls of an impregnable
fortress, suffering heavy losses and landing himself in an
impasse, unable either to advance or retreat. It is now already
October and winter is coming; the third stage of the war will
soon come to an end and its fourth stage begin. There is not
one of Hitler's strategic attempts to attack the Soviet Union
that has not met with failure. In this period, Hitler, seeing that
his defeat last summer was due to the division of his forces, has
concentrated his forces on the southern front. Yet the forces still
have to be divided because he attempted to achieve the twofold
aim of cutting off the Volga in the east and seizing the Caucasus

in the south at a single stroke. He has not yet taken into consideration the discrepancy between his desire and his strength, with the result that, like "a carrier whose loads slip off both ends of his pole because there are no pegs on it", he has landed himself in the present impasse. On the other hand, the Soviet Union grows stronger and stronger with fighting. By brilliant strategic direction Stalin places himself entirely in the initiative and every one of his moves leads Hitler to ruin. The fourth stage of war beginning this winter will mark Hitler's approach to extinction.

Comparing Hitler's situation in the first stage of the war with that in the third stage, we can see that Hitler is on the threshold of final defeat. At present both in Stalingrad and in the Caucasus the Red Army has practically halted the German offensive; thus Hitler has failed in his attack on Stalingrad and on the Caucasus and is on the verge of exhaustion and collapse. Those forces which he had managed to mobilise in the winter, from last December to May this year, have already been used up. Now that another winter will descend on the Soviet-German front in less than a month, Hitler will have to turn hastily to the defensive. The whole area west and south of the Don river is his most vulnerable spot, because there the Red Army will turn to the counter-offensive. In this winter, Hitler, driven into desperation, will once more try to reinforce his army. To cope with the desperate situation on both the eastern and western fronts, he may manage to sweep together the tattered remnants of his forces and equip them and form them into a few new divisions and, in addition, extort some more cannon fodder from his fascist partners Italy, Rumania and Hungary. But while he must be prepared for enormous attrition in winter campaigns on the Eastern Front and for coping with the second front in the West, the Italians, the Rumanians and the Hungarians, feeling pessimistically that all is up with Hitler, will be daily drifting further away from him. In short, after October 9 only one road is open to Hitler: the road to extinction.

There is a point of similarity between the Red Army's defence of Stalingrad in the forty-eight days and its defence of Moscow last year. That is, Hitler's plan of this year has been foiled just as that of last year. What distinguishes the two,

however, is that although the Soviet people followed up their
defence of Moscow with a winter counter-offensive, they had
yet to face the summer offensive of the Germans this year,
partly because the Germans and their European accomplices
could still screw up courage for another offensive and partly
because the British and the Americans delayed the opening of
the second front. But after the battle of the defence of
Stalingrad the situation will be completely different. On the
one hand the Soviet Union will launch a second winter
counter-offensive on a vast scale, the British and the Americans
can no longer delay the opening of the second front (though
no one can tell definitely when it will be opened), and the
people in Europe will be ready to start uprisings in response.
On the other hand, as Germany and her European accomplices
are no longer capable of launching a large-scale offensive,
Hitler can only turn completely to strategic defensive. When
Hitler is compelled to do that, the fate of fascism is as good as
sealed. From its birth a fascist country like Hitler's builds its
political and military life on aggression, so that once its
aggression is stopped its life is ended. The Battle of Stalingrad
will stop fascist aggression and therefore bears a decisive
character. It is so decisive as to affect the world war as a whole.

The three strong foes confronting Hitler are: the Soviet
Union, Great Britain and the United States, and the common
people of the German-occupied areas. On the eastern front
he has to face the Red Army standing like an unshakable
fortress, and he has to endure a second winter and withstand
the successive counter-offensives of the Red Army—these are
factors that will decide the outcome of the whole war and the
destiny of mankind. On the western front, even if the British
and the Americans continue to wait and stall, when the time
comes and they have the opportunity of belabouring the dead
tiger, they will eventually open the second front. And then
there is the home front against Hitler: a great uprising is
brewing among the people in Germany, in France and in other
parts of Europe, who will start a third front in response the
moment the Soviet Union launches an all-out counter-offensive
and the guns roar on the second front. Such converging attacks
upon Hitler on three fronts will constitute the great historical
course of events after the Battle of Stalingrad.

Napoleon's political life ended at Waterloo, but it was his Moscow fiasco that sealed his fate. Hitler today is moving along Napoleon's track and the Battle of Stalingrad has spelled his ruin.

Such a situation will directly affect the Far East. The coming year will also not be a lucky year for the Japanese fascists. They will have more and more headaches as time goes on, until they step into their graves.

All those who are pessimistic about the world situation ought to change their viewpoint now.

October 12, 1942

IN CELEBRATION OF THE TWENTY-FIFTH ANNIVERSARY OF THE OCTOBER REVOLUTION

It is with the greatest optimism that we celebrate this anniversary of the October Revolution. I firmly believe that this anniversary not only marks the turning-point in the Soviet-German war, but is also a turning-point for the world anti-fascist front to defeat the fascist front.

Formerly, it was the Red Army alone that resisted fascist Germany and her accomplices in Europe, hence Hitler could continue his advance and stave off his defeat. Now, the Soviet Union has grown more powerful in the course of the war, and Hitler's second summer offensive has come to nothing. From now on, the task of the world anti-fascist front is to start an offensive against the fascist front in order to bring about the final defeat of fascism.

The warriors of the Red Army at Stalingrad have achieved a feat of heroism that will determine the fate of mankind. They are the sons and daughters of the October Revolution. The banner of the October Revolution is the symbol of invincibility and all fascist forces are doomed to extinction.

In celebrating the Red Army's victory, we, the Chinese people, are also celebrating our own. Our Anti-Japanese War has been going on for upwards of five years, and although difficulties still lie ahead of us, the dawn of victory is already in sight. The defeat of the Japanese fascists is not only certain but is also drawing near.

It is the task of the Chinese people to concentrate all their efforts to defeat the Japanese fascists.

November 6, 1942

ECONOMIC AND FINANCIAL PROBLEMS DURING THE ANTI-JAPANESE WAR

Originally entitled "A Basic Summing-Up of Our Work in the Past", the following article forms the first chapter of the report, *Economic and Financial Problems*, delivered at the conference of the senior cadres of the Shensi-Kansu-Ningsia border region. In the course of the Anti-Japanese War, 1941 and 1942 were the years of greatest difficulty for the liberated areas. The Japanese invaders' savage attacks and the Kuomintang's encirclement and blockade combined to put the liberated areas in an extremely difficult financial situation. Comrade Mao Tse-tung pointed out that the Party must exert itself to lead the people to develop agriculture as well as other branches of production, and called upon the government bodies, schools and troops throughout the liberated areas to engage as much as possible in production for self-support so that the financial and economic difficulties could be overcome. His report, *Economic and Financial Problems*, and such articles as *Spread in the Base Areas the Campaign for Rent Reduction, for Production and for the Army's Support of the Government and Protection of the People* and *Let Us Get Organised* contain the Party's basic programme for the campaign of production in the liberated areas. In *Economic and Financial Problems*, Comrade Mao set forward the Party's correct line of "securing supplies through economic development", and severely criticised the erroneous view which is concerned only with public revenue and expenditure and leaves economic development out of account, as well as the wrong style in work which consists in demanding things from the people while neglecting to mobilise and help them to develop production and surmount difficulties. Developed along the line mapped out by the Party, the campaign of production in the Shensi-Kansu-Ningsia border region and the liberated areas in the enemy rear achieved great results, which not only enabled the army and the people in the liberated areas to tide over successfully the most difficult period of the Anti-Japanese War, but also provided a rich store of experience for the Party to guide the economic construction in the years to come.

To secure supplies through economic development is the main aim guiding our economic and financial work. Many of our comrades, however, are aware only of the importance of public finance, and have no idea of the importance of the economy as a whole; they are engrossed only in problems of public revenue and expenditure as such and, hard as they try, they fail to solve a single problem. This is because an antiquated and conservative view is doing mischief in their minds. They do not know that, while a good or bad financial policy may affect the economy, it is economic development that determines the financial situation. We can never overcome financial difficulties unless we have a sound economy, and we can never attain financial abundance without economic development. The financial problem in the Shensi-Kansu-Ningsia border region is a problem of securing funds for the living and working expenses of scores of thousands of military and civilian personnel; *i.e.* funds for waging the war against the Japanese invaders. All these funds are to be obtained through taxes collected from the people and through productive activities carried on by the military and civilian personnel themselves. If we do not develop both the private and public economic enterprises, we shall be doomed to ruin. Financial difficulties can be overcome only through substantial and effective economic development. The conservative view which overlooks economic development or fails to exploit financial resources, but is concerned with overcoming financial difficulties by cutting down indispensable expenditure, can solve no problem at all.

We have passed through several stages in the last five years. The greatest difficulty arose in the years 1940 and 1941 when the Kuomintang's two anti-Communist drives took place. For a while we were reduced almost to the state of having no clothes to wear, no oil to cook with, no paper, no vegetables, no footwear for the soldiers and, in winter, no bedding for the civilian personnel. The Kuomintang tried to wreck us by cutting off our allowance and imposing economic blockade, and we were indeed in great straits. But we managed to pull through. This we owed not only to the people of the border region who provided us with foodstuffs but especially to our determination to build up with our own hands the public sector of our economy. The government in the border region established many industries to meet our needs; the troops carried out an extensive campaign for production and developed agriculture, industry and commerce in order to become self-supporting; and the tens of thousands of the personnel in schools and government bodies also developed similar economic activities for self-support. Such economic activities for self-support, carried out by the armed units, public agencies and schools, are a special development under today's special conditions; they are at present perfectly reasonable and absolutely necessary, although unreasonable and inconceivable under other historical conditions. It is by such means that we have overcome our difficulties. Have not indubitable historical facts proved to us the truth that supplies can be secured only through economic development? Although we are still confronted with many difficulties, the foundation of the public sector of our economy has already been laid. In another year, by the end of 1943, the foundation will become even more consolidated.

It is a correct line to develop the economy, but we should not pursue it recklessly or unrealistically. Some comrades, over-looking the specific conditions here and now, pointlessly clamour for development, demanding, for example, the estab-lishment of heavy industry and putting forward plans for gigantic salt and armament industries, all of which are unrealistic and impracticable. The Party's line envisages a correct course of development, which opposes on the one hand the antiquated and conservative viewpoint and, on the other, grandiose plans of an empty and unrealistic character. Such is the Party's two-front struggle in financial and economic work.

While we must develop the public sector of our economy, we should not overlook the importance of help from the people. They have given us grain to consume, 90,000 piculs in 1940, 200,000 in 1941, and 160,000 in 1942,[1] thus ensuring the food supply for our troops and civilian personnel. Up to the end of 1941, the food output of our publicly-operated farms was quite meagre; we had to rely on the people for food. Although we must henceforth urge our army to increase food production, yet for the time being we still have to rely mainly upon the people. Though vast in area and so situated in the rear as to be safe from any direct war damage, the Shensi-Kansu-Ningsia border region is sparsely populated and it is not easy for its 1,500,000 inhabitants to provide large quantities of grain. Besides, the people who transport salt for us pay the salt tax in cash, and in 1941 subscribed to government bonds to the value of five million silver dollars, which is no light burden. To meet the needs of the War of Resistance and national reconstruction, the people must bear burdens, and they realise this necessity quite well. When the government is in the utmost difficulty, it is also necessary to ask the people to bear a heavier burden, and they will understand this too. But while taking from the people we should help them to recoup and develop their economy. That is to say, we ought to take appropriate measures and steps to help the people develop agriculture, stock-breeding, handicrafts, salt-making and commerce, enabling them to make gains there while taking losses here and, moreover, to gain more than they lose, so that the protracted War of Resistance can be sustained.

It is a mistake for some comrades, regardless of the requirements of war, to stress the necessity for the government to adopt "a policy of benevolence". For if we should lose the Anti-Japanese War, such a "policy of benevolence" would benefit none but the Japanese imperialists and would have nothing to do with the people. Conversely, although the people's burden is fairly heavy for the time being, if we can thereby overcome the difficulties confronting the government and the troops, sustain the War of Resistance and defeat the enemy, the people will see better days, and only thus can there be realised the great benevolence of a revolutionary government.

Another mistaken view is to take into consideration only the needs of the government and the troops but not the difficulties of the people, to make endless demands on the people in the manner of "draining a pond to catch all the fish". That is the Kuomintang's idea which we must never adopt. Although we have for the moment increased the people's burdens, we have at once applied ourselves to the building of the public sector of our economy. In the years 1941 and 1942 the greater part of our total needs was met through the toil of our armed units, offices and schools. This is a miracle unknown in Chinese history and provides for us an unshakable material basis. The further we advance along the line of economic self-support, the lighter will be the tax burden we impose on the people. In the first stage, from 1937 to 1939, we took very little from the people, thus enabling them to recuperate to a very large extent. In the second stage, from 1940 to 1942, the burden on the people was increased. With the year 1943 will begin the third stage. If in the coming two years, 1943 and 1944, the public sector of our economy continues to develop and if all, or a great part of, our troops in the Shensi-Kansu-Ningsia border region are given opportunities to engage in farming, then by the end of 1944 the people will again be eased of their burden and will be able once more to recuperate. This is a possibility which we should be ready to turn into reality.

We must refute one-sided views of all kinds and put forward the correct slogan of our Party, namely, "secure supplies through economic development". In the matter of relations between public and private interests, our slogan is "due consideration to both public and private interests" or "due consideration to both troops and civilians". In our opinion, only such slogans are correct. Only by developing both public and private economic enterprises in accordance with the actual circumstances can we secure our financial resources. Even in times of difficulty we must take care to set a limit to taxation so that the burden, though heavy, will not exhaust the people. And whenever we can manage, we should lighten the people's burden so that they can recuperate.

The Kuomintang die-hards regard construction in the border region as hopeless and the difficulties confronting it as insurmountable; they are every day expecting a "collapse" in the border region. It is not worth while arguing with such people, for they will never see the day of our "collapse" and we shall only become more prosperous. They do not understand that under the leadership of the Communist Party and the border region's revolutionary government the masses of the people always give their support to the Party and the government. The Party and the government, for their part, will never fail to take economic and financial measures effective enough to tide over difficulties however serious. As to our recent difficulties, some we have pulled through already, others we soon shall. In the past we met much greater difficulties, yet we surmounted them just the same. With intense fighting going on every day, our bases in North and Central China are now facing difficulties much greater than those of the Shensi-Kansu-Ningsia border region, yet we have already held out there for five years and a half, and can certainly continue to hold out till victory. For us there is no pessimism; we can conquer any kind of difficulty.

After this conference of the senior cadres of the Shensi-Kansu-Ningsia border region we shall immediately enforce the policy of "picked troops and simplified administration".[2] This time the policy must be enforced strictly, thoroughly and extensively, and not perfunctorily, superficially or on a restricted scale. By enforcing this policy we must attain the following five objectives: simplification, unity, efficiency, economy and struggle against bureaucracy. These five objectives have important bearings upon our economic and financial work. Once this policy is implemented, the outlay for consumption will be cut down and the revenue from production will be increased; this will not only have a direct and salutary influence on the state of our finance, but will also lighten the people's burdens and improve their economic conditions. In our economic and financial set-up, such evil phenomena as disunity, clamour for independence, and each going his own way must be eliminated; and we must establish a working system that is unified, flexible and capable of carrying out our policies and programmes to the letter. With the establishment of such a unified system, working efficiency will be increased. Economy deserves the attention of all our organisations, and particularly those engaged in economic and financial work. As a result of practising economy, a large sum to the tune of tens of millions of dollars of unnecessary and wasteful expenses can be cut down. Furthermore, the personnel engaged in economic and financial work should get rid of the bureaucracy which is still found among them and is in some cases of a very serious nature, such as corruption and graft, empty formality, meaningless "standardisation" and red tape. If we can fully attain all the above-mentioned five objectives in the Party, the government and the army, then the aim of our policy of "picked troops and simplified administration" will be achieved, our difficulties will surely be overcome and those who gibe at our approaching "collapse" will be silenced.

December 1942

ON METHODS OF LEADERSHIP

This is a resolution on methods of leadership drafted on behalf of the Central Committee of the Communist Party of China.

1. The two methods which we Communists should employ in carrying out any task are, first, the linking of the general with the specific and, second, the linking of the leadership with the masses.

2. We cannot mobilise the broad masses for a particular task unless we publicise those general directives which are applicable to all. But there is no possibility of testing the correctness of such general directives and of making them more specific and concrete, and there is a danger of their coming to nothing, unless the leaders, instead of contenting themselves with issuing directives, personally carry out the tasks on hand in a concrete and thorough manner in some of their organisations until initial success is achieved in one place, and then use the experience so gained to direct the work in the rest of the organisations. For example, in the course of the 1942 campaign to rectify the style in work, success was achieved wherever the method of linking general directives with specific guidance was used and failure occurred wherever it was ignored. In the rectification campaign of 1943 all bureaux and sub-bureaux of the Central Committee of the Party, all regional and district Party Committees should, in addition to issuing general directives (*i.e.* the year's plan for the campaign), endeavour to gain experience in the following way: Select two or three units (but not too many) in their own organisations or other near-by organisations, schools or troops, and thoroughly investigate them to get acquainted in detail with the way they are carrying on the campaign; pick a few of their typical members (again, not too many), and make a detailed study of their political records, their outlook, their attitude to study and the records of their work and, furthermore, give direct personal guidance to the leaders of the selected units to help them effectively solve the practical problems which crop up in their respective units. As an office, a school or an army unit

is also composed of a number of sub-units, its leaders should do the same. This is also the method of giving leadership while learning how to lead. No leading worker can possibly give general guidance to all the units under his direction if he does not get actual experience in working on specific tasks with individual workers in particular units. This method should be widely popularised so that leading workers at all levels can learn to apply it.

3. The experience gained in the rectification campaign of 1942 also proves that, to achieve success in the campaign, it is essential that within each unit a leading group should be formed comprising a small number of active workers united around the head of the given unit and that this group should maintain close contact with the masses taking part in the campaign. The activity of this leading group, unless combined with that of the masses, will dissipate itself in the fruitless efforts of a handful of people. On the other hand, mass activity, unless well organised by a strong leading group, can be neither sustained long nor be developed in the right direction and raised to a higher level. The masses in all cases are by and large composed of three groups of people: the active, the relatively passive and those who are betwixt and between. The leadership must therefore be skilled in drawing the small number of active individuals into the leading group and in relying on them to enhance the activity of the betwixt and between and draw the passive into the work. A leading group that is genuinely united and firmly linked with the masses can be gradually formed only in the course of a mass campaign, not apart from it. In most cases, the composition of the leading group should not and cannot remain entirely unchanged throughout the initial, intermediate and final stages of a great campaign. The active people who emerge in the course of the struggle should be constantly promoted to replace those members of the leading group who cannot keep up the pace or have become demoralised. The fundamental reason for failure to advance our work in various places and organisations is precisely the absence of such a permanently healthy leading group firmly united and linked with the masses. A school with about a hundred students cannot be run properly unless it has a leading group comprising a few or a dozen or more people,

which has emerged naturally (and not been formed artificially) from among the most active, staunch and capable members of its faculty, staff and student body.

The principles concerning the creation of a basic leading group which J. V. Stalin set forth in the ninth of his twelve conditions for building up a Bolshevik Party[1] should be applied in every office, school, military unit, factory or village, whether large or small. In creating such a leading group the criteria should be those four for choosing cadres given in Georgi Dimitrov's discussion on cadres policy (namely, absolute devotion to the cause, close contact with the masses, ability to find one's orientation independently and strict observance of discipline).[2] In any case, whatever the task, whether a central task connected with the war, production or education (including the rectification campaign) or such a task as checking up work or examining cadres, etc., we must not only link general directives with specific guidance, but also link the leading group with the broad masses.

4. In all practical work of our Party, correct leadership can only be developed on the principle of "from the masses, to the masses". This means summing up (*i.e.* co-ordinating and systematising after careful study) the views of the masses (*i.e.* views scattered and unsystematic), then taking the resulting ideas back to the masses, explaining and popularising them until the masses embrace the ideas as their own, stand up for them and translate them into action by way of testing their correctness. Then it is necessary once more to sum up the views of the masses, and once again take the resulting ideas back to the masses so that the masses give them their whole-hearted support. . . . And so on, over and over again, so that each time these ideas emerge with greater correctness and become more vital and meaningful. This is what the Marxist theory of knowledge teaches us.

5. In order to correct the wrong views obtaining among our cadres, we should, during the present campaign to rectify the style in work, widely publicise the idea that, whether in an organisation or in a campaign, proper relations must be established between the leading group and the broad masses; that the leadership can work out correct ideas only if it sums up the views of the masses and takes the resulting ideas back

to the masses so that they can gain firm mass support; and that, in putting the ideas of the leadership into practice, general directives must be linked with specific guidance. Many comrades neither care nor know how to rally active people to form a leading group, nor do they care or know how to link such a leading group closely with the broad masses; as a result, their leadership becomes bureaucratic and divorced from the masses. Many other comrades neither care nor know how to sum up the experience of a mass struggle, but are fond of proclaiming their own subjective opinions with an air of great profundity, as a result of which their judgements become empty talk divorced from reality. Still others content themselves with giving out general directives on various questions and, having done that, do not bother and, in fact, do not know how to go on immediately to give specific guidance on the tasks on hand; as a result their directives remain mere words, directives only put down on paper or issued at the conference table, and their leadership becomes bureaucratic. During the present campaign to rectify the style in work, we must get rid of these defects; in the course of rectifying our style in work, checking up our work and examining our cadres, we must learn how to maintain close contact between the leadership and the masses and also how to link general directives with specific guidance, and we must apply these methods consistently in all our future work.

6. The basic method of leadership is to sum up the views of the masses, take the results back to the masses so that the masses give them their firm support and so work out sound ideas for leading the work on hand. In summing up the opinions of the masses and mobilising them to uphold the ideas so adopted, the leadership should use the method of combining general directives with specific guidance, which is an organic part of the method "from the masses, to the masses". On the basis of numerous cases of giving specific guidance we work out general ideas (general directives) for action, then put these general ideas to the test in many individual units (not only by ourselves, but by others acting on our advice), and finally generalise (*i.e.* sum up) the new experience so gained so as to work out new directives for the general guidance of the masses. This is the way all comrades should carry on their work, not

only in the present rectification campaign, but also in every other kind of work. The better one grasps this method, the better his leadership proves.

7. In assigning a task (such as prosecution of the revolutionary war, production, education, the rectification campaign, checking up work, examining cadres, propaganda, organisational or anti-espionage work, etc.) to a subordinate unit, the higher leading organisation and its departments should act through the leader who has overall responsibility for the lower organisation concerned, so that he can undertake the assignment with a full sense of responsibility, thereby achieving a division of duties under unified leadership (centralised authority). It is inadvisable for one department of a higher organisation to have contacts only with its counterpart in lower organisations (for example, the organisational, propaganda or anti-espionage departments of a higher organisation to have contacts only with the corresponding departments of lower organisations), leaving the responsible head of a lower organisation (for example, the secretary, chairman, director or school principal, etc.) uninformed and unable to answer for the work assigned. It is essential that the leader of a lower organisation concerned as well as the heads of its particular departments should be informed of the assigned task and held answerable for its fulfilment. Such a centralised authority, *i.e.* division of duties under unified leadership, permits the leader at the top to mobilise a large number of people—on occasion even the entire personnel of an organisation—to carry out a particular task; in this way, shortage of workers in particular units can be remedied and a large number of people can be drawn in as active participants in a given task. This is also a form of linking up the leadership with the masses. If, for example, a check-up on personnel is carried out by only a few members of such a leading body as the Organisation Department, there is little doubt that it will not be done successfully; if on the other hand, through the head of an institution or school principal we can secure the participation of a considerable number of the personnel of that institution or of the students, or, perhaps, even the entire staff or the whole student body, while the leadership of the organisational department concerned gives adequate guidance and actually

applies the principle of linking the leadership with the masses, then it is certain that the objectives of the check-up can be fully achieved.

8. Not more than one main task should be assigned at any one time to any one locality; at any given time there can be only one central task, though it may be supplemented by tasks of secondary and third-rate importance. So the leader of a locality should put each kind of work in its proper place according to the history and the circumstances of the struggle in that locality, rather than act without plan and rush from task to task as higher organisations assign them, thereby causing havoc and confusion with a bewildering number of "central tasks". Nor should a higher organisation on its part simultaneously hand down a lot of assignments to organisations at a lower level, irrespective of their relative importance and urgency and without specifying which is the main task, because this will disorganise the work of the lower organisations and prevent them from achieving the desired end. The art of leadership is for a leader to take into account the situation as a whole in accordance with the historical conditions and immediate circumstances of each specific locality, correctly determine the central task and programme of work in a given period, then steadfastly carry out this decision, and see to it that results are achieved. This also is a question of methods of leadership which must be carefully solved in applying the principles of linking the leadership with the masses and combining the general with the specific.

9. We have not gone into the details of the question of methods of leadership, and we hope that comrades everywhere can, in the light of the principles and directives here set forth, think over the details carefully and use their own initiative. The harder the struggle, the greater is the necessity of closely linking Communist leadership with the demands of the masses, of closely combining general Communist directives with specific guidance and thus completely ending subjective and bureaucratic methods of leadership. All the leading comrades of the Party must at all times oppose and overcome subjective and bureaucratic methods of leadership with scientific Marxist methods of leadership. The development of Party work is greatly impeded by subjectivists and bureaucrats who ignore

the principles of linking the leadership with the masses and of combining the general with the specific. In order to combat subjective and bureaucratic methods of leadership, we must extensively and thoroughly promote scientific, Marxist methods of leadership.

SOME QUESTIONS PUT TO THE KUOMINTANG

This is an editorial written for the *Liberation Daily*, published in Yenan.

Within the last few months something abnormal and shocking has happened within the camp of resistance to the Japanese invaders, namely, the campaign started by many Kuomintang-led party, government and army organisations with a view to disrupting solidarity and resistance. This campaign takes the form of opposing the Communist Party, but actually sets itself against the Chinese nation and the Chinese people.

First, let us look at the Kuomintang troops. Out of the country's troops under Kuomintang leadership, as many as three group armies of the main forces are stationed in the north-west: the Thirty-fourth, the Thirty-Seventh and the Thirty-eighth, all under Hu Tsung-nan, Deputy Commander of the Eighth War Zone. Two of them were used to encircle the Shensi-Kansu-Ningsia border region, while the remaining one manned the defences along the Yellow river from Ichwan to the Tung pass against the Japanese invaders. Such was the situation for more than four years, and people got used to it so long as no military conflict arose. Unexpectedly, a change took place a few days ago: of the three armies on defence duty along the river, *i.e.* the First, the Sixteenth and the Ninetieth, two have been moved away, the First Army dispatched to the area of Pinchow and Chunhwa and the Ninetieth Army to the area of Lochwan, and are actively making preparations for an attack on the border region, leaving large gaps in the river defence line facing the Japanese invaders.

This cannot but make people raise the question: What exactly are the relations between these Kuomintang people and the Japanese?

Day in, day out many Kuomintang people have outrageously carried on their propaganda about the Communist Party's "undermining the Resistance" and "disrupting solidarity". Can the complete evacuation of the main forces for the river defences be described as strengthening the Resistance? Can the attack on the border region be described as strengthening solidarity?

We should like to raise a question to those Kuomintang people who are doing these things: As you are turning your back on the Japanese who, however, do not turn their face away, what if they should march on your back?

You have abandoned a large section of the river defence, and the Japanese are watching quietly from the other bank without bestirring themselves; all they do is to gaze in high spirits through a telescope at the gradually receding view of your back. Why is all this? Why do the Japanese so much enjoy looking at your back, and what makes you feel so much at ease, paying no heed to the river defence and leaving large gaps in it?

In a society of private ownership, a person must bolt the doors of his house before going to bed at night. He is not being fussy; he is, as everybody knows, protecting himself against burglars. Now leaving the doors wide open, are you not afraid of the burglar's visit? When the doors are wide open and yet the burglar does not come, what is the reason indeed?

As you put it, in China the Communists alone are "undermining the Resistance", while you yourselves are in all possible ways devoted to the cause of "the nation above all". Now what do you consider to be "above all" when you turn your back on the enemy?

As you put it, the Communists are also "disrupting solidarity", while you yourselves are in all possible ways devoted to the cause of "solidarity in good faith". Now you are ordering a huge force of three group armies, only short of one army, to advance on the people of the border region with fixed bayonets and heavy artillery: can this be regarded as promoting "solidarity in good faith"?

Or as you put it another way: you do not really care about solidarity, but are very fond of "unification", therefore you want to wipe out the border region, eliminate what you call "a feudal independent régime" and kill all Communists. Very well. But why are you not afraid that the Japanese may "unify" the Chinese nation, with you yourselves thrown in?

Suppose you could, with flying colours, "unify" the border

region and crush the Communists, while the Japanese, immobilised by your "sleeping draught" or under your "spell", failed to "unify" the nation including yourselves, then, would you gentlemen of the Kuomintang kindly give us some hints about your "sleeping draught" or "spell"?

If, however, you have got no such sleeping draught and no such spell for the Japanese, and if, furthermore, you have not reached a secret understanding with them, then let us tell you solemnly: You ought not to attack the border region and you must not attack it. There is truth in these two parables: "If a snipe and a clam are locked in fight, it is only to the advantage of the fisherman," and "the mantis stalks the cicada, unaware of the oriole lurking behind". The proper thing for you to do is to join forces with us to "unify" the areas occupied by the Japanese, and drive out the Japanese invaders. Why should you be in such a hurry to "unify" this small strip of land of the border region? Vast stretches of our beloved country have fallen into the hands of the enemy, and you feel no worry, show no hurry, while you hasten to attack the border region and knock down the Communist Party. What a pity! What a shame!

Next, let us look at the Kuomintang's party affairs. To oppose the Communist Party the Kuomintang has organised several hundred detachments of secret agents, into which scoundrels of all descriptions are recruited. On July 6, 1943, the thirty-second year of the Chinese Republic, *i.e.* on the eve of the sixth anniversary of the War of Resistance, the Kuomintang's *Central News Agency* circulated a release, saying that in Sian, Shensi, a certain "cultural association" held a meeting and resolved to send a telegram to Mao Tse-tung, requesting him to take the opportunity of the dissolution of the Communist International to "dissolve" the Communist Party of China, and, furthermore, requesting him to "abolish the independent régime of the border region". This may seem "news" to the readers; but actually it is an old story.

The whole thing was started by one of hundreds of detachments of Kuomintang secret agents. Acting on the orders of its head offices (*i.e.* the Bureau of Investigation and Statistics of the Military Council of the National Government and the Bureau of Investigation and Statistics of the Central Executive

Committee of the Kuomintang), this detachment gave instructions to a Trotskyite traitor Chang Ti-fei—now Director of Discipline in the Labour Camp in Sian, notorious for his anti-Communist articles published in *Resistance and Culture*, a traitorous periodical financed by the Kuomintang—to call a ten-minute meeting of nine persons on June 12, twenty-five days before the *Central News Agency* circulated the release, and it was at this meeting that the text of the so-called telegram was "unanimously endorsed".

Up till now the said telegram has not reached Yenan, though we already know what it is all about; it says, so we are told, that since the Third International has been dissolved, the Communist Party of China should likewise be "dissolved", and that "Marxism-Leninism has become bankrupt", etc., etc.

So this is what the Kuomintang people have said! We have always known that anything may issue from the mouths of such Kuomintang people (who are banded together, like attracting like) and, just as we expected, what wonderful stuff has now issued from them!

In China there are now many parties and groups; there are two Kuomintangs, not to mention others. One is the Kuomintang of Wang Ching-wei's brand, set up in Nanking and other places, flying also the Kuomintang standard of the "white sun in the blue sky", and possessing its so-called Central Executive Committee as well as numerous detachments of secret agents. Besides, everywhere in the occupied areas there are the fascist parties created by the Japanese.

Dear gentlemen of the Kuomintang: Why is it that after the dissolution of the Third International you are entirely taken up with plotting the "dissolution" of the Communist Party, but do not choose at all to make some effort for the dissolution of certain traitorous and Japanese-sponsored parties? When you directed Chang Ti-fei to draft the telegram, why didn't you, besides demanding the dissolution of the Communist Party, add a single phrase to say that the traitorous and Japanese-sponsored parties likewise deserve to be dissolved?

Could it be that you think there are too many Communist parties in the country? In the whole of China there is only one Communist Party, while there are two Kuomintangs. After all, of which of the parties is there one too many?

Gentlemen of the Kuomintang: Have you ever given this matter a thought? Why is it that, besides you, the Japanese and Wang Ching-wei together are also making frantic efforts to overthrow the Communist Party, unanimously declaring that the Communist Party alone is superfluous and must therefore be overthrown? And why is it that they never think that there are too many Kuomintangs (but that there are only too few), and that everywhere they are fostering the Kuomintang of Wang Ching-wei's brand?

Gentlemen of the Kuomintang, we shall take the trouble of telling you something. The reason why the Japanese and Wang Ching-wei are particularly fond of the Kuomintang and the Three People's Principles is that in both they find something which they can turn to good account. It was only after the First World War, during 1924-7, when the Kuomintang, reorganised by Dr. Sun Yat-sen, admitted the Communists into its ranks and formed a national alliance based on Kuomintang-Communist co-operation, that it aroused the hatred and animosity of all the imperialists and traitors, who thus plotted desperately for its overthrow. And it was in the same period when the Three People's Principles were personally revised by Dr. Sun Yat-sen into the revolutionary Three People's Principles as given in the Manifesto of the First National Congress of the Kuomintang, that they aroused the hatred and animosity of all the imperialists and traitors, who thus plotted desperately for their overthrow. Save for that period, this party and these principles, by expelling the Communists and betraying the revolutionary spirit of Dr. Sun Yat-sen, have won the heart of all imperialists and traitors, and consequently the Japanese fascists and Wang Ching-wei the traitor also give their hearts to them, cherishing and nurturing them as something extremely precious. Formerly, as a distinctive sign, a yellow patch appeared on the left corner of the flag of Wang Ching-wei's brand of Kuomintang, but now even this sign has been removed and everything is made to look the same, so as not to offend the eye. How great is their affection for the Kuomintang!

The Kuomintang of Wang Ching-wei's brand multiplies not only in the occupied areas but also in the big rear area. Some of its members operate underground, being fifth-columnists sent by the enemy. Others operate in the open, *i.e.* people who turn the Kuomintang into a racket and make a profession out of the secret service, who do not resist Japan at all but specialise in anti-Communism. They are really Wang Ching-wei's men, though not ear-marked as such. They too are fifth-columnists sent by the enemy, but they appear in a somewhat different guise to conceal their identity and escape detection.

The matter has by now become perfectly clear. The reason why, in directing Chang Ti-fei to draft the telegram, you absolutely refused to add a single phrase to say that, in addition to demanding the "dissolution" of the Communist Party, the traitorous and Japanese-sponsored parties should likewise be dissolved, is that in ideology, in policy, as well as in organisation you have many things in common with them, the most fundamental idea common to you all being opposition to the Communist Party and the people.

We want to ask you Kuomintang people another question: Is it true that in China and indeed in the world, only one doctrine, namely, Marxism-Leninism, has become "bankrupt", while all other doctrines remain good stuff? We have mentioned above Wang Ching-wei's Three People's Principles; what about Hitler's, Mussolini's or Tojo's fascism? Or Chang Ti-fei's Trotskyism? And what about the counter-revolutionary doctrine of the various brands of counter-revolutionary secret services?

Dear gentlemen of the Kuomintang: When you instructed Chang Ti-fei to draft the telegram, why did you not put in even a single phrase or add the smallest proviso about these various so-called "doctrines" which plague the world like a pest, infest it like vermin, and befoul it like dog's droppings? Could it be that in your eyes all these counter-revolutionary doctrines are faultless and perfect to the last degree, while Marxism-Leninism is the only doctrine that has become completely "bankrupt"?

To be frank, we rather suspect that because you are collaborating with the Japanese-sponsored and traitorous parties, you chime in with them in everything; in what you do and what you say, you and the Japanese and the traitors are alike, undifferentiated and indistinguishable. The Japanese and the traitors wanted to disband the New Fourth Army, and you disbanded it; they want to dissolve the Communist Party, so do you; they want to abolish the border region, so do you; they do not want you to defend the Yellow river, so you abandon its defence; they attack the border region (for the last six years the enemy forces along the bank opposite the counties of Suiteh, Micheh, Chiah, Wupu and Tsingkien have never for one moment ceased shelling the river defences of the Eighth Route Army), and you too contemplate an attack on it; they are anti-Communist, so are you; they bitterly revile communism and liberal ideas, so do you;[1] if they catch a Communist they force him to make a recantation in the newspapers, so do you; they send counter-revolutionary secret agents to sneak into the Communist Party, the Eighth Route Army and the New Fourth Army to carry out disruptive activities, so do you. How can you be like them, undifferentiated from them and indistinguishable from them to such a degree? Since in so many of your views and actions you are like them, undifferentiated from them and indistinguishable from them, how can people help suspecting that you are in league with them or that you have come to some sort of secret understanding with them?

To the Central Executive Committee of the Kuomintang we hereby make this formal protest: The evacuation of the huge forces for the river defence as a preparatory step for attacking the border region and starting civil war is a grossly erroneous act which cannot be tolerated. The news released on July 6 by the *Central News Agency* which disrupts solidarity and insults the Communist Party represents a grossly erroneous view which cannot be tolerated either. Both the erroneous action and the erroneous view are enormities in no way distinguishable from what the Japanese and the traitors do or say; you must correct them.

To Mr. Chiang Kai-shek, *Tsungts'ai*[2] of the Kuomintang, we hereby make this formal demand: That you order Hu Tsung-nan's troops to return to defence duty along the river, reprimand the *Central News Agency* and punish the traitor Chang Ti-fei.

To all those Kuomintang members who are true patriots and are opposed to the withdrawal of the forces defending the

River for an attack on the border region and opposed to the demand for the dissolution of the Communist Party, we hereby make this appeal: Please take action to avert the danger of a civil war. We are willing to work together with you to the very end to save the nation.

We consider these demands entirely just.

July 12, 1943

SPREAD IN THE BASE AREAS THE CAMPAIGN FOR RENT REDUCTION, FOR PRODUCTION, AND FOR THE ARMY'S SUPPORT OF THE GOVERNMENT AND PROTECTION OF THE PEOPLE

A directive written on behalf of the Central Committee of the Chinese Communist Party to the membership.

1. As the time for autumn harvest is come, leading bodies in all base areas must instruct Party and government organisations at all levels to check up on how the policy of rent reduction is being carried out. Rent must be reduced this year in all those places where it has not yet been actually reduced. And rent must be thoroughly reduced this year in all those places where it has been reduced but not thoroughly. Party committees should issue directives on rent reduction in accordance with the agrarian policy of the Central Committee of the Party and the actual conditions in various areas, make first-hand investigations in a few villages and pick out exemplary cases in order to expedite reduction elsewhere. At the same time, they should publish in the press editorials on rent reduction and accounts of its exemplary cases. Rent reduction is a mass struggle of the peasants; Party directives and government decrees are intended to guide and help this mass struggle and not to bestow favours on the masses. Any reduction is improper and its result not enduring if it is granted as a favour without the active spirit of the masses being aroused. In the struggle for rent reduction, peasant organisations should be formed or reconstituted. The government's stand is to enforce the decree on rent reduction and adjust the interests of the landlords and the tenants. As the base areas have now shrunk, it is of a more immediate significance now than in the past six years for our Party to win over the masses in these areas patiently, conscientiously and thoroughly and cast in our lot with them. If during this autumn we can find out how much has been done in rent reduction and carry out the reduction to the fullest

extent, then we shall be able to arouse the active spirit of the peasant masses and, in the coming year, intensify our struggle against the enemy and expedite the production campaign.

2. Most cadres in the various base areas in the enemy's rear do not know how, for the purpose of developing production extensively, to mobilise the personnel of the Party, army and government organisations and the masses of the people (including, without any exception, all men and women, the old and young, soldiers and civilians, those in public service as well as those engaged in civilian pursuits). The Party committee, government and army in each base area must make full preparations during this autumn and the coming winter for launching throughout the area next year a campaign of extensive production in both public and private farming as well as in industry, handicrafts, transport, stock-breeding and commerce, but mainly in farming—a campaign for the people to overcome difficulties with their own hands (the slogan of ample clothing and sufficient food should not be raised for the time being, except in the Shensi-Kansu-Ningsia border region). There are to be household production plans and mutual aid in labour (i.e. work-exchange teams in northern Shensi[1] and the ploughing teams or mutual-aid working groups which once existed in the Red areas in Kiangsi), reward of labour heroes, emulation in production and development of co-operatives that are in the service of the masses. In tackling financial and economic problems, Party and government personnel in counties and districts should devote nine-tenths of their energy to helping the peasants to increase production and only the remaining one-tenth to collecting taxes from them. If great pains have been taken with regard to the former, the latter will be a light and easy job. All public bodies, schools and army units should, under war conditions, make great efforts to grow vegetables and breed pigs, collect firewood, make charcoal, develop handicrafts and raise a part of the grain they need. Apart from the development of collective production in all the big and small units, all individuals (except those in the army) should at the same time be encouraged to devote their spare time to minor agricultural or handicraft production (but mercantile operation is forbidden), and be allowed to keep the proceeds. In various places training

courses of seven to ten days should be given on vegetable growing and pig farming, and to cooks for preparing better food. In all the organisations of the Party, the government and the army, economy should be stressed, waste combated and corruption forbidden. The leadership at all levels in the Party, government and army and in the schools should master the skill of guiding the masses in production. Any leader who does not study carefully the ways and means of production cannot be considered a good leader. Any soldier or civilian who neglects production and is lazy and self-indulgent cannot be considered a good soldier or a good citizen. All Party members in the rural districts who have not detached themselves from production should look upon the development of production as one of the qualifications for making themselves models among the masses. In the production campaign, the conservative, purely fiscal view is wrong which knows only the curtailment of expenditure but neglects economic development. The view is also wrong which neglects organising the enormous labour power of the rank and file of the Party, the government and the army, and the masses of the people to spread a mass campaign for production, but stresses one-sidedly that it is the duty of a small number of government personnel to collect taxes in grain or cash, and to get food supplies and money. The view (characteristic of the Kuomintang) is wrong which neglects making the utmost efforts to help the masses to develop production but knows only the exaction of grain and money from them. The view is wrong which neglects launching an all-out production campaign of the masses but leaves only a few economic organisations to organise a small number of people in production. The view is wrong which considers it disgraceful and immoral that Party members, in order to further the cause of revolution, should engage in household production to support their families (in the case of our members in rural districts) or to engage individually in side-production to improve their own living conditions (in the case of our members in public bodies and schools). It is a wrong approach when there are base areas, not to encourage the development of production and efforts to improve the conditions of material life by increasing production, but merely to exhort people to bear with hardships for the sake of the struggle. The view is wrong which regards the co-operatives not as economic organisations in the service of the masses, but as money-making concerns for a small number of functionaries or as government stores. The view is wrong which, instead of promoting in various places the model methods of production (*e.g.* mutual aid in labour, frequent ploughing and hoeing, and abundant manuring) employed by some of the labour heroes in agriculture in the Shensi-Kansu-Ningsia border region, maintains that such methods are not applicable in certain base areas. The view is wrong which maintains that the task of production should be entrusted only to the heads of the departments of construction, of supply and of general affairs; and that the production campaign can go on without the leading cadres assuming responsibility and personally taking part in it, without integrating the core of leadership with the broad masses, without linking general directives with specific guidance, without carrying out investigation and study, without putting first priorities first, without securing the participation of all men and women, the old and young, including vagabonds, or without training the cadres or educating the masses. Under the present conditions the pivot in the development of production is the organisation of labour power. In each of the base areas, even under present war conditions, it is possible and absolutely necessary to organise for production the labour power of tens of thousands of Party members, government personnel and troops, and of hundreds of thousands of the people (*i.e.* to organise on a voluntary basis all people who can fulfil the standard quota of work or fulfil only half the quota, according to the principle of equal pay for equal work, and in the forms of a production plan for each household, of work-exchange teams, transport teams, mutual-aid working groups or co-operatives). Every Party member must fully grasp the whole set of policies and methods for organising labour power. The universal and thorough reduction of rent in all the base areas this year will give a stimulus to the extensive development of production next year. And a material basis will be laid for steadfastly maintaining the anti-Japanese base areas when in the coming year all people, men and women, old and young, including those in the Party, government and army, will carry out the great production campaign to increase the supply of foodstuffs and articles of daily use and to prepare for the fight against natural calamities. Otherwise, grave difficulties will confront us.

3. To make the Party, the government and the army become one with the people and to facilitate thereby both the struggle against the enemy and the campaign for production in the coming year, the Party committees and leading bodies of the army and the government in all the base areas should prepare to launch, all-inclusively and without any exception, a broad mass campaign in the first month of the coming lunar year, a campaign for the army's support of the government and protection of the people and for the people's support of the army and taking care of the families of the fighters against the Japanese invaders. In this campaign the troops should renew their pledge to support the government and protect the people, hold meetings for criticism and self-criticism, invite the inhabitants to socials (also attended by members of the local Party organisation and government) and apologise and offer compensation for infringement, if any, on the interests of the masses. The masses should, under the leadership of the local Party, government and mass organisations, renew the pledge to support the army and take care of the families of the fighters against the Japanese invaders, and launch a fervent campaign to comfort and honour the troops. In this campaign, the army on the one hand and the Party and the government on the other should thoroughly examine the shortcomings that were found in their work and the mistakes they made in 1943 and resolutely rectify them in 1944. In the first month of every lunar year from now on such a campaign should be universally launched, during which the pledges of the army to support the government and protect the people, and of the masses to support the army and take care of the families of the fighters against the Japanese invaders, should be proclaimed over and over again; and open self-criticism (*i.e.* each side criticising itself and not the other side) should be made in large gatherings over and over again, taking into account the shortcomings and mistakes found in the various base areas, whether the bullying of the Party, the government or civilians by the army, or the lack of concern for the army on the part of the Party, the government or civilians, so as to rectify thoroughly these mistakes.

October 1, 1943

A COMMENT ON THE ELEVENTH PLENARY SESSION OF THE KUOMINTANG'S CENTRAL EXECUTIVE COMMITTEE AND THE SECOND SESSION OF THE THIRD PEOPLE'S POLITICAL COUNCIL

This is an editorial written for the *Liberation Daily*, published in Yenan.

The Eleventh Plenary Session of the Kuomintang's Central Executive Committee was held from September 6 to 13, and the Second Session of the Third People's Political Council called by the Kuomintang government was held from September 18 to 27; now with all the documents of both sessions in hand, we can make a general comment.

The international situation is on the eve of a tremendous change, and the imminence of this change is sensed by everyone. The European Axis powers have sensed it, and Hitler is now adopting a policy which amounts to a dying kick. The change is being brought about mainly by the Soviet Union. The Soviet Union is making the most of the change; the Red Army, sweeping everything before it, has fought its way to the Dnieper river, and with another winter offensive it will push on to Russia's old frontiers, if not the new ones. Great Britain and the United States are also making the most of the change; Roosevelt and Churchill are waiting for the first sign of Hitler's downfall to penetrate into France. In short, the German fascist war machine will soon collapse, the problem of anti-fascist war in Europe is on the eve of total solution, and the Soviet Union is the main force in annihilating fascism. The central point of the world-wide anti-fascist war is in Europe; once the problem is solved in Europe, the fate of the two camps in the world, fascist and anti-fascist, will be decided. The Japanese imperialists despair of finding any way out; their policy can only amount to one of mustering up all their strength for a dying kick. In China, they will try to "mop up" the Communists and tempt the Kuomintang to capitulate.

The Kuomintang has also sensed the change. Faced with

this situation, it feels joy as well as fear. It feels joy because it imagines that the solution of the problem in Europe will leave the hands of Great Britain and the United States free to attack Japan on its behalf so as to enable it to return to Nanking without much ado. It feels fear because, as the three fascist powers topple down together, the world will enter a great age of liberation unprecedented in human history, and the Kuomintang's fascist dictatorship of comprador capitalism and feudalism will dwindle to a small islet in the vast ocean of world democracy and freedom; it fears that its fascism of "one party, one doctrine and one leader" will be buried beneath the waves.

The Kuomintang originally intended, above everything else, to make the Soviet Union fight it out single-handed with Hitler, to induce the Japanese invaders to attack the Soviet Union so that, in a war of attrition, the socialist country would be destroyed or at least badly damaged, and to ask Great Britain and the United States, instead of fussing about the so-called second and third fronts in Europe, to shift all their forces to the Far East and first smash Japan and then wipe out the Chinese Communist Party. It was for this unmentionable reason that the Kuomintang cried first for "Asia before Europe" and then "equal attention to Europe and Asia". When towards the end of the Quebec Conference last August, Roosevelt and Churchill summoned T. V. Soong, foreign minister of the Kuomintang government, to have a little talk, the Kuomintang again clamoured that "Roosevelt and Churchill have now turned their eyes to the Far East and changed their plan of 'Europe before Asia'," or that "the Quebec conference is a conference of the three big powers, Great Britain, the United States and China", etc., and indulged in a bout of self-congratulation and self-glorification. But this was already the Kuomintang's last fit of jubilation. Since then its feelings have undergone a certain change; with the proposals of "Asia before Europe" and "equal attention to Europe and Asia" becoming hopelessly out-of-date, the Kuomintang is probably thinking of other plans. The Eleventh Plenary Session of the Kuomintang's Central Executive Committee and the second session of the Kuomintang-controlled People's Political Council mark perhaps the beginning of those plans.

The Eleventh Plenary Session of the Kuomintang's Central Executive Committee slanderously accused the Communist Party of "undermining the Resistance and endangering the state", and announced at the same time that "a political solution should be sought" and that "preparations will be made for realising a constitutional government". The last Session of the Third People's Political Council, manipulated and controlled by its Kuomintang majority, passed resolutions about the Communist Party which are on the whole similar to those of the Eleventh Plenary Session of the Kuomintang's Central Executive Committee. Besides, the Eleventh Plenary Session also "elected" Chiang Kai-shek chairman of the Kuomintang government to strengthen the dictatorial machine.

What plan is the Kuomintang cooking up now, after the Eleventh Plenary Session? There are only three possibilities: 1. capitulating to Japanese imperialism; 2. stalling along its old line; 3. changing its political objective.

Adapting themselves to the Japanese imperialists' demand of "attacking the Communists and tempting the Kuomintang", the defeatists and capitulators within the Kuomintang have all along advocated capitulation. All the time they have endeavoured to instigate an anti-Communist civil war which, once started, will naturally make the Resistance impossible, leaving only one way out, namely, capitulation. The Kuomintang has concentrated in north-western China troops 400,000 to 500,000 strong, and is stealthily sending more troops there from other fronts. It is reported that the Kuomintang generals are in high spirits, saying: "The problem of taking Yenan is no problem." They made this assertion after they heard Mr. Chiang Kai-shek's speech at the Eleventh Plenary Session on the Communist problem, to the effect that "this is a political problem, and should be solved through political channels", and after the plenary session passed resolutions more or less similar in drift. Similar resolutions were made last year by the Tenth Plenary Session of the Kuomintang's Central Executive Committee; but before the ink recording those resolutions was dry, the Kuomintang generals had mapped out under orders military plans for liquidating the border region, and in June and July this year they actually appointed commanders and deployed troops, ready to start a blitz on the border region;

the plot was only shelved temporarily in consequence of the opposition of public opinion, domestic and foreign. Now again, no sooner were the resolutions of the Eleventh Plenary Session put down in black and white than people learned of the generals' boastful announcement and the deployment of their troops. "The problem of taking Yenan is no problem"—what does this signify? It signifies simply a decision to capitulate to Japanese imperialism. Not all the Kuomintang people in favour of "taking Yenan" are determined capitulators. Some of them perhaps reason like this: "We fight the Communists on the one hand and resist the Japanese on the other." Many officers who came from the Whampoa Military Academy[1] probably think so. To these gentlemen we Communists wish to pose some questions: Have you already forgotten the experience of the ten years' civil war? Once another civil war starts, will the determined capitulators allow you to continue the Resistance? Will the Japanese and Wang Ching-wei allow you to continue the Resistance? Are you really capable enough to fight at the same time the domestic enemy and the foreign foe? You claim that you have three million troops, but actually the morale of your soldiers has struck bottom; they have been compared to two basketfuls of eggs on the ends of a carrier's pole, and the slightest collision will result in a mess. The campaigns of the Chungtiao mountains, of the Taihang mountains, of Chekiang and Kiangsi, of western Hupeh, of the Tapieh mountains—all had the same result. The reason is simply that you have followed the two fatal policies of "actively opposing the Communists" and "passively resisting the Japanese". The enemy of the nation has penetrated deep into our country, and the more actively you oppose the Communists and the more passively you resist the Japanese, the lower will the morale of your troops sink. If you fight so badly against the foreign enemy, then do you think that in the struggle against the Communists, against the people, your troops will suddenly become brave? And, once you start a civil war, you will have to devote yourselves whole-heartedly to it, abandon the "simultaneous Resistance" and, in the end, sign with Japanese imperialism a treaty of unconditional surrender, "capitulation" being the only policy left to you. Those of you in the Kuomintang who do not really wish to capitulate will inevitably become capitulators once you actively instigate or participate in a civil war. If you listen to the instigations of the capitulators, and take the resolutions of the Eleventh Plenary Session and the People's Political Council as the means to mobilise public opinion and prepare the anti-Communist civil war, you will inevitably come to that pass. Even if originally you are unwilling to capitulate, you will, by listening to the instigations of the capitulators and taking the wrong steps, finally have to surrender in the wake of the capitulators. This is the first possible direction for the Kuomintang after its Central Executive Committee's Eleventh Plenary Session, and forms an extremely serious danger. From the standpoint of the capitulators, the "political solution" and "preparations for realising a constitutional government" are excellent means for throwing dust in the people's eyes while they are preparing civil war, *i.e.* preparing to capitulate; all Communists, all patriotic Kuomintang people, all anti-Japanese parties and groups, and all our anti-Japanese countrymen should keep a sharp look out and pay close attention to this extremely grave situation and not be bewildered by the dust thrown by the capitulators. It must be borne in mind that the danger of civil war has never been so great as after the Eleventh Plenary Session of the Kuomintang's Central Executive Committee.

The resolutions of the Kuomintang's Central Executive Committee's Eleventh Plenary Session and the People's Political Council point also to a possible development in another direction, that of "stalling for the time being and fighting the - Communists in the future". This, somewhat different from the line of the capitulators, is the line of those who still want to keep up the appearance of continuing to resist the Japanese but are absolutely unwilling to renounce their anti-Communist stand and dictatorship. They may follow this direction because they see that a great change in the international situation is inevitable; that Japanese imperialism is bound to fail; that civil war means capitulation; that the Chinese people support the Resistance and oppose civil war; that they are facing the grave crisis of being isolated as never before because the Kuomintang has severed itself from the masses and lost the allegiance of the people; and that the United States, Great Britain and the Soviet Union are all at one in opposing the Chinese government's attempt to start civil war—all these things have forced them to postpone the civil war they have been plotting and to find a means for stalling by resort to such empty talk as "political solution" and "preparations for realising a constitutional government". Hitherto the stratagem of which these people are past masters has consisted in "deceiving" and "stalling". Even in their dreams they do not forget the desire to "take Yenan" and "annihilate the Communist Party". On this point they are entirely at one with the capitulators. However, because they still want to sail under the false colours of Resistance so as not to impair the international prestige of the Kuomintang, and at times still fear the censure of public opinion, domestic and foreign, they may stall for a time behind the smoke-screen of "political solution" and "preparations for realising a constitutional government", waiting for favourable conditions to turn up in the future. They are not really serious about "political solution" and "realisation of a constitutional government", at least not at all serious now. Last year, about the time of the Tenth Plenary Session of the Kuomintang's Central Executive Committee, the Central Committee of the Communist Party sent Comrade Lin Piao to Chungking to confer with Mr. Chiang Kai-shek; he was kept in Chungking for ten long months and neither Mr. Chiang Kai-shek nor the Kuomintang party centre was willing to discuss even a single specific problem. In March this year, Mr. Chiang Kai-shek published his book *China's Destiny* in which he emphasises his hostility to communism and liberalism, lays the blame of the ten years' civil war on the Communists, slanders the Communist Party, the Eighth Route Army and the New Fourth Army as "new-type warlords", "new-type independent régime", and hints that he has made up his mind to finish off the Communist Party within two years. On June 28, Mr. Chiang Kai-shek permitted Comrades Chou En-lai, Lin Piao and the others to return to Yenan, but at the same time he ordered the Kuomintang troops defending the banks of the Yellow river to shift their position and advance towards the border region, and ordered all the local authorities throughout the country to seize the opportunity of the dissolution of the Third International to petition in the name of "the people's organisations" for the dissolution of the Communist Party of China. Under such circumstances, we Communists are obliged to appeal to the Kuomintang and all the people of the country to prevent civil war, and are obliged to expose the Kuomintang's various sinister plots and conspiracies aimed at undermining the Resistance and endangering the state. Our patience has been taxed to the limit, as historical facts can prove. Ever since the fall of Wuhan, anti-Communist battles, big or small, have never ceased in Central and North China. It is now two years since war broke out in the Pacific, and for two years the Kuomintang has been attacking the Communists in Central and North China; apart from troops originally stationed there, the Kuomintang has also dispatched Wang Chung-lien's and Li Hsien-chou's group armies to Kiangsu and Shantung to attack the Communists. P'ang Ping-hsun's group army stationed in the area of the Taihang mountains is ordered to attack exclusively the Communists; so are the Kuomintang troops in Anhwei and Hupeh. For a long time in the past we did not even make these facts public. The Kuomintang newspapers and periodicals of all sizes have been vilifying the Communists without a moment's pause, but for a long time we did not reply a word. The Kuomintang, for no reason whatsoever, ordered the disbandment of the New Fourth Army which was so heroically resisting the Japanese, and organised a massacre in which more than nine thousand men of its contingents in southern Anhwei were wiped out, while Yeh T'ing was arrested, Hsiang Ying was killed[2] and hundreds of leading personnel were imprisoned; this was a monstrous example of turning traitor to the people and to the nation, but we, apart from protesting to the Kuomintang and proposing certain remedial measures, still persevered in forbearance for the country's sake. During the audience he gave Comrade Chou En-lai, representative of the Communist Party, at Kuling in June and July 1937, Mr. Chiang Kai-shek promised to issue a decree giving appointments to the officials of the Shensi-Kansu-Ningsia border region and granting to the region the status of an administrative district under the direct jurisdiction of the Executive Yuan of the National Government; he not only went back upon his own words, but even dispatched troops numbering 400,000 to 500,000 men to encircle the border region and enforced a military and economic blockade; he could feel happy only when both the people of the border region and the rear headquarters of the Eighth Route Army were annihilated. As for cutting off the supplies of the Eighth Route Army, abusing the Communist Party as the "traitors' party", the New Fourth Army as the "rebels' army" and the Eighth Route Army as the "traitors' army", such facts are known to everybody. In a word, the Kuomintang people who have perpetrated such deeds regard the Communist Party as the enemy. In the Kuomintang's eyes, the Communist Party is ten times, nay, a hundred times more hateful than the Japanese. It has concentrated its bitter hatred against the Communist Party; as for the Japanese, it has very little hatred, if any, to spare for them. This is quite in keeping with the difference in the attitude of the Japanese fascists towards the Kuomintang and the Communist Party respectively. Concentrating their bitter hatred against the Chinese Communist Party, the Japanese fascists have become daily milder and blander towards the Kuomintang; of their two slogans, "Oppose the Communists" and "Annihilate the Kuomintang", only the first remains still in force. The newspapers and periodicals controlled by the Japanese and Wang Ching-wei no longer mention such slogans as "Down with the Kuomintang" and "Overthrow Chiang Kai-shek". Japan brings 58 per cent of her forces in China to bear upon the Communists, but only 42 per cent to keep watch on the Kuomintang, and has lately withdrawn many of her troops from Chekiang and Hupeh to relax her watch a little in order to further her scheme of inducing the Kuomintang to capitulate. Japanese imperialism dares not breathe a word to induce the Communist Party to capitulate, but it boldly and ceaselessly sends forth reams and reams of verbiage to persuade the Kuomintang to capitulate. The Kuomintang is fierce only towards the people and the Communist Party, but drops all its ferocity before the Japanese. Not only in the matter of action has it changed from fighting the Japanese into standing aside to watch the Communists fight the Japanese, but in the matter of speech, it dares not utter even a single sharp word to rebut the coaxing or insulting pronouncements made by the Japanese imperialists. "There is no mistake in the drift of the argument in Chiang

Kai-shek's *China's Destiny*", say the Japanese. Have Mr. Chiang Kai-shek and his followers ever refuted that statement? No, they have not and they dare not. The Japanese imperialists have witnessed how Mr. Chiang Kai-shek and the Kuomintang refer only the Communists to "military order and government decree" and "discipline", but have neither the wish nor the courage even to mention such things in connection with the twenty members of the Kuomintang's Central Executive Committee and fifty-eight Kuomintang generals who have capitulated to the enemy—how can the Japanese imperialists help despising the Kuomintang? To all the Chinese people and all the friendly nations in the world is presented only the spectacle of Mr. Chiang Kai-shek and the Kuomintang disbanding the New Fourth Army, attacking the Eighth Route Army, encircling the border region, spreading such calumnies about them as "traitors' party", "traitors' army", "new-type warlords", "new-type independent régime", "undermining the Resistance" and "endangering the state", and constantly harping upon "military orders and government decrees" and "discipline", while never enforcing any military order and government decree in connection with, or applying any disciplinary measure to, the twenty members of the Kuomintang's Central Executive Committee and fifty-eight Kuomintang generals who have capitulated to the enemy. Even on this occasion, the Eleventh Plenary Session of the Kuomintang's Central Executive Committee and the People's Political Council passed only resolutions directed against the Communist Party, but not a single one on measures to deal with the large numbers of that same Kuomintang's Central Executive Committee members and Kuomintang generals who have betrayed the country and capitulated to the enemy—what will all the Chinese people and the friendly nations in the world think of the Kuomintang? Just as we had expected, catchwords like "political solution" and "preparations for realising a constitutional government" came up again at the Eleventh Plenary Session of the Kuomintang's Central Executive Committee; very well, we welcome such catchwords. But judging by the political line the Kuomintang has consistently followed for many years, such catchwords are merely empty talk to dupe the people and, indeed, to gain the time necessary for preparing civil war and perpetuating the anti-popular dictatorship.

Is there a third direction in which the current situation can develop? Yes, this is what a number of Kuomintang members, the people throughout the country and we Communists all hope. What is this third direction? It is to settle justly and reasonably by political means the issues between the Kuomintang and the Communist Party, to establish in good faith a real constitutional government of democracy and freedom, to abolish the fascist dictatorship of "one party, one doctrine and one leader" and to convoke during the Resistance a national assembly truly elected by the people. We Communists have advocated this policy from the very beginning. A section of the Kuomintang will also agree to this policy. For a long time in the past we even hoped that Mr. Chiang Kai-shek and the Kuomintang factions under his direct control would pursue the same policy. But to judge by what has actually taken place in the last few years and what is actually happening now, Mr. Chiang Kai-shek and the majority of the Kuomintang people who are in power have done nothing to show their willingness to carry out such a policy.

The implementation of this policy requires a number of conditions, international and domestic. The international conditions (with fascism in Europe on the eve of complete collapse) are favourable to China's War of Resistance, and the capitulators are striving all the more to instigate civil war at this moment so that they can capitulate, and the Japanese and Wang Ching-wei are striving to do the same so as to facilitate their baiting for capitulation. Wang Ching-wei said (according to the report of the *Domei News Agency* on October 1): "Loving brothers will always remain brothers; the Chungking régime will certainly follow the same path as we do, and the sooner the better, we sincerely hope." What affection, confidence, and eager invitation in these words! That is why one can at best expect from the Kuomintang a policy of dragging things out, while there exists a grave danger of a sudden deterioration in the situation. Conditions are not yet present for going in the third direction, and patriots in all parties and groups and the people throughout the country must make every effort to bring them about.

At the Eleventh Plenary Session of the Central Executive Committee of the Kuomintang Mr. Chiang Kai-shek announced:

"We should declare that our party centre makes no other demand upon the Communist Party than that it should abandon the attempt to seize territory by force of arms and cease its surprise attacks on the National Army, which undermine the Resistance; that it should actually carry out the declaration it made in 1937 calling for united efforts to save the nation, and put into effect the four pledges in the said declaration."

When Mr. Chiang Kai-shek talks of "the attack on the National Army, which undermines the Resistance", he ought to be referring to the Kuomintang itself, and it is a pity that he should have slandered the Communist Party with bias and malignancy. Ever since the fall of Wuhan, the Kuomintang has engineered three anti-Communist upsurges all characterised by the surprise attacks its troops sprang on the Communist troops. In the first, from the winter of 1939 to the spring of 1940, the Kuomintang troops attacked and captured, even by means of bombing from the air, the five cities of Chunhwa, Sunyi, Chengning, Ninghsien and Chenyuan in the Shensi-Kansu-Ningsia border region, cities garrisoned by the Eighth Route Army. In North China, Chu Huai-ping's troops were dispatched to attack the Eighth Route Army in the region of the Taihang mountains and the Eighth Route Army fought back only in self-defence. The second was in January 1941. Previously Ho Ying-ch'in and Pai Ch'ung-hsi had issued a telegraphic order, dated October 19, 1940, to Chu Teh, P'eng Teh-huai, Yeh T'ing and Hsiang Ying, that the Eighth Route Army and the New Fourth Army south of the Yellow river must move in their entirety to the north of it within a month. We agreed to move our troops in southern Anhwei northward and, while not finding it feasible to move the other troops, promised to move them to their assigned stations after the victory of the Anti-Japanese War. When in pursuance of the order our troops of more than 9,000 men were moving from southern Anhwei on January 5, they had no idea of the fact that Mr. Chiang Kai-shek had already issued an order to "catch them all by a dragnet". From January 6 to 14, the Kuomintang troops in southern Anhwei really succeeded in "catching" that contingent of the New Fourth Army "by a dragnet" and, moreover, on the seventeenth, Mr. Chiang Kai-shek issued an order to disband the whole New Fourth Army and court-martial Comrade Yeh T'ing. Since then, in all the bases of the resistance against the Japanese invaders in Central and North China where the Kuomintang troops are stationed, the Eighth Route Army and the New Fourth Army have been subject to their attacks and have fought back only in self-defence. The third anti-Communist upsurge began in March this year and is still going on. Apart from the fact that the Kuomintang troops continue their attacks on the Eighth Route Army and the New Fourth Army in Central and North China, Mr. Chiang Kai-shek has published his anti-Communist and anti-popular book *China's Destiny*, dispatched large numbers of the Kuomintang troops defending the banks of the Yellow river to prepare a blitz on the border region, set in motion the so-called "popular organisations" throughout the country to demand the dissolution of the Communist Party, and mobilised the Kuomintang majority in the People's Political Council to accept Ho Ying-ch'in's military report calumniating the Eighth Route Army and to adopt anti-Communist resolutions, thereby turning the People's Political Council, a symbol of unity against the Japanese invaders, into the Kuomintang's private tool for concocting anti-Communist "public opinion" and preparing civil war; thus the Communist member of the Council, Comrade Tung Pi-wu, had to walk out in protest. In sum, the Kuomintang has deliberately launched these three anti-Communist upsurges. If these are not "activities which undermine the Resistance", then what are they?

The Central Committee of the Communist Party of China issued on September 22, 1937 a declaration calling for unity in face of the national calamity. It reads in part:

"To remove the pretext for the enemy's designs and to eliminate the cause of misunderstanding among all well-meaning doubters, the Central Committee of the Communist Party of China finds it necessary to express its heartfelt devotion to the cause of national liberation. Therefore it

solemnly reiterates the following to the whole nation:
1. That the Three People's Principles of Dr. Sun Yat-sen
being what China needs today, our Party pledges itself to
fight for their complete realisation; 2. That the Communist
Party will discontinue completely its policy of insurrections
aimed at overthrowing the Kuomintang régime and its
policy of forcible confiscation of the land of the landlords;
3. That the present Red government will be reorganised as
the democratic government of the special district to facilitate
the unification of political power throughout the country;
4. That the Red Army will change its name and designation,
will be reorganised as the National Revolutionary Army
and placed under the command of the Military Council of
the National Government and will be ready for orders to
march to the anti-Japanese front to carry out its duty."

We have completely fulfilled these four pledges; neither
Mr. Chiang Kai-shek nor any other Kuomintang people can
charge us with having defaulted on any of them. In the first
place, all the policies the Communist Party has carried out in
the Shensi-Kansu-Ningsia border region and all the anti-
Japanese base areas in the enemy's rear correspond to the
policies of Dr. Sun Yat-sen's Three People's Principles; there
is not a single policy that runs counter to those principles.
Secondly, on the condition that the Kuomintang does not
capitulate to the national enemy, disrupt the Kuomintang-
Communist co-operation or start an anti-Communist civil war,
we will always adhere to our pledge of not seeking to overthrow
the Kuomintang régime or confiscate the land of the landlords
by force. We adhered to it in the past, we are doing so at
present and we shall do so in the future. This means that only
if the Kuomintang should capitulate to the enemy, disrupt
co-operation and prosecute civil war should we be compelled
to cease carrying out our pledge, that is, only then should we
find it impossible to fulfil it. Thirdly, the original Red government was reorganised as early as the first year of the Anti-
Japanese War, and the "tripartite system" of democratic
government has been already put into effect, though the
Kuomintang has not yet fulfilled its promise of giving recognition to the Shensi-Kansu-Ningsia border region and,

furthermore, has accused us of setting up a "feudal independent régime". Mr. Chiang Kai-shek and the Kuomintang people ought to know that such a status of the Shensi-Kansu-Ningsia border region and all other anti-Japanese base areas to which the Kuomintang government has refused recognition, the status of what they call "independent régime", is not what we want but has entirely been forced upon us by them. They have broken their promise, refused to recognise what they pledged themselves to recognise, refused recognition of this democratic system, while accusing us of setting up an "independent régime" —what logic is all this? Day in day out we have asked for their recognition, but they persist in refusing recognition—which side should be held responsible for this? In *China's Destiny*, even Mr. Chiang Kai-shek, in his capacity as the *tsungts'ai* of the Kuomintang and the man at the helm in the Kuomintang government, becomes scurrilous about the "independent régime" without showing the slightest sense of his own responsibility—what justification is there for this? Availing ourselves of the occasion of the Eleventh Plenary Session of the Kuomintang's Central Executive Committee at which Mr. Chiang Kai-shek again demands that we fulfil our pledge, we now demand that he fulfils his: we ask him to give legel recognition to the Shensi-Kansu-Ningsia border region, where the Principle of Democracy has already been put into effect, and all democratic anti-Japanese base areas in the enemy's rear. If the Kuomintang should persist in the policy of non-recognition, that would mean it would force us to continue the "independent régime", and the responsibility will, as in the past, rest entirely on the Kuomintang and not on us. Fourthly, it is long since "the Red Army" changed its "name and designation", underwent "reorganisation as the National Revolutionary Army" and came "under the command of the Military Council of the National Government"; this pledge we have long fulfilled. Only the New Fourth Army of the National Revolutionary Army remains directly under the command of the Central Committee of the Communist Party instead of the Military Council of the National Government, because on January 17, 1941 the Military Council of the National Government issued a counter-revolutionary order which undermined the Resistance and endangers the state, declaring the New Fourth Army to be a "rebels' army" and "disbanding" it and moreover subjecting the army to daily attacks of the Kuomintang troops. But this army has not only all along fought the Japanese in Central China, but has also consistently fulfilled the first three pledges; moreover it is willing to come again "under the command of the Military Council of the National Government" and asks Mr. Chiang Kai-shek to repeal the order for its disbandment and restore its designation, so that it can fulfil the fourth pledge.

Besides the above-mentioned points, the documents concerning the Communist Party issued by the Eleventh Plenary Session of the Kuomintang's Central Executive Committee also say:

> "As to the other problems, since the present session has resolved that within one year after the conclusion of the war the national assembly should be convoked and the constitution drawn up and promulgated, they can be raised at the national assembly for discussion and solution."

The "other problems" are: abolition of the Kuomintang dictatorship, abolition of the fascist secret service, realisation of a nation-wide democratic government, abolition of economic control and of the exorbitant taxes and miscellaneous assessments which prevent the improvement of the people's welfare, and nation-wide implementation of the agrarian policy of reducing rent and interest as well as the economic policy of helping medium and small-scale industries and improving the workers' living conditions. In our declaration calling for unity in face of national calamity on September 22, 1937, we said:

> "A democratic government should be set up and a national assembly convoked to draw up a constitution and make policies for national salvation. To enable the Chinese people to lead a prosperous and happy life, we must first of all give effective help to those who suffer from natural calamities, put the people's welfare on a secure basis, develop an economy for national defence, deliver the people from suffering and improve their living conditions."

Since Mr. Chiang Kai-shek made a statement on the very next day (September 23) subscribing to our declaration wholesale, he should not only ask the Communist Party to fulfil the four pledges in the declaration, but should also ask himself, the Kuomintang and the Kuomintang government to fulfil the aforesaid programme. At present Mr. Chiang Kai-shek, besides being the *Tsungts'ai* of the Kuomintang, has become the chairman of the Kuomintang government (officially called the "National Government") and ought conscientiously to put into effect the aforesaid programme for democracy and the people's welfare and make good the innumerable pledges he has made to us Communists as well as to the people throughout the country; he should never again allow any of his pledges to sink into oblivion and should not indulge himself in the use of pressure, in saying one thing and doing another. We Communists and the people throughout the country want to see deeds and are unwilling to hear any more empty words uttered to deceive us. Deeds, if there are any, are welcome; without deeds, empty words cannot deceive people for long. Our requests of Mr. Chiang Kai-shek and the Kuomintang are: to resist the Japanese to the end, to avert the danger of capitulation, to continue co-operation, to forestall the danger of civil war, to recognise the democratic government in the border region and all the anti-Japanese base areas in the enemy's rear, to reinstate the New Fourth Army, to stop the anti-Communist upsurge, to withdraw the troops 400,000 to 500,000 strong now encircling the Shensi-Kansu-Ningsia border region, to stop turning the People's Political Council into the Kuomintang's private tool for concocting anti-Communist "public opinion", to grant freedom of speech, of assembly and of association, to abolish the one-party dictatorship of the Kuomintang, to reduce rent and interest, to improve the living and working conditions of the workers, to help medium and small-scale industries, to abolish the secret service, to put an end to the fascisation of school education and to put into effect education for democracy. The majority of these requests are precisely their own pledges. If they fulfil such requests and pledges, we assure them that we will continue to fulfil our own pledge. We are willing to renew parleys at any time with the Kuomintang if only Mr. Chiang Kai-shek and the Kuomintang are willing.

In short, among the three possible orientations for the

Kuomintang, the first, that of capitulation and civil war, will lead Mr. Chiang Kai-shek and the Kuomintang to their extinction. The second, that of deceiving people with empty words so as to play for time while stealthily and steadfastly clinging to fascist dictatorship and actively preparing civil war, will not lead to their survival. Only the third, the orientation of leaving for good the wrong path of fascist dictatorship and civil war and taking the right path of realising democracy and co-operation, will lead to their survival. But up till now Mr. Chiang Kai-shek and the Kuomintang have not yet done anything to convince the people that they will orient themselves in the last direction, therefore the people throughout the country must be on the lookout for the extremely grave danger of capitulation and civil war.

All patriotic members of the Kuomintang ought to unite and forbid the Kuomintang authorities to take the first direction, stop them from continuing on the second and demand that they turn to the third.

All patriotic parties and groups and all citizens fighting against the Japanese invaders ought to unite and forbid the Kuomintang authorities to take the first direction, stop them from continuing on the second, and demand that they turn to the third.

An unprecedented great change in the world is imminent; we hope Mr. Chiang Kai-shek and the Kuomintang people know wl at to do at this turning-point of a great era; we hope all patriotic parties and groups and all patriotic people know what to do at this turning-point of a great era.

October 5, 1943

LET US GET ORGANISED

A talk at a reception given to the labour heroes of the Shensi-Kansu-Ningsia border region.

Today the Central Committee of the Communist Party is giving a reception to the labour heroes and heroines and model workers in production elected from among the peasants, from the armed forces, offices, schools and factories in the Shensi-Kansu-Ningsia border region, and I should like to say a few words on behalf of the Central Committee. What I want to say can be summed up in a few words, "Let us get organised". According to the resolutions adopted at the meeting of senior cadres convened last winter by the North-west Bureau of the Central Committee of the Chinese Communist Party, the masses of the border region—the peasants and the people in the armed forces, offices, schools and factories—have carried on a production campaign this year. Every aspect of this year's production shows great achievements and progress and gives the border region an entirely new look. Facts have fully proved that the policy adopted by the meeting of senior cadres is correct. The gist of that policy is: to get the masses organised, to mobilise and organise into a big army of labour all the forces—so far as conditions permit—of the armies, offices and schools, of the common people, all men and women, old and young, all those who can fulfil the standard quota of work or fulfil only half the quota. We have troops for fighting and troops of labour. The Eighth Route Army and the New Fourth Army are our fighting troops, but they should serve a twofold purpose, both to fight and to engage in production. We have both kinds of troops and our fighting troops can do both things; if in addition we can also do mass work, we shall certainly overcome difficulties and crush the Japanese imperialists. If the achievements of our production campaign in the border region in the past years were not great or remarkable enough to prove this conclusively, our achievements this year, as we have all seen with our own eyes, have fully proved it.

In all the armed units of the border region that have been allotted land this year, the soldiers have on the average cultivated eighteen *mou* per person, and can make or produce practically everything—foodstuffs like vegetables, meat and cooking oil; things to wear like cotton and woollen clothing, shoes and socks; shelters like caves, houses, big and small meeting halls; articles for daily use like tables, chairs, benches and stationery; and fuel like firewood, charcoal and coal. With our own hands we have attained the end of being "well-clad and well-fed". In each year every soldier needs only to spend three months in production and can devote the remaining nine months to training or fighting. Our troops depend for their pay neither on the Kuomintang government, nor on the border region government, nor on the people, but can provide for themselves. Of what great significance this innovation is to our cause of national liberation! During the past six years and a half of the War of Resistance, the enemy has carried out the policy of triple atrocity—of "burning all, killing all and looting all"—in the anti-Japanese base areas, while the Shensi-Kansu-Ningsia border region, surrounded by rings of the Kuomintang's blockade, was financially and economically in the greatest straits; if our troops could do nothing else except fight, we would never have been able to solve our problems. Now the troops of our border region have acquired skill in production and some of the troops at the front have also acquired it while others are learning. If in our Eighth Route and New Fourth Armies, so heroic and resourceful on the battlefield, every one is not only able to fight and do mass work, but is also skilled in production, we need not fear any difficulty and shall be, in the words of Mencius, "invincible under the sun".[1] Our offices and schools have also made great strides forward this year: only a small part of their expenses is paid by the government while the greater part comes from the proceeds of their own production; they have grown this year 100 per cent of the vegetables they consume as compared with 50 per cent last year; the pigs and sheep they have raised increase considerably their meat consumption and they have established many workshops for making articles of daily use. As the armed forces, offices and schools have themselves wholly or for the most part solved the problem of material supplies, less tax is collected from the people, who can therefore retain more of the fruits of their labour for their own enjoyment. As the soldiers and the civilians are alike developing production, so all are well-clad, well-fed and happy. In our factories, too, production has been stepped up, secret agents combed out and efficiency in production greatly increased. Throughout the border region, labour heroes have emerged in agriculture and industry, in schools and offices, and also in the army; we can say that production in the border region has been set on the right path. All this comes from organising the forces of the masses.

To organise the forces of the masses is one kind of policy. But is there a policy contrary to this? Yes, there is. It consists in rejecting the standpoint of the masses and refusing to rely on them or to organise them; in paying attention only to organising a handful of persons in the financial, supply or trading organisations, and neglecting the broad masses in the villages, the armed forces, offices, schools and factories; and in thinking that economic work is not a broad movement or a struggle on a broad front, but merely an expedient for meeting fiscal deficits. This is the other kind of policy, and a wrong policy. The Shensi-Kansu-Ningsia border region pursued this policy in the past, but after it had been repeatedly criticised throughout all these years, especially after the senior cadres' meeting last year and the mass movement this year, the number of people entertaining this wrong notion has probably dwindled. In the base areas of North and Central China, where bitter fighting is taking place and the leading bodies have not paid enough heed to this matter, the production movement of the masses has not yet developed extensively. But after the directive of the Central Committee of October 1[2] this year, preparations have been made in various places to start the movement next year. Conditions at the front are more difficult than those in the border region, because there is not only bitter fighting but also, in many places, serious famine. Nevertheless, in order to support the war, to cope with the enemy's policy of "triple atrocity" and to relieve famine, we have to mobilise everyone in the Party, government, army and the civilian population to combat the enemy on the one hand and to engage in production on the other. As to production at the front, with the experiences of the past years and the ideological, organisational and material preparations this winter, a wide-spread movement can and must be started next year. Under the conditions in the front-line areas it is not yet possible for the people there to become "well-clad and well-fed", but perfectly possible and in fact necessary that they should "overcome difficulties with their own hands".

At present, the most important form in which we should organise the masses along economic lines is the co-operative. Although one need not mechanically attach the name of co-operative to all branches of production of the masses in our armed forces, offices and schools, yet such productive activities of the masses carried on under a centralised leadership with the aim of satisfying the material wants of certain depart-ments, units or individuals by means of mutual help and joint labour, are really of the nature of co-operatives. They form a kind of co-operative.

For thousands of years a system of individual production has prevailed among the peasant masses, under which a family or a household makes a productive unit; this scattered, individual form of production was the economic foundation of feudal rule and has plunged the peasants into perpetual poverty. The only way to change this state of affairs is gradual collectivisation, and the only way to bring about collectivisation is, according to Lenin, through co-operatives.[3] Here in the border region many peasants' co-operatives have been set up, but they are at present only co-operatives of a rudimentary form, and must undergo several stages of development before they can turn into co-operatives of the Soviet type known as collective farms. Our economy is new-democratic, and our co-operatives are at present still organisations of collective labour founded on the basis of individual ownership (*i.e.* the basis of private property). Such co-operatives, again, fall into several types. One of the types is organisation for mutual aid in agricultural work such as the "work-exchange teams" and "labour-for-hire teams",[4] which were once called "mutual-aid working groups" or "ploughman teams"[5] in the Red areas in Kiangsi and are now called "mutual-aid groups" in some places at the front. No matter what names they have; no matter whether they are each composed of a few, or dozens or hundreds of people, or whether they are formed entirely by people who can fulfil the standard quota of work or include some people who can fulfil only half the quota; no matter whether their mutual aid is rendered in terms of man-power, animal power or implements, or whether their members may or may not live and board together during the busy season; and no matter whether they are of a temporary or permanent nature—all are good so long as they are collective mutual-aid organisations in which the masses take part of their own free will (no compulsion whatsoever is allowed). This method of collective mutual aid was discovered by the masses themselves. We summed up such experiences of the masses once in Kiangsi and now we are doing the same in northern Shensi. Advocated at the senior cadres' meeting last year and put into practice throughout this year, the method of mutual aid in the border region is now more systematic and better developed. This year there are in the border region many work-exchange teams for collective ploughing, planting, weeding and reaping, and the harvest is double that of the last year. Having seen such substantial results, certainly more and more people will follow this practice next year. Though at present we do not expect in the next year to organise into co-operatives all the hundreds of thousands of people in the border region who can fulfil the standard quota of work or can fulfil only half the quota, this aim can be realised within a few years. The masses of women, too, should all be mobilised to take a definite part in production. All the loafers must be remoulded and take part in production so that they become good citizens. In all the anti-Japanese base areas in North and Central China such collective mutual-aid producers' co-operatives should also be extensively organised by the masses on a voluntary basis.

Besides this type of mutual-aid co-operatives in agricultural production, there are three other types of co-operatives: the synthetic co-operative, the type of co-operatives now found in southern district of Yenan, which is a combination of producers', consumers', transport (salt transportation) and credit co-operatives; the transport co-operative (salt transport team); and the handicraft co-operative.

With these four types of co-operatives of the masses of the people and the collective labour co-operatives in the armed forces, offices and schools, we can organise all the forces of the masses into a huge army of working people. This is the only road to lead the masses of the people to liberation, to lead them from poverty to prosperity and to the victory of the War of Resistance. Every Communist must learn to organise the labour of the masses. Those Communists who come from the intelligentsia must also try to learn to do so; once they have made up their minds, they can thoroughly learn it in a year or even half a year. They can help the masses to organise their production and sum up their experiences. When our comrades have acquired among other things the abilities of organising the labour of the masses, helping the peasants to make production plans on a family basis, forming work-exchange teams, salt-transport teams and synthetic co-operatives, carrying on production in the army, offices, schools and factories, conducting emulation campaigns in production, encouraging the emergence of labour heroes, organising produce exhibitions, and developing the creative power and initiative of the masses, we shall certainly be able to expel the Japanese imperialists and, together with the people of the whole country, build up a new China.

We Communists must be able to carry out any kind of work in close unity with the masses. If our Party members spend their whole life sitting indoors and never go out to weather the storm and see the world, can they be of any use to the Chinese people? No, not at all; we do not want such people to be members of our Party. We Communists ought to weather the storm and see the world, the storm being the big storm of mass struggle, and the world being the big world of mass struggle. The old saying, "Three cobblers with their wits combined would equal Chukeh Liang the master mind",[6] simply means that the masses have great creative power. Among the Chinese people there are in fact thousands upon thousands of "Chukeh Liangs", every village, every town having its own. We should go into the midst of the masses, learn from them, sum up their experiences so that these experiences will become well-defined principles and methods, and then explain them to the masses (through agitation work), and call upon the masses to put them into practice in order to solve their problems and lead them to liberation and happiness. If those comrades doing civilian work isolate themselves from the masses and do not understand their feelings or help them to organise their production and improve their living conditions; if they care only to collect "grain for national salvation" from the masses and do not know that, if 90 per cent of their energy had been devoted to helping the masses to solve the problem of producing "grain for the people's own salvation", the remaining 10 per cent of their energy would be quite enough to solve the problem of collecting "grain for national salvation", then they are contaminated by the Kuomintang's style in work and covered with the dust of bureaucracy. The Kuomintang only demands things from the people and never gives them anything in return. If a member of our Party should act likewise, then his style in work would be that of the Kuomintang, and his face would be thickly covered with the dust of bureaucracy and need a good wash in a basin of hot water. In my opinion, in all of our anti-Japanese base areas such bureaucratic style in work can be found in the civilian field as well as a number of comrades who isolate themselves from the masses because they do not view things from the standpoint of the masses. We must therefore resolutely do away with this style in work before we can unite closely with the masses.

In addition, there remains the warlordist style in work in the army, which is also the style of the Kuomintang, for the Kuomintang troops always isolate themselves from the masses. Our troops must adhere to correct principles in their relationship with the people, the government and the Party, and in the relationship between officers and men, between military work and political work and among the cadres, and should never fall into the errors of warlordism. Officers must take good care of their men, and must not be indifferent to them or inflict corporal punishment on them; the army must take good care of the people and must never encroach upon their interests; it must respect the government and the Party, and must not assert independence. Our Eighth Route and New Fourth Armies are armed forces of the people; they have always been good and are, in fact, among the best troops in the country. But in recent years the evil of warlordism has certainly infected them; some comrades in army work have become haughty and behave badly towards the soldiers, the people, the government and the Party; they never admit their own mistakes but always find fault with the comrades in civilian work, seeing their own achievements but not shortcomings, and listening only to flattery but not to criticism. Such things are found, for example, in the Shensi-Kansu-Ningsia border region. As a result of the senior cadres' meeting and the conference of military and political cadres held last year, and the campaigns to "support the government and protect the people" and "support the army" carried out in the Spring Festival[7] of this year, this tendency towards warlordism has been fundamentally curbed, but further effort is needed to clear it up. This evil is also found in the base areas of Central and North China, and the Party organisations and the armed units there must endeavour to eradicate it.

Whether it is bureaucracy in civilian work or warlordism in army work, the evils are of the same nature, namely, isolation from the masses. The overwhelming majority of our comrades are good. Comrades affected by the bad tendency can rectify it once they are subjected to criticism and their errors pointed out. But we must encourage self-criticism, face the wrong tendencies squarely and rectify them in earnest. If one does not criticise the tendency to bureaucracy in our civilian work or the tendency to warlordism in our army work, that means that one is willing to preserve the Kuomintang's style in work, to retain the dirt of bureaucracy or warlordism on his otherwise clean face, and that one is not a good Communist. If we can eliminate these two tendencies, then all tasks will proceed smoothly, including, of course, production.

The border region has taken on a totally new look, because great results have been achieved here in production, whether among the peasant masses, in the offices, armed forces, schools or factories; and because the relation between the army and the people has also been greatly improved. All this indicates that our comrades are now more firmly adhering to the standpoint of the masses and have made a great advance in uniting themselves with the masses. Nevertheless we should not be self-complacent, but must continue with self-criticism and seek further progress. In production, too, we must seek further progress. As our faces are apt to be covered with dust, we must wash them every day; as the floor is apt to be covered with dust, we must sweep it every day. Although at present the tendencies towards bureaucracy in our civilian work and warlordism in our army work have been fundamentally curbed, such evils may arise again. As we are surrounded by the forces of the Japanese imperialists and the Chinese re-actionaries cordon upon cordon, and by the undisciplined petty bourgeoisie, extremely foul dust-storms of bureaucracy and warlordism are making daily assaults on our faces. Therefore, we must never become self-complacent at our achievements. We should check our self-complacency, constantly criticise our own shortcomings, just as we should daily wash our faces or sweep the floor to remove the dust and keep them clean.

Labour heroes and heroines and model workers in production: you are the leaders of the people and have achieved a good deal in your work; I hope you too will not grow self-complacent. I hope that, when you get back to the counties of the sub-regions of Kwanchung, Lungtung, Sanpien, Suiteh and Yenan,[8] when you get back to your military units, offices, schools or factories, you will lead the people, the masses, to do better work, and first of all, organise the masses on a voluntary basis into co-operatives, organise them in greater numbers and in a better way. I hope that when you get back, you will put this into practice and propagandise it, so that by the time of next year's meeting of labour heroes and heroines you will have achieved greater results.

November 29, 1943

OUR STUDY AND THE CURRENT SITUATION

The Chinese Communist Party's central leading body and senior cadres held during 1942-4 discussions on the Party's history, especially the period from the beginning of 1931 to the end of 1934, which helped greatly to bring about within the Party ideological unity on a Marxist-Leninist basis. Although the enlarged meeting of the Political Bureau called by the Central Committee at Tsunyi, Kweichow, in January 1935 rectified the "Left" erroneous line which prevailed from early 1931 to late 1934, changed the composition of the Party's central leading body, established a leadership headed by Comrade Mao Tse-tung and set the Party's policy on the right track of Marxism-Leninism, many cadres failed to understand thoroughly the nature of the erroneous line of the past. In order to promote the cadres' understanding of Marxism-Leninism, the Central Political Bureau held during 1942-3 several discussions on the Party's history, and then directed the Party's senior cadres to hold similar discussions during 1943-4. These discussions constituted an important preparatory step for the Seventh National Congress of the Party, because they enabled the Party to achieve at that Congress an ideological and political unity unprecedented in its history. The present article was originally Comrade Mao's speech at a discussion on the subject held by senior cadres in Yenan. For the Central Committee's detailed conclusions on the mistakes of the "Left" opportunist line which held sway from early 1931 to late 1934, see the appendix to this article, *Resolution on Some Historical Problems*, adopted by the enlarged plenary session of the Central Committee of the Chinese Communist Party (the seventh plenary session since the Sixth National Congress).

I

Since last winter, the Party's senior cadres have studied the problem of the two lines in the Party's history. This study has raised considerably the political level of large numbers of senior cadres. Comrades brought up many problems in the course of this study, and the Central Political Bureau has formulated its conclusions on some of the important ones. They are as follows:

(1) On the attitude to be adopted in the study of our past experience. The Central Committee of the Party is of the opinion that we should give the cadres a perfectly clear idea of the problems in the Party's history and adopt a lenient attitude

157

in forming conclusions about those who committed mistakes in the past, so that on the one hand the cadres understand thoroughly our Party's past experience and avoid repeating their mistakes and, on the other, all comrades are united for our common endeavour. In our Party's history there were the great struggles against the erroneous lines of Ch'en Tu-hsiu and of Li Li-san, struggles which were absolutely necessary. But the methods employed therein were defective: on the one hand, the cadres were not brought to a full understanding of the causes of these errors, the conditions under which they arose or the detailed ways and means to rectify them, so much so that similar mistakes were repeated later; on the other hand, personal responsibility was over-stressed, so that we failed to unite as many people as we could for our common endeavour. We should take warning from these two defects. In taking up historical problems this time we should not stress the responsibility of certain individual comrades, but devote ourselves to the analysis of the situation in which the particular mistakes were committed, their nature, and their social, historical and ideological roots; and this should be done in the spirit of "learning from past experience in order to avoid similar mistakes in the future" and of "treating the illness in order to save the man", thereby achieving the twin objectives of clarifying our ideas and uniting our comrades. The cautious handling of cases of individual comrades without glossing over their mistakes or doing them injustice is a gauge of the growth and development of our Party.

(2) Treat all problems analytically instead of negating everything. For instance, we should make a twofold analysis of the leading line of the Central Committee during the period from the January 1931 plenary session[1] to the Tsunyi meeting.[2] On the one hand we must point out that the political as well as military tactics and the cadres policy of the central leadership during that period were essentially erroneous, while on the other we should indicate that on such fundamental issues as opposing Chiang Kai-shek and supporting the Agrarian Revolution and the Red Army's struggle there was no disagreement between ourselves and those comrades who committed mistakes. We should also be analytical on tactics. For example, on the agrarian problem, the mistake of those

comrades consisted in their "Left" policies of allotting no land to the landlords and only poor land to the rich peasants; but in the confiscation of the land of the landlords to be distributed among the peasants who have no land or only a little land they were all at one with us. Concrete analysis of concrete conditions is, Lenin said, "the most essential thing in Marxism, the living soul of Marxism".[3] Many of our comrades, lacking an analytical mind, love to form on complex matters simple conclusions, either absolutely affirmative or absolutely negative, and are unwilling to analyse and study them over and over again in order to understand them thoroughly. This defect is borne out by the fact that few analytical articles appear in our press and that analysis of problems is not yet an established practice in the Party. From now on we should remedy this situation.

(3) On discussion of the documents of the Sixth National Congress of the Party. We should point out that the line adopted by the Sixth National Congress was basically correct because it defined the character of the present revolution as bourgeois-democratic, affirmed the then situation as one between two revolutionary upsurges, criticised opportunism and adventurism, and promulgated the Ten-Point Programme.[4] It had, however, its shortcomings or mistakes, among which was the failure, for instance, to point out the unusual pro-tractedness of the Chinese revolution and the vital importance of our rural base areas. For all that, the Sixth National Congress marked a forward step in our Party's history.

(4) The legality of the Party's provisional Central Committee formed in 1931 in Shanghai and the plenary session[5] held after its formation. The present Central Committee regards both of them as legal, but it should be pointed out that the election procedure was inadequate and that the case should serve as a historical lesson.

(5) On the question of inner-Party sectarianism in the past. It should be pointed out that after a series of changes in the situation since the Tsunyi meeting, the factions that appeared in our Party and produced bad effects no longer exist. In our present study of the two lines within the Party, it is absolutely necessary to point out that these factions did exist and produce bad effects. But it is incorrect to suppose that there still exist

in the Party factions with the same erroneous political programmes and organisational forms, after all the changes
brought about by the inner-Party struggles—the Tsunyi
meeting in January 1935, the Central Committee's plenary
session (the sixth since the Sixth National Congress) in October
1938, the enlarged session of the Central Political Bureau in
September 1941,[6] the all-Party campaign to rectify the style
in work in 1942, and the study begun in the last quarter of
1943 concerning the struggles between the two lines in the
Party's history. Those old factions have now disappeared.
What is left now is only the remnant of doctrinaire and
empiricist ideology, which we can overcome by continuing
and intensifying our campaign to rectify the style in work.
What now exists in our Party to a serious degree and to an
almost universal extent is the mountain-stronghold mentality,[7]
which is a kind of bigotry. For example, there are cases of
mutual misunderstanding or disrespect and lack of unity
among comrades of different units, all of which arise from
differences—differences in the experience of struggles, in the
locality of work (such as the differences between one base area
and another, and between the enemy-occupied areas or
Kuomintang-controlled areas and the revolutionary base areas),
and in the nature of the work (such as the differences between
one section of the army and another, and those between one
kind of work and another)—and all seem quite commonplace,
but they really constitute a serious obstacle to the unity of the
Party and to the growth of its fighting capacity. The social-
historical cause of the sentiment of the mountain-stronghold
lies in the fact that the Chinese petty bourgeoisie among whom
we live is a particularly big class and that the rural base areas
where we do our work have been for long cut off from each
other by the enemy, while its subjective cause is that there is
not enough of inner-Party education. It is our important task
at present to point out these causes, to persuade our comrades
to overcome their bigotry, to enhanced their awareness, to
break down the ideological barriers that separate them, and
to promote their mutual understanding and mutual respect
so as to bring about the all-inclusive unity of the Party.

Once the whole Party attains a clear and definite understanding on the above problems, not only will our present

study programme in the Party succeed, but the Chinese revolution will also achieve victory.

II

There are two features in the present situation: one is the growth of the anti-fascist front and the decline of the fascist front, and the other is the growth of the people's forces and the decline of the anti-popular forces within the anti-fascist front. The first is quite obvious and can be easily seen. Hitler will be defeated before long and the Japanese invaders are already on the decline. The second feature is not so obvious and cannot yet be easily seen by people in general, but it is becoming every day more and more prominent in continental Europe, in Britain and the United States and in China.

In an account of the growth of the forces of the Chinese people, our Party occupies the central position.

The growth of our Party in the period of the Anti-Japanese War can be divided into three phases. The first phase began in 1937 and ended in 1940. In the first two years, *i.e.*, in 1937 and 1938, the Japanese militarists, setting store by the Kuomintang and slighting the Communist Party, employed their main forces in attacking the Kuomintang front, and adopted towards the Kuomintang a policy of military blows as the chief means with political baits for capitulation as the supplementary; to the anti-Japanese base areas under the leadership of the Communist Party, however, they paid little attention, thinking that only a handful of Communists were fighting a guerrilla war there. But after occupying Wuhan in October 1938, the Japanese imperialists began to change their policy, starting to set store by the Communist Party and to slight the Kuomintang; they changed their policy towards the Kuomintang to one of political baits for capitulation as the chief means with military blows as the supplementary, and gradually turned their main forces against the Communist Party. For they came to feel that the menace was no longer the Kuomintang but the Communist Party. In 1937 and 1938, the Kuomintang fought the Japanese more or less energetically and maintained more or less good relations with our Party and, in spite of the many restrictions it imposed, it allowed the people's anti-Japanese movement a certain latitude. Since the fall of Wuhan, however, the Kuomintang, because of its defeats in the war and its increasing hostility towards the Communist Party, began to turn reactionary, growing more and more energetic in its anti-Communist activities and more and more lethargic in its resistance to the Japanese invaders. Owing to the reverses sustained in the civil war period, the Communist Party had in 1937 only about 40,000 organised members and an army of 30,000 odd; hence it was slighted by the Japanese militarists. But by 1940 Party membership had risen to 800,000 and the army to nearly 500,000 strong; the population in the base areas, including both those paying taxes to us alone and those paying taxes to us and the Japanese,[8] totalled about 100,000,000. In a few years our Party opened such an extensive theatre of war in the liberated areas that we succeeded in drawing the Japanese main forces to our environs, stopping them from launching strategic offensives on the Kuomintang front for five years and a half, saving the Kuomintang front from a crisis and keeping up the War of Resistance. During that phase, however, some comrades of our Party erred by under-estimating the Japanese imperialists (consequently overlooking the protractedness and ruthlessness of the war and maintaining that we should chiefly carry on mobile warfare by large army formations while neglecting guerrilla warfare), pinned all their hopes on the Kuomintang, and failed to pursue soberly an independent policy (hence capitulationism towards the Kuo-mintang, and vacillation in pursuing such policies as boldly and freely arousing the masses to establish anti-Japanese democratic base areas in the enemy's rear, and considerably expanding the armies under the Party's leadership). In the meanwhile, the Party had recruited a large number of new members who were still inexperienced, and the base areas in the enemy's rear, which were all newly established, were not yet consolidated. In this phase, because of the favourable develop-ment of the general situation and the expansion of the Party and its army, many members became arrogant and got swelled heads. In this phase, however, we overcame the Right devia-tion in the Party and adopted an independent policy; and we not only dealt blows at the Japanese imperialists, established base areas and expanded the Eighth Route and the New

Fourth Armies, but also repulsed the Kuomintang's first anti-Communist upsurge.

The years 1941 and 1942 form the second phase. In order to prepare and launch the war against Britain and the United States, the Japanese imperialists, pursuing more actively the policy which they had adopted since the fall of Wuhan, i.e. the policy of concentrating their attack on the Communist Party instead of the Kuomintang, massed a good deal more of their main forces round the base areas under Communist leadership and carried out "mopping-up" operations in succession and the ruthless policy of "triple atrocity"; under the heavy blows of the enemy, our Party for two years, 1941–2, was in an extremely difficult situation. During this phase our base areas shrank in size, the population was reduced to under 50,000,000, the Eighth Route Army to about 300,000 men, the casualties among cadres were very heavy and our finance and economy were in great straits. At the same time the Kuomintang, thinking that it had been relieved, opposed our Party in a thousand and one ways, engineered a second anti-Communist upsurge and attacked us in co-ordination with the Japanese imperialists. Such difficulties, however, only served to educate us Communists and we have learnt thereby a great many things. We have learnt how to counteract the enemy's "mopping-up" campaigns, his policy of "nibbling up" our territory,[9] his campaign to "strengthen the measures for public safety",[10] his policies of "triple atrocity" and of inducing voluntary surrender; we have learnt or begun to learn the "tripartite system" of political power in the united front, the agrarian policy, the campaign to rectify the style in work in three fields,[11] the way to accomplish the task of picked troops and simplified administration, and of unifying leadership, of promoting the army's support of the government and protection of the people, of developing production, etc.; we have overcome many of our defects, including the arrogance of those who got swelled heads in the first phase. Although we suffered heavy losses during this phase, we have held our own and repulsed the Japanese invaders' offensives as well as the Kuomintang's second anti-Communist upsurge. However, the Kuomintang's anti-Communist policy and the necessity of our waging struggles against it in self-defence gave rise to a

"Left" deviation in the Party, as may be found in the excessive measures against the landlords and inattention to uniting with people outside the Party, both resulting from the supposition that the break-up of the Kuomintang-Communist co-operation was imminent. But we have also overcome this "Left" deviation. We set forth the principle of justifiability, expediency and restraint in our struggle against friction, pointed out the necessity of alliance alongside struggle, and of alliance through struggle in the united front, and preserved the Anti-Japanese National United Front in the base areas as well as throughout the country.

The third phase extends from 1943 up to the present. Our various policies have proved more efficacious than ever; in particular, the campaigns of rectifying the style in work in three fields and developing production have yielded substantial results, thereby making our Party invincible both ideologically and materially. Moreover, since last year we have learnt or begun to learn the policies of examining our cadres and of combating espionage. Under these circumstances our base areas have again expanded, and the population, including both those paying taxes to us alone and those paying taxes to us and the Japanese, has risen again to over 80,000,000, with an army of 470,000, a militia of 2,270,000 and a Party membership of over 900,000.

In 1943, the Japanese militarists made no appreciable change in their policy towards China, and continued to direct their attacks mainly upon the Communist Party. For more than three years, from 1941 to the present, over 60 per cent of the Japanese troops in China have borne down on the various anti-Japanese base areas under the leadership of our Party. In this period, the Kuomintang troops in the enemy's rear, totalling several hundred thousand, could not withstand the blows of the Japanese imperialists, and about half of them surrendered and the other half was completely annihilated, those who survived or made good their withdrawal being very small in number. As the Kuomintang troops who surrendered to the enemy have turned against us, we have to bear the additional burden of resisting over 90 per cent of the puppet troops. The Kuomintang has only to face less than 40 per cent of the Japanese forces and less than 10 per cent of the puppet troops. For five years and a half after the fall of Wuhan in October 1938 the Japanese militarists have launched no strategic offensive on the Kuomintang front; there have been only a few fairly big campaigns (like those of Chekiang-Kiangsi, of Changsha, of western Hupeh, of southern Honan and of Changteh), and even in these the Japanese, too, made only very brief sorties or onslaughts while focusing their attention on the anti-Japanese base areas under the leadership of our Party. This being the case, the Kuomintang adopted a policy of "going into the mountains" and watching others fight, exchanging a few blows with the enemy when he came and standing by with folded arms when he went away. In 1943 the Kuomintang became even more reactionary in its domestic policy and instigated the third anti-Communist upsurge, but we repulsed it as before.

In 1943 and up to this spring the Japanese invaders began to suffer reverses in the Pacific theatre, the American counter-offensive was intensified and in the West Hitler was tottering under the violent assaults of the Soviet Red Army. To avert their doom the Japanese imperialists sought complete control over the Peiping-Hankow[12] and Hankow-Canton railways and, as their policy of baiting for capitulation had not yet borne fruit, found it necessary to deal the Kuomintang in Chungking another blow; hence their plan for major offensives on the Kuomintang front this year. The campaign in Honan[13] has been going on for over a month. The enemy, with a few divisions, has routed without battle several hundred thousand Kuomintang troops; only the troops of miscellaneous brands have put up a fight. Under T'ang En-po's command utter disorder prevails, officers isolating themselves from men and the troops from the people, and the army has suffered a loss of more than two-thirds of its strength. The divisions dispatched by Hu Tsung-nan to Honan collapsed at the first encounter with the enemy. All this is entirely due to the Kuomintang's reckless pursuit of reactionary policies in the past years. In the five years and a half since the fall of Wuhan, the theatre of war of the Communist-led liberated areas has borne the burden of combating the main forces of the enemy and the puppet régime; though from now on some changes may set in, they can only be of a temporary nature because the Kuomintang, rendered utterly degenerate by its reactionary policy for the last five years and six months of passive resistance to Japan but active opposition to the Communists, will suffer serious reverses, and then the responsibility of our Party to combat the enemy and his puppets will be further increased. For five years and six months the Kuomintang has been standing by with folded arms, completely deprived of fighting capacity. For five years and six months the Communist Party has carried on hard combat and bitter struggle and thus increased its fighting capacity. Such a situation will determine China's destiny.

Comrades can see for themselves that in the seven years from July 1937 to the present the people's democratic forces under the leadership of our Party have gone through the three phases of rising, falling and rising again. Our Party has beaten off the ferocious attacks of the Japanese invaders, established extensive revolutionary base areas, expanded greatly the Party and its army, repulsed three times the Kuomintang's large-scale anti-Communist upsurge, overcome erroneous Right and "Left" ideologies and acquired much valuable experience. This is a summary of our work in the past seven years.

Our task at present is to prepare ourselves to shoulder an even greater responsibility than in the past. We should prepare to drive out the Japanese invaders from China under any circumstances. To enable our Party to shoulder this responsibility we must further develop and consolidate our Party, our army and our base areas, attend to our work in the big cities and along main communication lines and attach as much importance to our work in the cities as to that in the base areas.

Great progress was made in our work in the base areas during the first phase, but the achievements were not consolidated; hence in the second phase the base areas shrank under the severe blows of the enemy. In the second phase all anti-Japanese base areas under our Party's leadership went through a process of severe steeling and came out much better than they had been in the first phase; the cadres and Party members made great advances in their ideology and in their under-standing of policies, and learnt to do many more things. But the attainment of ideological unity and the study of policies still requires time, and we have still many things to learn. Our Party is not yet sufficiently strong, not yet sufficiently unified or consolidated and consequently not yet able to shoulder a responsibility greater than that of the present. Our job is further to develop and consolidate our Party, our army and our base areas as the War of Resistance goes on, and that is the first item in our ideological and material preparation necessary for shouldering gigantic responsibilities in the future. Without such an item we cannot drive out the Japanese invaders or liberate the whole of China.

Our work in the big cities and along main communication lines has all along been deficient. If we still neglect to win over the masses of tens of millions of workers and other inhabitants in the big cities and communication centres now under the oppression of Japanese imperialism, rally them round our Party and prepare them for armed insurrection, our army and rural base areas will meet with all sorts of difficulties for lack of co-ordination with the cities. For more than ten years we have lived in the countryside and it has been necessary to promote an intimate understanding of the conditions in the countryside and the building of rural base areas. For over ten years the task of preparing insurrections in the cities which was set by the Sixth National Congress was not and could not be carried out. The situation is now different, and the decision of the Sixth National Congress is to be carried out after the Seventh National Congress. Our Party will soon hold its Seventh National Congress, at which discussions will be held on the questions of strengthening our work in the cities and winning victory throughout the country.

The industrial conference of the Shensi-Kansu-Ningsia border region now in session is of great significance. Factory workers in the border region numbered only 700 in 1937, increased to 7,000 in 1942, and now total 12,000. These figures are not to be taken lightly. We must learn, while we are still in the base areas, how to manage industry and commerce and the communications in the big cities, or else we shall be at a loss when the time comes. To prepare armed insurrection in the big cities and communication centres and to learn how to manage industry and commerce form, therefore, the second item in our indispensable ideological and material preparation: Without it, we still cannot drive out the Japanese invaders or bring about the complete liberation of China.

III

In order to win more victories we urge the Party's cadres to "lay down the bundle" and "set the brain working". To "lay down the bundle" means to relieve ourselves of the mental burden. Things may easily become our burden or bundle if we hold on to them blindly without critical awareness. For instance, having committed a mistake, one may despair of oneself and become dispirited; on the other hand, having committed no mistakes at all, one may pique oneself on that account and thus become conceited. Failure in work may cause pessimism and depression, while success in work may engender arrogance and haughtiness. Comrades with a short record of struggle may shirk responsibilities because of the shortness of their record, while veterans with a long record of struggle may become self-opinionated because of their long record. Pluming themselves on their glorious class origin, workers and peasants may look down upon intellectuals, while intellectuals may take pride in their stock of knowledge in certain fields and despise workers and peasants. Expertise of any kind can become the wherewithal for a person to be arrogant and contemptuous towards others. Even age can be the source of self-conceit; the young, because of their cleverness and efficiency, may despise the old, while the old, because of their rich experience, may despise the young. All such things, if one is not critically aware of them, may become a burden or a bundle. An important reason why some comrades, taking their ease in their high positions and isolating themselves from the masses, commit mistakes repeatedly is that they are burdened with such bundles. Thus, to take stock of the bundles on our backs, to get rid of them and become free spiritually is one of the prerequisites for our maintaining close contact with the masses and making fewer mistakes. There have been several instances in the past in which our Party succumbed to pride and consequently incurred great damage. The first instance occurred in the earlier part of 1927. The Northern Expedition Army had reached Wuhan and some comrades became so proud and overweening that they forgot that the Kuomintang was getting ready to spring an attack on us. The result was the mistake of Ch'en Tu-hsiu's line which brought defeat to the revolution. The second instance occurred in 1930. The Red Army took advantage of the big war between Chiang Kai-shek on the one hand and Yen Hsi-shan and Feng Yu-hsiang on the other,[14] and scored a few victories; again some comrades became proud and overweening. The result was the mistake of Li Li-san's line which caused losses to the revolutionary forces. The third instance occurred in 1931. The Red Army had smashed the third campaign of "encirclement and annihilation", and immediately the people throughout the country, faced with the Japanese invasion, started the stirring, heroic anti-Japanese movement; again some comrades became proud and overweening. The result was an even more serious mistake of political line which cost us about 90 per cent of the revolutionary forces which we had built up with so much toil. The fourth instance occurred in 1938. The War of Resistance had been set afoot and the united front successfully established; again some comrades became proud and overweening and the result was a mistake more or less similar to Ch'en Tu-hsiu's line. This time, revolutionary work suffered serious damage in all places where the effects of these comrades' erroneous ideas were most pronounced. Comrades throughout the Party should take warning from these instances of pride and error. We have recently issued a reprint of Kuo Mo-jo's essay on Li Tzu-ch'eng[15] in order to warn comrades against repeating the mistake of feeling proud at the moment of success.

To "set the brain working" means to become adept in the use of the organ of thinking. Some people have no bundles on their backs and are good at keeping in close contact with the masses, yet they fail to accomplish any work because they do not know how to reflect and are unwilling to use their brains to think much and to think hard. Others refuse to use their brains because they have bundles on their backs which weigh down their intellect. Lenin and Stalin often exhort people to learn to use their brains, and we shall advise the same. The special function of such an organ as the brain is to think. Mencius said, "To the mind belongs the office of thinking".[16] He has given a correct definition of the function of the brain. We must use our brains to think carefully over everything. As the common saying goes, "Knit the brows and some stratagem flashes upon the mind". In other words, wisdom comes after much thought. To remove the profound mental blindness prevalent among our Party members, we must encourage thinking, learn the method of analysis and cultivate the habit of analysis. In our Party, we still have far too little of this habit. Once we lay down our bundles and set the brain working, we, light of foot and quick in brain, shall be sure of victory.

April 12, 1944

APPENDIX: RESOLUTION ON SOME QUESTIONS IN THE HISTORY OF OUR PARTY

ADOPTED BY THE ENLARGED PLENARY SESSION OF THE CENTRAL COMMITTEE OF THE CHINESE COMMUNIST PARTY (THE SEVENTH SINCE THE SIXTH NATIONAL CONGRESS) ON APRIL 20, 1945

I

Ever since its birth in 1921, the Chinese Communist Party has set as the guiding principle for all its work the integration of the universal truth of Marxism-Leninism with the actual practice of the Chinese revolution, and Comrade Mao Tse-tung's theory of and his practical work in the Chinese revolution form an example of such integration. The founding of our Party immediately ushered in a new stage in the Chinese revolution which, as defined by Comrade Mao Tse-tung, is the stage of new-democratic revolution. In the twenty-four years (1921–45) of the struggle to realise New Democracy, throughout the three historical periods of the First Great Revolution, the Agrarian Revolution and the Anti-Japanese War, our Party consistently and unswervingly led the broad masses of the Chinese people to wage, amid untold difficulties and with surpassing bravery, revolutionary struggles against imperialism and feudalism, the enemies of the Chinese people, and scored great achievements and acquired rich experience. In the course of the struggles, Comrade Mao Tse-tung emerged from the Party as its leader. On behalf of the Chinese proletariat and the Chinese people, Comrade Mao Tse-tung has creatively applied human wisdom of the highest order, the scientific theory of Marxism-Leninism, to the big, semi-feudal and semi-colonial country of China whose principal section of the masses is the peasantry, whose immediate task is to fight against imperialism and feudalism, whose area is vast and population enormous, whose situation is extremely complicated and whose struggles are extremely hard; and he has thus brilliantly developed Lenin's and Stalin's teachings on the revolutionary movement in the colonial and semi-colonial countries as well as Stalin's teachings on the Chinese revolution. It is only because the Party has strictly adhered to the correct line of Marxism-Leninism and fought victoriously against all erroneous ideas opposed to this line, that it has scored great achievements in the three periods of the revolution, secured such an unprecedented ideological, political and organisational unity and solidarity, and developed into such a gigantic revolutionary force; and, possessing a membership of over 1,200,000 and exercising its leadership over the Chinese liberated areas with a population of nearly 100,000,000 and an army of nearly 1,000,000, it has become the great rallying centre of the whole people in the Anti-Japanese War and in the case of liberation.

II

In the first period of China's new-democratic revolution, *i.e.* during 1921–7, and especially during 1924–7, thanks to the correct guidance of the Communist International and to the influence it exerted, and to the impulse given and the agitation and the organisational work done under the Chinese Communist Party's correct leadership, the great anti-imperialist and anti-feudal revolution of the Chinese people made rapid progress and scored great victories. During this great revolution the entire membership of the Party undertook stupendous revolutionary work, developed movements of the workers, youth and peasants through the country, gave impetus and rendered assistance to the reorganisation of the Kuomintang and the founding of the National Revolutionary Army, supplied political backbone to the Eastern Campaign[1] and the Northern Expedition, gave •leadership to the great national struggle against imperialism and feudalism, and thus wrote a chapter of dazzling glory in the history of the Chinese revolution. Nevertheless, the revolution ended in defeat because the reactionary clique in the Kuomintang, then our ally, betrayed it in 1927; because the combined force of that clique and the imperialists was very strong; and particularly because in the concluding period of the revolution (about six months) the Right viewpoint in our Party, with Ch'en Tu-hsiu as its exponent, developed into a line of capitulation, and the Party's leading body, in thrall to this view, refused to carry out the wise directives of the Communist International and Comrade Stalin on the one hand and rejected the correct proposals of Comrade Mao Tse-tung and other comrades on the other, with the result that when the Kuomintang turned against the revolution and launched an assault on the people, our Party and the people failed to organise an effective resistance.

In the ten years from the defeat of the revolution in 1927 to the outbreak of the Anti-Japanese War in 1937, the Chinese Communist Party, and it alone, despite the counter-revolutionary reign of intense terror, continued with perfect solidarity to hold aloft the great banner of anti-imperialism and anti-feudalism and led the broad masses of workers, peasants, soldiers, revolutionary intellectuals and other revolutionary people to wage great political, military and ideological struggles. In the course of these struggles it built up the Red Army, established governments of the councils of workers', peasants' and soldiers' representatives, set up revolutionary bases, allotted land to the poor peasants and resisted the attacks of the reactionary Kuomintang government and, after September 18, 1931, the aggression of the Japanese imperialists, so that the Chinese people's national and social liberation achieved great success along the lines of New Democracy. With the same perfect solidarity the Party fought against the counter-revolutionary activities of the Trotskyite Ch'en Tu-hsiu clique[2] and of Lo Chang-lung[3] and Chang Kuo-t'ao,[4] who all aimed at splitting the Party and betraying it, and thus ensured its own unity on the basis of the general principles of Marxism-Leninism. This general line of our Party and the militant fight for its realisation over these ten years were entirely correct and necessary. Countless members of the Party, countless people and non-Party revolutionaries heroically carried on revolutionary struggles on divers fronts, never yielding or flinching and never hesitating to step into the breach left by fallen comrades; they have won immortality in the nation's history by their fighting spirit and self-sacrifice. Without all this, the Anti-Japanese War could not have been started, and, even though started, it could not have been continued to victory without such a mainstay as the Chinese Communist Party well-seasoned in a people's war. This is beyond any doubt.

We rejoice especially in the fact that in these ten years our Party, with Comrade Mao Tse-tung as its representative, took a big stride forward in the creative application of the revolutionary theories of Marx, Engels, Lenin and Stalin to the actual conditions in China. Towards the end of the Agrarian Revolutionary War, Comrade Mao Tse-tung's leadership was at last definitely established in the Central Committee and throughout the Party. This was the Chinese Communist Party's greatest achievement in the period and is the surest guarantee of the liberation of the Chinese people.

We must point out, however, that in these ten years our Party, as well as achieving great successes, also committed a number of mistakes. The gravest of all was the "Left" deviation in the political, military and organisational lines in the period from the Central Committee's plenary session (the fourth since the Sixth National Congress) in January 1931 to the enlarged meeting of the Central Political Bureau (the Tsunyi meeting) in January 1935. This mistake caused serious losses to our Party and the Chinese revolution.

In order to take stock of the historical lessons of the Chinese revolution, "to learn from past experience in order to avoid similar mistakes in the future and to treat the illness in order to save the man", and to make "the overturning of the cart in front a lesson for the cart behind"; in order to consolidate the entire membership on the ideological basis of Marxism-Leninism and unite it like a family living in harmony and a solid piece of steel to fight for complete victory in the Anti-Japanese War and the total liberation of the Chinese people; this enlarged plenary session of the Central Committee considers it profitable and necessary to draw up proper conclusions on certain questions in the Party's history in these ten years, particularly on the leading line of the Central Committee during the period from its plenary session in January 1931 (the fourth since the Sixth National Congress) up to the Tsunyi meeting.

III

After the defeat of the revolution in 1927, both "Left" and Right deviations occurred in our Party.

Pessimistic about the future of the revolution, a handful of capitulators in the First Great Revolution, with Ch'en Tu-hsiu as their representative, eventually became liquidationists. Adopting the reactionary standpoint of Trotskyism, they held that the Chinese bourgeoisie had already won victory over the imperialist and feudal forces after the revolution in 1927, that its rule over the people had been stabilised, and that capitalism was already playing a dominant role in Chinese society and was developing peacefully; and they therefore dogmatically asserted that the Chinese bourgeois-democratic revolution had already been concluded, that the Chinese proletariat must postpone the "socialist revolution" to a future date, and that for the time being it could only carry on so-called legal movements centring round the slogan for a "National Congress" and should give up its revolutionary movement; hence they opposed all revolutionary struggles waged by the Party and slandered the Red Army movement as a "movement of roving insurgents". They not only rejected the Party's advice to abandon such an opportunist, liquidationist anti-Party viewpoint, but even went to the length of forming an anti-Party faction in league with the reactionary Trotskyites; and as a result they had to be expelled from the Party and subsequently degenerated into counter-revolutionaries.

On the other hand, the ultra-revolutionism of the petty bourgeoisie, aggravated by hatred of the Kuomintang's policy of massacre and indignation at Ch'en Tu-hsiu's capitulationism, also found its expression in the Party and led to a rapid rise of "Left" sentiment. This sentiment reared its head as early as the emergency conference of the Central Committee on August 7, 1927. The August 7 meeting achieved something in the history of the Party. At a critical moment of the Chinese revolution, it resolutely rectified the capitulationism of Ch'en Tu-hsiu and brought it to an end, it laid down the general line of carrying on the Agrarian Revolution and putting up armed resistance to the Kuomintang reactionaries' policy of massacre, and it rallied the Party and the masses of the people to continue their revolutionary struggle—all this was correct and constituted the main feature of the meeting. While combating the Right deviation, however, the August 7 meeting paved the way for a "Left" deviation. Politically, it failed to realise that at that time, according to the different conditions in different areas, it should have organised either proper counter-attacks or necessary tactical retreats, so that revolutionary positions could be preserved and revolutionary forces mustered in a planned manner; on the contrary, it tolerated and even fostered tendencies towards adventurism and authoritarianism (especially as regards forcing the workers to strike). Organisationally, it initiated an excessive, sectarian inner-Party struggle, overstressed the importance of the working-class origin of leading cadres to the exclusion of other considerations, and brought about a serious state of extreme democratisation in the Party. At the enlarged meeting of the Central Committee in November 1927, this "Left" sentiment, which continued to rise after the August 7 meeting, became a "Left" line of reckless action (adventurism) and for the first time brought the "Left" line to a dominant position in the Party's central leading body. The advocates of reckless action characterised the Chinese revolution as a "permanent revolution" (confusing the democratic revolution with the socialist revolution) and the situation of the Chinese revolution as a "permanent upsurge" (denying the defeat of the revolution in 1927), and consequently, heedless of the fact that the enemy was powerful and the people had just suffered defeat in the revolution, they still refused to organise an orderly retreat, but commanded handfuls of Party members and the Party's followers to undertake local insurrections all over the country without the slightest hope of success. Along with political adventurism, the organisational policy of sectarian persecution also developed. However, as this erroneous line had from the very beginning met with just criticism and objection on the part of Comrade Mao Tse-tung and many comrades working in the White areas, and as it had caused a great deal of damage in practical work, it was abandoned in many places at the beginning of 1928; in April (less than six months from its start) it virtually came to an end in all practical work throughout the country.

The line of the Party's Sixth National Congress, held in July 1928, was basically correct. It correctly asserted that Chinese society was a semi-feudal and semi-colonial society, pointed out that none of the basic contradictions which give rise to the contemporary Chinese revolution had been resolved, and therefore affirmed that the Chinese revolution in the present stage remained a bourgeois-democratic revolution and proclaimed a ten-point programme for the democratic revolution. It correctly pointed out that the political situation of that time was one lying between two revolutionary upsurges, that the revolution was uneven in its development, and that the general task of the Party consisted not in launching attacks or organising insurrection but in winning over the masses. It carried out a two-front struggle in refuting both Right Ch'en Tu-hsiu-ism and "Left" adventurism, and pointed out particularly that the main danger in the Party consisted of reckless action, military adventurism and authoritarianism, all of which result in isolation from the masses. All this was completely necessary. But the Sixth National Congress also had its defects and made certain mistakes. It failed to work out a correct estimate as well as a correct policy regarding the double-faced character of the intermediate classes and the internal contradictions among the reactionary forces, and failed to reach an adequate understanding either on the tactics of an orderly retreat necessary for the Party after the setback of the Great Revolution or on the importance of rural bases and the protractedness of the democratic revolution. Although these defects and mistakes prevented a thorough rectification of the "Left" ideas existing since the August 7 meeting, which were to become even more pronounced and extremely widespread in the "Left" line of a later period, they in no way eclipsed the correctness of the Congress in its main aspect. For some time after the Congress the Party's work was fruitful. During this period, Comrade Mao Tse-tung not only developed in practical work the correct aspect of the line of the Congress and found correct solutions to many problems which the Congress had not solved or correctly solved, but also, in the theoretical field, provided in a more specific and comprehensive way the scientific basis of Marxism-Leninism for the orientation of the Chinese revolution. Under his guidance and influence, the Red Army movement eventually developed into an important political factor in the nation. In the White areas the Party organisations were revived and their work resumed to a certain extent.

But, during the second half of 1929 and the first half of 1930, certain "Left" ideas and policies surviving in the Party gained some ground. They culminated into the second "Left" line as

soon as events turned in favour of the revolution. Spurred on
by the domestic situation after war broke out in May 1930
between Chiang Kai-shek on the one side and Feng Yu-hsiang
and Yen Hsi-shan on the other, the Central Political Bureau
of the Party, with Comrade Li Li-san at its head, adopted on
June 11 the "Left" resolution of "The New Revolutionary
Upsurge and the Winning of Victory First in One or Several
Provinces", whereupon for the second time the "Left" line
prevailed in the leading body of the Party. This erroneous line
(Li Li-san's line) came into being because Comrade Li Li-san
and others, denying the necessity for the revolution being fully
prepared for by the growth of its own organisational strength,
thought that "the masses want big actions, not small ones",
and consequently believed that, since the warlords were fighting incessantly among themselves while the Red Army movement was beginning to make progress and our work in the
White areas was being resumed, conditions were already ripe
for "big actions" (armed insurrections) throughout the country.
It came into being also because these comrades, denying the
uneven development of the Chinese revolution, considered that
the revolutionary crisis was mounting in all parts of the country
at the same rate, that preparations for immediate insurrections
must be made throughout the country and that, in particular,
the major cities should take the lead so as to form centres
of the revolutionary upsurge, and hence slanderously labelled
as "absolutely erroneous" and "localism and conservatism of
peasant ideology" Comrade Mao Tse-tung's idea that for a
long time we should employ our main forces to create rural
bases, surround the cities from the countryside and use the bases
to expedite the nation-wide revolutionary upsurge. It came
into being because these comrades, denying the uneven
development of the world revolution, thought that the general
outbreak of the Chinese revolution would inevitably lead to the
general outbreak of the world revolution, and that that alone
would make the victory of the Chinese revolution possible.
Finally it came into being because these comrades, denying the
protracted nature of China's bourgeois-democratic revolution,
held that as soon as we had won victory in one or several
provinces the transition to the socialist revolution would begin,
and consequently formulated a number of untimely "Left"

policies. Misled by these erroneous ideas, the leaders of Li Li-san's line mapped out an adventurist plan for organising armed uprisings in major cities throughout the country and concentrating all the nation's Red Army forces for attacking them; later on they merged the leading bodies at each level of the Party, the Youth League and the trade unions, into an action committee to prepare armed insurrections, thus bringing all regular work to a standstill. In making and executing these erroneous decisions, Comrade Li Li-san rejected the correct criticisms and suggestions of many comrades, stressed the fight against the so-called Right deviation in the Party and, under the slogan of combating the Right deviation, unjustly persecuted cadres who disagreed with him, thus giving rise to inner-Party sectarianism. Hence Li Li-san's line took a more full-fledged form than the first "Left" line.

But the reign of Li Li-san's line in the Party was also short-lived (less than four months). Since the Party and the revolutionary forces invariably suffered losses wherever the line was put into practice, great numbers of cadres and Party members demanded its rectification. Comrade Mao Tse-tung, in particular, never supported it but, on the contrary, rectified with much patience the "Left" mistakes found in the First Front Army of the Red Army,[5] with the result that in this period the Army, stationed in the revolutionary base in Kiangsi, not only incurred no losses but also expanded its ranks by utilising the favourable situation arising from the war of Chiang Kai-shek, Feng Yu-hsiang and Yen Hsi-shan and successfully smashed the enemy's first campaign of "encirclement and annihilation" in late 1930 and early 1931. With a few exceptions the same was true of the Red Army forces in other revolutionary bases. Many comrades engaged in practical work also voiced their opposition to Li's line through organisational channels.

In putting an end to the execution of Li's line, an active role was played by the Central Committee's plenary session (the third since the Sixth National Congress) held in September 1930 and the Central Committee formed by this session. Although the documents of the plenary session revealed a conciliatory and compromising attitude towards the line (*e.g.* regarding it not as a wrong line but only as a piece of "wrong tactics"), and although the plenary session repeated the mistakes of sectarianism in organisation, yet, as it rectified the line's extremely "Left" appraisal of the revolutionary situation in China, as it put an end to the execution of the plan of organising insurrections throughout the country and concentrating all the nation's Red Army forces to attack major cities, and as it re-established the Party, the Youth League and the trade unions as independent organisations carrying on their usual activities, it did bring to an end the characteristic mistakes of the line. At the plenary session Comrade Li Li-san admitted the mistakes pointed out to him and subsequently left his leading post in the Central Committee. After the plenary session, in the supplementary resolution of November and Circular No. 96 of December 1930, the Central Committee further pointed out that the line of Comrade Li Li-san and his supporters was wrong and that the conciliatory attitude of the plenary session was wrong too. True, neither during nor after this plenary session did the Central Committee undertake to liquidate and rectify the ideological essence of Li's line, and consequently certain "Left" ideas and policies that had existed since the meeting of August 7, 1927, and especially since 1929, constituted a serious problem at the session and after it. However, since both during this plenary session and after it the Central Committee did take the positive measures mentioned above to put an end to Li Li-san's line, all comrades in the Party should, on the basis of these measures, have made further efforts to bring the campaign against the "Left" deviation to its completion.

But at this juncture a number of comrades who had no experience in actual revolutionary struggle and were victims of "Left" doctrinairism, with Comrade Ch'en Shao-yu (Wang Ming) at their head, rose to oppose the Central Committee after the plenary session under the banners "Combat Li Li-san's line" and "Combat the line of conciliation", adopting a stand even more sectarian than that of Li Li-san. They waged struggles not to help the Central Committee to liquidate thoroughly the ideological essence of Li Li-san's line, or the "Left" ideas and policies that had existed and remained unrectified since the August 7 meeting of 1927 and particularly since 1929, but, as indicated in Comrade Ch'en Shao-yu's pamphlet *The Two Lines—A Struggle for the Further Bolshevisation of the Chinese Communist Party*, actually to put forward a new political programme which in one way or another continued, restored and developed in a fresh form Li Li-san's line as well as other "Left" ideas and policies. In this manner, "Left" ideas were revived in the Party and developed into a new "Left" line.

Although this new "Left" line initiated by Comrade Ch'en Shao-yu also criticised the "Left" mistakes of Li Li-san's line and the erroneous conciliatory attitude of the Central Committee's plenary session (the third since the Sixth National Congress), its chief characteristic was that it criticised in the main the Right deviation of Li Li-san's line, and blamed the plenary session for "doing nothing to expose or combat the persistent Right opportunist theory and practice of Li Li-san's line", and censured Circular No. 96 for its failure to note that "the Right deviation remains the principal danger in the Party at present". With regard to the nature of society and the class relations in China, the new "Left" line exaggerated the weight of capitalism in China's economy, over-stressed the significance of fighting the capitalists and rich peasants and of "the factors of socialist revolution" in the present stage of the Chinese revolution and denied the existence of an intermediate camp or third group. With regard to the revolutionary situation and the tasks of the Party, it continued to emphasise the nation-wide "revolutionary upsurge" and the need of a national "line of offensive" for the Party, believing that a "situation of immediate revolution" would soon prevail in one or several important provinces, including their major cities. It slanderously declared from a "Left" viewpoint that there was as yet no "genuine" Red Army or government of councils of workers', peasants' and soldiers' representatives in China, and announced with particular emphasis that the main danger in the Party lay in the so-called "Right opportunism", "opportunism in practical work" and "the line of rich peasants". Organisationally, the exponents of this new "Left" line brought about a serious crisis in the Party because they violated Party discipline, refused to accept assignments from the Party and wrongly formed a number of comrades into a group to carry out factional activities against the Central Committee and called upon the Party membership to set up a provisional central leading body; they also demanded "the reform and replenishment of the leading bodies at all levels" by "militant cadres" who would "actively support and carry out" their line. Thus, although the new "Left" line did not stand for insurrections in major cities, nor did it, for some time, call for concentrating the Red Army to attack these cities, yet, compared to the "Left" deviation of Li Li-san's line, it was on the whole even more resolute, more overpowering, more fully "armed with theory" and more full-fledged in form.

Owing to the pressure applied from all directions by the doctrinaire sectarians with Comrade Ch'en Shao-yu at their head, and to the concessions and support accorded to them by some comrades in the Central Committee who were victims of empiricism, the Central Committee of the Party held another plenary session (the fourth since the Sixth National Congress) in January 1931. This session, accomplishing nothing positive or constructive, accepted the new "Left" line, which triumphed in the central leading body; thus began, for the third time during the Agrarian Revolutionary War, the domination of a "Left" line in the Party. The session itself put into effect two inter-related erroneous tenets of the new "Left" line, namely, the fight against "the Right deviation" as the "immediate main danger in the Party", and the "reform and replenishment of the leading bodies at all levels". Although to all appearances it raised the banner of combating Li Li-san's line and the "line of conciliation", yet in essence its main political programme consisted in "combating the Right deviation". Although in its resolutions it made no analysis of the current political situation or provisions for the concrete political tasks of the Party, contenting itself with vague opposition to the so-called "Right deviation" and "opportunism in practical work", yet actually it endorsed Comrade Ch'en Shao-yu's pamphlet embodying the "Left" ideas then existing in the Party, *The Two Lines—A Struggle for the Further Bolshevisation of the Chinese Communist Party*; that pamphlet, considered both at that time and for more than ten years afterwards to have played a "correct programmatic role", contained in fact, as witness the above analysis, a completely erroneous "Left" opportunist general programme for "combating Right deviation". On the basis of this programme both that plenary session and the Central Committee after it promoted "Left" doctrinaire-sectarian comrades to leading posts on the one hand, and, on the other, dealt excessively severe blows at comrades who had committed mistakes along Li Li-san's line, misdirected blows at comrades headed by Ch'u Ch'iu-pai[6] who had supposedly committed "mistakes along the line of conciliation" and, immediately after the session, misdirected blows at most comrades of the so-called "Right wing". As a matter of fact, the so-called "Rightists" at that time mainly emerged from the sectarian fight "against the Right deviation" at this session. Of course there were among them the few splitters headed by Lo Chang-lung, who later formed a real Right wing, degenerated into counter-revolutionaries and were expelled permanently from the Party, and who beyond any doubt should be resolutely opposed because their establishment and maintenance of a dual Party organisation was absolutely incompatible with Party discipline. But as to the twenty-odd important cadres of the Party, including Lin Yu-nan,[7] Li Ch'iu-shih[8] and Ho Meng-hsiung,[9] they did much useful work for the Party and the people, maintained excellent connection with the masses and, when arrested shortly afterwards, stood up firm to the enemy and became noble martyrs. Comrade Ch'u Ch'iu-pai, who was supposed to have committed "mistakes along the line of conciliation", was a Party leader of prestige and did much useful work (mainly cultural) even after blows were dealt to him, and died a hero's death in June 1935 at the hands of the Kuomintang executioners. The memory of the proletarian heroism of all these comrades will be kept green for ever. A "reform" similar to that of the central body undertaken by this session was effected in organisations in all revolutionary bases and in the White areas. More seriously and systematically than the previous plenary session and its subsequent Central Committee, the Central Committee after this plenary session sent representatives, agencies or new leading cadres to all parts of the country in order to carry out thoroughly its fight "against the Right deviation".

The resolutions issued shortly after this session by the Central Committee on May 9, 1931, showed that the new "Left" line was already being concretely applied and developed in practical work. Presently a chain of major events took place in China.

Under the correct leadership of Comrade Mao Tse-tung and through the active efforts of all comrades, and before the Central Committee constituted at this session had found time to carry out its erroneous line thoroughly, the Red Army of the Central areas in Kiangsi won great victories in smashing successively the enemy's second and third campaigns of "encirclement and annihilation"; and most of the other revolutionary bases and Red Army units scored many victories and developed considerably in the same period under the same circumstances. Meanwhile, with the invasion of Japanese imperialists, begun on September 18, 1931, the movements for democracy and national independence throughout the country reached a new climax. The new Central Committee from the very beginning made a completely mistaken appraisal of the new situation arising out of these events. It exaggerated the crisis of the Kuomintang's rule and the growth of the revolutionary forces and, neglecting the sharpening of the national contradictions between China and Japan and the demand of the intermediate classes since September 18, 1931, for resistance and democracy, stressed that Japan and other imperialist powers would unanimously attack the Soviet Union and that the imperialist powers and reactionary cliques and even the intermediate groups in China would unanimously attack the Chinese revolutionary forces, and asserted that the intermediate groups were the most dangerous enemy of the Chinese revolution. Hence it insisted on "down with everything", in the belief that at that time "a life-and-death struggle between the revolution and the counter-revolution forms the innermost centre of the political situation in China", and once again put forward a number of adventurist proposals, including the seizure of major cities by the Red Army to win victory first in one or several provinces and, in the White areas, the arming of workers and peasants everywhere and the declaration of a general strike in all enterprises. These mistakes first found expression in the Central Committee's "Resolution on the Urgent Tasks Arising from the Breaking Down of the Enemy's Third Campaign of 'Encirclement and Annihilation' by the Workers' and Peasant's Red Army and from the Approaching Climax of the Revolutionary Crisis", dated September 20, 1931, and were repeated and amplified in the following resolutions made either directly by the provisional Central Committee or under its leadership:

Resolution on the Seizure of Manchuria by Japanese Imperialism (September 22, 1931);

Resolution on Winning Victory of the Revolution First in One or Several Provinces (January 9, 1932);

Resolution on the Incident of January 28 (February 26, 1932);

The Vacillation of the Opportunists in the Chinese Communist Party in the Struggle to Win Victory of the Chinese Revolution First in One or Several Provinces (April 4, 1932);

Resolution of the Central Political Bureau of the Central Area on Our Leading Role in a Week's Campaign Against Imperialist Attack on the Soviet Union and Partition of China and for Extension of the National Revolutionary War (May 11, 1932); and

The Mounting Revolutionary Crisis and the Task of the Party Organisation in the North (June 24, 1932).

The period between the establishment of the provisional Central Committee headed by Comrade Ch'in Pang-hsien (Po Ku)[10] in September 1931 to the Tsunyi meeting in January 1935 was the period of the continuous development of the third "Left" line. During this period in early 1933, the provisional Central Committee, after causing serious damage to the work in the White areas with its erroneous line of leadership, moved its headquarters into the southern Kiangsi base area, and the result was that the erroneous line was carried out there and in the adjacent bases more thoroughly than before. Previously, the Party conference of the southern Kiangsi base area in November 1931 and the Ningtu meeting of the Central Committee in August 1932, in keeping with the erroneous programme adopted by the Central Committee's plenary session of January 1931 for "Combating the Right deviation" and "reforming the leading bodies at all levels", had maligned the correct line which had been followed in the base areas of southern Kiangsi and western Fukien, describing it as a "rich peasant line" vitiated by "serious mistakes of persistent Right opportunism", and had replaced the former correct Party and military leadership; but thanks to the profound influence of Comrade Mao

Tse-tung's correct strategic principles, the Red Army was still able to win victory in the fourth campaign against the enemy's "encirclement and annihilation" in the spring of 1933 before it was permeated with the influence of the provisional Central Committee's erroneous line. In the fifth campaign against "encirclement and annihilation" which started at the close of 1933, however, an utterly erroneous strategy became dominant. "Left" mistakes became fully manifest in many other policies, particularly the policy regarding the Fukien Incident.

The plenary session (the fifth since the Sixth National Congress) called by the provisional Central Committee in January 1934 marked the height of the third "Left" line. Disregarding the setbacks in the Chinese revolutionary movement caused by the "Left" line and those in the people's anti-Japanese and democratic movements in the Kuomintang-controlled areas since the events of September 18, 1931, and January 28, 1932, this session blindly affirmed that "the revolutionary crisis in China has reached a new acute stage—the situation for an immediate revolution now exists in China", and that the fifth campaign against the enemy's "encirclement and annihilation" was a "fight for the complete victory of the Chinese revolution" which would determine "which is the victor and which the vanquished in the contest between the revolutionary way and the colonial way" in China. Recapitulating the viewpoint of Li Li-san's line, it declared that "when we have spread the democratic revolution of the workers and peasants over important sections of China, the basic task for the Communist Party will be to carry out a socialist revolution, and that only on this basis can China be unified and the Chinese people achieve their national liberation", etc. Putting forward slogans like: "Down with Right opportunism, the main danger", "No compromise with Right opportunism" and "Down with double-dealing in practical work to sabotage the Party line", it furthered the development of excessive sectarian struggles and persecution.

The most disastrous consequence of the third "Left" line in the revolutionary bases was the failure of the fifth campaign against the enemy's "encirclement and annihilation" and the withdrawal of the main forces of the Red Army from the area where the headquarters of the Central Committee was located. In addition, the "Left" line gave rise to the mistake of flight-ism in the military operations during the retreat from Kiangsi and the Long March, thereby bringing further losses to the Red Army. Similarly, on account of the dominance of the "Left" line, Party work in most of the revolutionary bases (the Fukien-Chekiang-Kiangsi area, the Hupeh-Honan-Anhwei area, the Hunan-Hupeh-Kiangsi area, the Hunan-Kiangsi area, the western Hunan-Hupeh area and the Szechwan-Shensi area) and in the vast White areas ended in defeat. Besides its general "Left" features, the line of Chang Kuo-t'ao which was once dominant in the Hupeh-Honan-Anhwei and the Szechwan-Shensi areas manifested itself as a particularly serious case of war-lordism and, when confronted by the enemy's offensive, of flight-ism.

The above were the main features of the erroneous "Left" line which, led by two doctrinaires, Comardes Ch'en Shao-yu and Ch'in Pang-hsien, was the third one to dominate in the Party.

Decked up with "Marxist-Leninist theory" and relying on the prestige they had built up politically and organisationally at the Central Committee's plenary session of January 1931 (the fourth since the Sixth National Congress), the comrades who had committed the mistake of doctrinairism succeeded in making the third "Left" line dominant in the Party for four long years, giving it the fullest and most integral expression ideologically, politically, militarily and organisationally, so much so that it exerted a most profound influence in the Party, and therefore caused the greatest damage. However, the comrades responsible for this erroneous line had for a long time completely distorted the Party's history, doing their utmost, in the teeth of the facts, to brag about the "correctness" and "immortal achievements" of the leading line of the Central Committee since that session, as witness their dogmatic assertions of "the further bolshevisation of the Communist Party of China", or "hundred per cent bolshevisation".

Comrades upholding the correct line, with Comrade Mao Tse-tung as their representative, totally opposed the third "Left" line during the period of its dominance. Since they disapproved of it and demanded its rectification, their correct leadership in various districts was removed by the Central Committee reconstituted at the plenary session of January 1931 or by the agencies or representatives sent by it. But the repeated failures in practical work met by the "Left" line and especially the repeated defeats in the fifth campaign against the enemy's "encirclement and annihilation" in the area where the Central Committee had its headquarters began to reveal this line's erroneousness to more and more leading cadres and Party members and aroused their doubts and discontent. These doubts and discontent reached such a height after the Red Army of the Central Committee's area embarked on the Long March that some comrades who had once committed "Left" mistakes began to awake and turned against them. The broad ranks of cadres and Party members who were opposed to the "Left" line rallied round Comrade Mao Tse-tung as their leader; and this made it possible for the enlarged meeting of the Central Political Bureau, convened at Tsunyi, Kweichow, in January 1935 under the leadership of Comrade Mao Tse-tung, to succeed in terminating the rule of the "Left" line in the Central Committee and in saving the Party at a most critical juncture.

The Tsunyi meeting was entirely correct in concentrating all its effort on rectifying the military and organisational mistakes of a decisive significance. The meeting inaugurated a new leadership in the Central Committee with Comrade Mao Tse-tung at the head, and this was a change of paramount historical importance in the Chinese Party. It was owing to this change that the Party could victoriously conclude the Long March, preserve and steel its own backbone and that of the Red Army under the most difficult and dangerous conditions during the march, overcome the line of Chang Kuo-t'ao that insisted on taking to flight and led to the establishment of a second Party, save the northern Shensi revolutionary base from the crisis brought about by the "Left" line,[11] give correct leadership to the Movement for National Salvation of December 9, 1935, settle correctly the Sian Incident of 1936, organise the Anti-Japanese National United Front, and set afoot the sacred Anti-Japanese War.

Since the Tsunyi meeting the Central Committee's political line directed by Comrade Mao Tse-tung has been a perfectly correct one. The "Left" line has been gradually overcome politically, militarily and organisationally. Since 1942, under the leadership of Comrade Mao Tse-tung, the Party-wide rectification campaign against subjectivism, sectarianism and the Party "eight-legged essay" and the campaign to study the Party's history have led to the liquidation of the ideological roots of the "Left" and Right deviations which had been repeated again and again in the history of our Party. The overwhelming majority of comrades who once committed Right or "Left" mistakes have made considerable progress through a long period of reflection in practical work and have done a great deal of work beneficial to the Party and the people. With a common political understanding, they are now united with the broad ranks of other comrades. This enlarged plenary session of the Central Committee rejoices in pointing out that after successes and reverses our Party has finally, under the leadership of Comrade Mao Tse-tung, attained for the first time the present height of solidarity and unity ideologically, politically, organisationally and militarily. It is a Party approaching victory, a Party invincible before any force.

This enlarged plenary session considers that, since the Anti-Japanese War is not yet over, it would be appropriate to postpone until some future date the drawing of conclusions on certain historical problems in the Party during this period.

IV

To enable comrades to understand better the erroneousness of the "Left" line of different periods, particularly of the third period, so that they can "learn from past experience in order to avoid similar mistakes in the future", the main aspects in which it was opposed to the correct line politically, militarily, organisationally and ideologically are dealt with *seriatum* as follows:

1. Politically:

As pointed out by Comrade Stalin[12] and analysed in detail by Comrade Mao Tse-tung, China at the present stage is a semi-colonial and semi-feudal country (reduced in parts to a colony after September 18, 1931) and the revolution taking place in this country since the First World War is a national democratic revolution in the era of the victory of the international proletariat in the Soviet Union and of the political awakening of the Chinese proletariat. This determines the fact that the Chinese revolution at the present stage is a proletarian-led anti-imperialist and anti-feudal revolution in which the workers and peasants form the mainstay and the other broad social strata take part—a new democratic revolution differing from both the old democratic revolution and a socialist revolution. The extreme lack of evenness and uniformity in China's economic and political development, which is due to the fact that China at present is a big semi-colonial and semi-feudal country under the rule of a number of powerful and yet conflicting imperialist countries in conjunction with Chinese feudal forces, determines the extreme unevenness in the development of her new-democratic revolution, making it necessary for the revolution to carry on a protracted struggle along a tortuous path before it can win nation-wide victory, and yet at the same time providing this struggle with ample opportunities to make use of the enemy's contradictions first to set up and maintain armed revolutionary bases in the vast areas where the enemy's control is comparatively weak. This basic feature or basic law of the Chinese revolution, verified through practice, was not understood but contravened by all sorts of Right lines as well as by the "Left" line of different periods, especially the third "Left" line. Hence politically the "Left" line erred on three main issues.

First, the "Left" line of different periods erred on the issue of the tasks of the revolution and the relations between classes. Far back in the period of the First Great Revolution Comrade Mao Tse-tung, in line with Comrade Stalin, pointed out not only that the task of the Chinese revolution at its present stage is to fight imperialism and feudalism, but, in particular, that the peasants' fight for land is the basic feature of the anti-imperialist and anti-feudal struggle in China, that the Chinese bourgeois-democratic revolution is in essence a peasant revolution and that the basic task of the Chinese proletariat in the bourgeois-democratic revolution is therefore to give leadership to the peasants' struggle.[13] Early in the Agrarian Revolutionary War, he again made it clear that China remains in need of a bourgeois-democratic revolution and that only after "going through such a democratic revolution"[14] can we envisage the prospect of socialism; that the defeat of the revolution in the cities enhanced the significance of the agrarian revolution and that "the revolution in semi-colonial China will fail only if the peasant struggle is deprived of the leadership of the workers, and it will never suffer just because the peasants, through their struggle, become more powerful than the workers";[15] and that even though the big bourgeoisie had betrayed the revolution, there was still a difference between the liberal bourgeoisie and the comprador bourgeoisie, that there were still broad sections of people who demanded democracy and particularly a fight against imperialism, and that we must therefore deal correctly with the intermediate classes of all varieties and try our best to ally with them or neutralise them, and in the countryside deal correctly with the middle peasants and rich peasants (e.g. "take from those who have much to help those who have little, take from those who have fertile land to help those who have poor land", while firmly uniting with the middle peasantry, protecting the well-to-do middle peasantry and providing certain economic opportunities for the rich peasantry as well as enabling the ordinary landlord to make a living).[16] These are all the basic ideas of New Democracy, yet they were not understood but opposed by the "Left" deviationists. Although the "Left" line of different periods set many revolutionary tasks which were democratic in character, it invariably blurred the demarcations between the democratic and the socialist revolutions, giving expression to a subjective desire to go beyond the framework of the democratic revolution; it invariably underestimated the decisive role of the anti-feudal struggle of the peasants in the Chinese revolution, and invariably stood for a fight against the bourgeoisie as a whole, and even the upper stratum of the petty bourgeoisie. The "Left" line of the third period further placed the struggle against the bourgeoisie on an equal footing with the struggle against imperialism and feudalism, denying the existence of an intermediate camp or a third road and stressing in particular a fight against the rich peasants. Especially after the Incident of September 18, 1931, an obvious, momentous change took place in the class relations in China, but far from taking this into consideration the third "Left" line passed the verdict "the most dangerous enemy" on the intermediate groups that were in conflict with the reactionary rule of the Kuomintang and were taking positive action. It should be pointed out that exponents of the third "Left" line did attend to such correct tasks as giving leadership to the peasants in the redistribution of land, in the building up of political power and in armed resistance to the attacks of the Kuomintang government; but as a result of the aforesaid "Left" views, it was erroneously afraid to accept the Red Army movement as a peasant movement led by the proletariat; it erroneously opposed the so-called "peculiar revolutionary character of the peasants", "peasant capitalism" and "the line of the rich peasants", and carried out a number of so-called "class-line" policies exceeding the bounds of the democratic revolution, including the policy of eliminating the rich peasantry as a factor in national economy and other "Left" economic and labour policies, the policy of political power which excludes all exploiters from government, the policy of national education which lays its chief stress on inculcating communism, the "Left" policy towards the intellectuals, a movement among enemy troops for winning over only the men but not the officers, and the "Left" policy in liquidating counter-revolutionaries, etc.— all this led to the distortion of the present tasks of the revolution, the isolation of the revolutionary forces and setbacks in the Red Army movement. On the other hand, it should be noted that our Party did many things correctly in the Kuomintang-controlled areas after the defeat of the revolution in 1927: it gave persistent and firm leadership to the people's national and democratic movements, to the economic struggles of the workers and other sections of the people and to the revolutionary cultural movement, and it fought against the Kuomintang government's policy of oppressing the people and betraying the national interest; especially after September 18, 1931, it gave leadership to the Anti-Japanese Amalgamated Armies in the north-east, supported the military operations against the Japanese during the event of January 28, 1932 and extended help to the Allied Anti-Japanese Armies in northern Chahar. It formed an alliance with the People's Government in Fukien, which aimed at resisting the Japanese invaders and struggling for democracy, put forward three conditions on which the Red Army would unite with the Kuomintang troops against the Japanese invaders[17] and six conditions on which the Communist Party would form with all sections of the people a committee for national armed self-defence,[18] and issued on August 1, 1935, "An Appeal to All Fellow Countrymen for National Salvation and Resistance to Japan" which called for the formation of a national defence government and a united army to resist the Japanese. But in each of the periods when the "Left" line was dominant, especially in the third one, the erroneous guiding policies made it impossible to solve practical problems correctly, and so the Party's work in the Kuomintang-controlled areas either did not achieve such results as it should or ended in complete failure. Of course, in the matter of resisting the Japanese invaders, nobody could anticipate at that time the changes that would, after the North China Incident of 1935, particularly after the Sian Incident of 1936, take place in the Kuomintang's chief ruling clique—the clique representative of the main sections of China's big landlords and big bourgeoisie; but vast numbers of our Party members and of the people did sense the change by which the intermediate classes and some local groups of the big landlords and big bourgeoisie were turning into our allies against the Japanese; nevertheless, the third "Left" line either overlooked or denied this change, and thereby brought about serious closed-door sectarianism and lagged far behind the Chinese people in political life. The isolation and backwardness due to closed-door sectarianism remained basically unchanged until the Tsunyi meeting.

Secondly, the "Left" line of different periods erred also on the issue of revolutionary war and revolutionary bases. Comrade Stalin said: "In China, armed revolution is fighting against armed counter-revolution. This is one of the peculiarities and one of the advantages of the Chinese revolution."[19] Likewise, Comrade Mao Tse-tung pointed out correctly in the early period of the Agrarian Revolutionary War that, in the Chinese revolution, because semi-feudal and semi-colonial China is a big, loosely knit country which lacks democracy and where industry is poorly developed, armed struggle is the main form of struggle and an army composed mainly of peasants is the main form of organisation. He also pointed out that the indispensable, vital positions for the Chinese revolution are located in the vast rural areas which are the home of the broad masses of peasants (*i.e.* the revolutionary countryside can surround the cities while the revolutionary cities cannot detach themselves from the countryside), and that armed revolutionary bases *can* and must be built in China as a starting point for winning national victory (for a democratic national unification).[20] In the revolutionary period of 1924–7, when a coalition government was formed through Kuomintang-Communist co-operation, the bases had their centres in big cities, but even then they could be consolidated only if, under proletarian leadership, a people's army composed mainly of the peasants was established and the land problem in the rural areas solved. In the period of the Agrarian Revolutionary War, when all cities of the country were occupied by powerful counter-revolutionary forces, bases could only be built, expanded and consolidated first in the countryside (not in major cities) where the reactionary rule was weak, and mainly through guerrilla warfare (not positional warfare) of the peasants. Comrade Mao Tse-tung noted that the historical conditions for the existence of such armed revolutionary bases in China's countryside were China's "localised agricultural economy (instead of unified capitalist economy) and the imperialist policy of division and exploitation by marking off spheres of influence", and the resultant "prolonged splits and wars within the White régime".[21] Pointing out the historical significance of such bases for the Chinese revolution, he said:

> "Only thus can we win the confidence of the revolutionary masses throughout the country, just as the Soviet Union has done throughout the world. Only thus can we create tremendous difficulties for the reactionary ruling classes, shake their very foundations and precipitate their internal disintegration. And only thus can we really create a Red Army that will be our chief weapon in the coming great revolution. In short, only thus can we accelerate the revolutionary upsurge."[22]

As to the policy for mass work in the cities at that time, we should, as advocated by Comrade Liu Shao-ch'i, exponent of the correct line in our work in the White areas, mainly take the defensive (not the offensive) and develop our work by exploiting all possible legal opportunities (not by rejecting them) in order to make the Party organisation burrow deep among the masses, lie under cover for a long period of time and accumulate strength, dispatching part of our forces at the right time to the rural areas to develop the armed struggle there, so that the struggles in the cities could be co-ordinated with those in the rural areas and the revolution be pushed forward. Hence, until the general situation became such that conditions were again present for forming democratic governments in the cities, the Chinese revolutionary movement should devote itself mainly to rural work, with city work as its supplement; the revolution's victories in the countryside and its temporary inability to win victories in the cities, its offensive in the countryside and its general defensive in the cities, its victories and offensives in one rural area and its defeat, retreat and defence in another—these formed a picture indicating the crisscross of the nation-wide revolution and the nation-wide counter-revolution in this period and paved the way for the revolution to turn from defeat to victory under the existing conditions. But as the exponents of the various "Left" lines failed to understand the peculiarities of China's semi-feudal and semi-colonial society, the bourgeoise-democratic revolution in China as a peasant revolution in essence, and the unevenness, sinuosity and protractedness of the Chinese revolution, they underestimated the importance of military struggle, especially the importance of peasant guerrilla war and rural base areas, and directed their fight against the so-called "rule of the gun" and "localism and conservatism of peasant ideology", while invariably mapping out their activities on the basis of the illusion that with the struggles of the workers and other sections of the masses in the cities developing rapidly after suddenly breaking through the enemy's high-handed oppression, armed insurrections would be launched in the major cities, which would be followed by "victory won first in one or several provinces" and then by the so-called nation-wide revolutionary upsurge and nation-wide victory. In reality, however, the relative strength of the classes after the defeat of the revolution in 1927 being generally what it was, the first result of this illusion was nothing but the failure of city work. The first "Left" line having thus met with defeat, the second "Left" line repeated the same mistake, the difference being that it demanded support from the Red Army, which had by then grown into a significant force. The second one having ended in failure, the third "Left" line again insisted upon "real" preparations for armed insurrections in the big cities, the difference being that it chiefly demanded that the Red Army should seize the big cities, because by now the Red Army had grown even larger while city work had declined further. As a result of subordinating rural work to city work and not the other way round under the conditions then prevailing, our rural work largely failed following the failure of our city work. It ought to be pointed out that since 1932, because of the failure of the Red Army to seize or hold the major cities, and particularly because of the Kuomintang's large-scale offensives, attempts to capture such cities had been practically given up, and that since 1933, because of the further destruction of our city work, the provisional Central Committee effected a change, abandoning its headquarters in the city and moving it into a rural base. But this change, as far as the comrades of the "Left" line were concerned, was not effected wittingly or based on any correct conclusion reached through a study of the peculiarities of the Chinese revolution, and consequently they continued to direct the work in the Red Army and the rural bases from their mistaken urban viewpoint and damaged it. The following are the proofs: they advocated positional warfare and opposed guerrilla warfare or mobile warfare of a guerrilla character; they wrongly stressed so-called regularisation and opposed what they called the guerrilla-ism of the Red Army; they did not use human and material resources sparingly or take measures in keeping with a decentralised countryside and a protracted guerrilla war fought in a theatre intersected by the enemy; they put forward in the fifth campaign against the enemy's "encirclement and annihilation" such erroneous slogans as "Decisive fight between the two ways in China" and "Do not yield a single inch of territory of the bases".

This enlarged plenary session of the Central Committee emphatically points out that we are now approaching the change in the situation, the very change to be brought about by our rural work and waited for by our city work in the period mentioned above. Only at the present moment, at the final stage of the Anti-Japanese War, when the army under our Party's leadership has grown powerful and will become even more so, is it correct to give the same weight to the work in the enemy-occupied cities as the work in the liberated areas and to work hard for all the conditions necessary for annihilating the Japanese aggressors in the major cities from both within and without, and then shift the focus of our work to the cities. This will be a fresh change full of historical significance for our Party, which shifted with much difficulty the focus of its work to the countryside after the defeat of the revolution in 1927, and comrades of the whole Party must prepare for this change with full consciousness and must not repeat the mistake of the exponents of the "Left" line in regard to the shift from the city to the countryside during the Agrarian Revolutionary War, a mistake which consisted in raising objection to a proposed action and refusing to carry it out at first and reluctant, unwilling and blind acceptance of it afterwards. But the case is different in the Kuomintang-controlled areas where our present tasks are: freely mobilising the masses in both the countryside and the cities; resolutely opposing civil war and national split; striving for peace and unity and calling for redoubled effort in the war against Japan, abolition of the Kuomintang's one-party dictatorship and formation of a democratic coalition government for the whole nation. The rural bases will have accomplished their historical task when the enemy-occupied cities are liberated by the people themselves and a democratic coalition government for the whole nation is actually established and consolidated.

Thirdly, the "Left" line of every period erred also in its tactical directions for attack and defence. Correct tactical direction, as Comrade Stalin pointed out, requires a correct analysis of the situation (a correct estimate of the alignment of the class forces and a sound judgment as to the ebb and flow of the movement), correct forms of struggle and organisation based thereon, and the ability to utilise correctly "every fissure in the camp of the opponents, the ability to find allies"[23] for oneself; and all these are best exemplified in Comrade Mao Tse-tung's direction of the Chinese revolutionary movement. After the defeat of the revolution in 1927, Comrade Mao Tse-tung rightly pointed out that adventurous attacks would certainly court defeat because the revolutionary tide was ebbing low and nationally the enemy was stronger than we were; yet on the other hand, it was possible for "one or several small areas under Red political power" to "come into existence amid the encirclement of White political power"[24] under the general condition that splits and wars were going on incessantly within the reactionary political power and the people's demand for a revolution was being renewed and was growing, as well as under the specific condition that there were the masses that had gone through the struggles in the First Great Revolution, a Red Army of considerable strength and a Chinese Communist Party with correct policies. He also pointed out that, in a period when there are splits within the ruling classes, in order to expand the Red political power "we may adopt a strategy of comparatively rapid advance and expand the independent régime over a comparatively large area by armed force"; but when the ruling classes are in a period of relative stability, such expansion

> "must be one of gradual advance. We must then take the utmost care neither to divide up the forces for venturesome advance in military matters, nor to scatter our personnel in all quarters and neglect the laying of a solid foundation in the central districts in the matter of local work (including the distribution of land, the establishment of political power, the expansion of the Party and the organisation of local armed forces)."[25]

Even in one and the same period, our tactics should differ according to the difference in strength of different sections of the enemy; thus the independent régime in the Hunan-Kiangsi border area "adopted a defensive strategy for Hunan where the ruling power was comparatively strong and an offensive strategy for Kiangsi where the ruling power was comparatively weak".[26] Later, when the Red Army of the Hunan-Kiangsi border area reached the borders of Fukien and Kiangsi, Comrade Mao proposed a plan of "contending for Kiangsi while including also western Fukien and western Chekiang as the objectives of our endeavour".[27] An important basis for determining our tactics is the different way in which the revolution affects the interests of different groups in the enemy camp. This is why Comrade Mao always demands "the utilisation of every conflict inside the reactionary camp by taking active steps to widen its cleavage",[28] and stands "against isolationism and for the winning over of all possible allies".[29]

These tactical principles of "capitalising on contradictions in order to win over the majority, oppose the minority and crush the enemies separately"[30] have been applied and brilliantly developed under his leadership in the campaigns against the enemy's "encirclement and annihilation" and, especially after the Tsunyi meeting, in conducting the Long March and in building up an Anti-Japanese National United Front. Comrade Liu Shao-ch'i's tactics for our work in the White areas also serve as an excellent example. Having correctly appraised the glaring disparity between the enemy's strength and ours in the White areas, particularly in the cities, after the defeat of the revolution in 1927, he proposed to organise systematically our retreat and defence and to "avoid for the time being decisive engagements with the enemy when the circumstances are unfavourable to us, in order to prepare for revolutionary attacks and decisive engagements in future";[31] he also proposed to transform systematically and strictly the Party's open organisations in the 1924-7 revolution into underground organisations, while "fully utilising open, legal means" in carrying out mass work which would serve to conceal for a long time the strength of the Party's underground organisations and enable them to burrow deep among the masses to "accumulate and increase the strength of the masses and heighten their political consciousness."[32] Comrade Liu Shao-ch'i held that, in giving leadership to mass struggles, we should

"in conformity with the existing situation and conditions of a given place at a given time and the degree of the political consciousness of the masses, propose slogans, demands and forms of struggle of a limited nature that are acceptable to the masses in order to arouse them into action and then, on the basis of the changes brought about thereby, either gradually push the fight to a higher stage or call a halt at the right moment and conclude it temporarily to prepare for greater and more advanced struggle in future".

He maintained that, in utilising the contradictions within the enemy camp and winning over temporary allies, we should

"precipitate an open conflict of these contradictions and form a temporary alliance against the principal members in the enemy camp with those of their colleagues who may co-operate with us or who have not yet become our principal enemies";

and that we should

"make necessary concessions to allies willing to co-operate with us, to draw them to unite with us and take joint actions and then to exert our influence on them and win over their rank-and-file".[33]

The success of the December 9 Movement testifies to the correctness of these tactical principles for the work in the White areas. Contrary to these correct tactical directions, comrades who followed the "Left" line of different periods did not know how to make an objective appraisal of the enemy's forces as compared with our own in order to adopt suitable forms of struggle and organisation, and denied or neglected the contradictions within the enemy camp; thus they met with defeat not only because they blindly carried out the so-called "line of offensive" when they should have taken the defensive, but also because they were incompetent in organising a victorious offensive even when an offensive should really have been taken. Their way of appraising the situation was to exaggerate what tended to support their view into something widespread, serious, direct, all-embracing and essential though it was only something isolated, incipient, indirect, one-sided and superficial, and they dared not accept or failed to notice the glaring realities that contradicted their view (such as the enemy's strength and temporary victory, our weakness and temporary defeat, the inadequate political consciousness of the masses, the contradictions in the camp of the enemy and the progressive aspect of the intermediate forces). Ignoring the most difficult and complex circumstances that might possibly emerge, they always dreamed about the most favourable and simplest situation that could not possibly arise. In the Red Army movement, they constantly described the enemy surrounding the revolutionary bases as "utterly unstable", "extremely panicky", "approaching final extinction", "collapsing at an accelerating speed", and "totally collapsing". The exponents of the third "Left" line even held that the Red Army enjoyed a superiority over the entire Kuomintang army which outnumbered it many times, and thus always demanded that it make reckless advances unconditionally and even without any intermission. Denying the unevenness in revolutionary development of South and North China which resulted from the 1924–7 revolution (a situation that was to be reversed only during the Anti-Japanese War), they erroneously opposed the so-called "theory of the backwardness of the North", demanding that Red political power be built up throughout the countryside in the North and mutinies be organised throughout the White troops so as to form units of the Red Army. They also denied the unevenness in the development of the central and border section of the revolutionary bases and erroneously opposed the so-called Lo Ming's line.[34] They refused to exploit the contradictions among the warlords attacking the Red Army and to reach compromises with the troops willing to stop their attacks. In the work in the White areas, in the cities where the reactionary ruling forces had become formidable after the ebbing of the revolutionary tide, they refused to take necessary steps for retreat and defence or to utilise all possible legal means but, continuing to employ the forms of an offensive impermissible under the situation, set up huge, unprotected Party agencies as well as so-called Red mass organisations of the nature of a second Party, unconnected with the broad masses, and made it a regular practice to call for and organise, regardless of the circumstances, political strikes, general strikes, strikes of the students, merchants, troops and policemen, parades and demonstrations, lightning meetings and even armed insurrections—actions which could not easily or possibly win the participation or support of the masses; yet they misinterpreted the failures of all these actions as successes. To sum up, comrades who followed the "Left" line of different periods, particularly that of the third period, knew nothing but closed-door sectarianism and adventurism and continuously suffered unnecessary and avoidable defeats in their fanatical conviction of "struggle above all, all for struggle" and "incessant expansion and intensification of the struggle".

2. Militarily:

At the present stage of the Chinese revolution, military struggle is the main form of political struggle. During the

Agrarian Revolutionary War this became the most urgent question concerning the Party line. By applying Marxism-Leninism, Comrade Mao Tse-tung laid down not only the correct political line for the Chinese revolution but, from the days of the Agrarian Revolutionary War, also the correct military line subordinate to the political line. Comrade Mao's military line has two basic points of departure: first, our army is and must be one which subordinates itself to the ideological leadership of the proletariat and places itself at the service of the people's struggle and the building of revolutionary bases; and secondly, our war is and must be one in which we, admitting the enemy's strength and our weakness, as well as his bigness and our smallness, strive for existence, victory and expansion by fully exploiting the enemy's defects and our strong points and by relying completely on the strength of the masses of the people. With the first view as a point of departure, the Red Army (at present the Eighth Route Army, the New Fourth Army and other armies of the people) must fight wholeheartedly for the Party's line, programmes and policies, that is, for all aspects of the interests of the people, and must oppose all kinds of warlordism which are in contradiction with them. Therefore it must oppose the pure military approach and the view of the roving insurgents who refuse to subordinate military affairs to political or even place political affairs under the direction of the military; it must shoulder the threefold task of fighting, carrying on mass work and raising funds (the last means production at present, and by mass work is meant that the Red Army must become an agitator and organiser for the Party and the people's political power), help the local populace in redistributing land (for the present, reducing rent and interest) and in building up their armed forces, political power and even Party organisations; hence, in its relations with the government and the people, the Red Army is strictly required to respect the organs of the people's political power and mass organisations, strengthen their prestige and rigorously observe the "Three Cardinal Rules of Discipline" and the "Eight Reminders";[35] within itself, it must establish a correct relationship between officers and men, practise democracy to a certain degree and enforce an authoritative, consciously accepted military discipline; and in its work among the enemy troops, it must have a correct policy to bring about their disintegration and win over the captives. With the second view as a point of departure, the Red Army must realise that guerrilla warfare and mobile warfare of a guerrilla character were the main forms of warfare during the Agrarian Revolution and that, to vanquish an enemy many times stronger than itself, it must wage a people's war in which the main forces are linked up with the local forces, the regular army with the guerrilla units and the militia and the armed sections with the unarmed sections of the masses. Thus the Red Army must reject the strategy of a war of quick decision and protracted campaigns but firmly adhere to the strategy of a protracted war and quick decision in campaigns, and reject the tactics of defeating the enemy by a numerically inferior force in a campaign or battle but firmly adhere to the tactics of defeating the enemy by a numerically superior force. Thus, the Red Army must carry out the following strategic and tactical principles: "disperse the forces among the masses to arouse them and concentrate the forces to deal with the enemy"; "enemy advances, we retreat; enemy halts, we harass; enemy tires, we attack; enemy retreats, we pursue"; "in an independent régime with stabilised territory, we adopt the policy of advancing in a series of waves. When pursued by a powerful enemy, we adopt the policy of circling around in a whirling motion";[36] "luring the enemy to penetrate deep";[37] and "amass superior forces to attack the enemy's weak spots so that we can assuredly eliminate a part, small or large, of the enemy forces by picking them off one at a time".[38] Militarily the "Left" line in each period took a stand diametrically opposed to Comrade Mao Tse-tung's. In the first period it resorted to reckless actions which consequently separated the Red Army from the masses of the people and in the second period it caused the Red Army to launch risky attacks. But in neither period did it draw up a complete set of military views. This it did in the third period. In building up the Red Army, the third "Left" line reduced the Army's threefold task to mere fighting, neglecting to instil ideas with regard to the correct relationship between the army and the people, between the army and the government and between the officers and men; it demanded that the Red Army be regularised to an improper extent, opposing the Army's sound guerrilla character and

calling it a manifestation of "guerrilla-ism"; and furthermore it
fostered the growth of formalism in the Army's political work.
In the operational aspect, rejecting the premise that the enemy
was strong and we were weak, the third "Left" line called for
positional warfare and for so-called regular warfare to be
waged solely by the main forces of the Red Army, for a strategy
of a war of quick decision and protracted campaigns and for
"an attack on all fronts" and "striking with both fists"; it
opposed "luring the enemy to penetrate deep", regarding the
necessary shifts of troops as "retreats and flight-ism"; and it
called for fixed front lines and an absolutely centralised command; in a word, it negated guerrilla warfare and mobile
operations of a guerrilla character and failed to understand
what makes a correctly conducted people's war. During the
fifth campaign against the enemy's "encirclement and annihilation", the "Leftists" first resorted to an adventurist offensive
and proposed to "halt the enemy beyond the gate", then turned
to conservative defence and proposed to divide the forces for
defence, to make "swift thrusts" and to engage the enemy in a
"contest of attrition", and ended up literally in flight-ism when
they were compelled to withdraw from the Kiangsi bases. Such
were the consequences of their attempt to replace guerrilla warfare and mobile warfare with positional warfare, and to replace a
correctly conducted people's war with a so-called regular war.

In the stages of strategic withdrawal and strategic stalemate
in the Anti-Japanese War, because of a greater disparity in
strength between the enemy and ourselves, the correct principle
for the Eighth Route Army and the New Fourth Army is:
"basically guerrilla warfare, but lose no chance for mobile
warfare under favourable conditions". And it is erroneous to
engage in too much mobile warfare. But in the coming stage of
strategic counter-offensive, just as the focus of the work of the
whole Party will necessarily be shifted from the countryside to
the cities, so in strategy a shift from guerrilla warfare to mobile
and positional warfare will also be required, provided that our
troops have secured modern equipment. Comrades throughout
the Party must therefore prepare themselves with full consciousness for this coming change.

3. Organisationally:

As Comrade Mao Tse-tung observed, a correct political line

should be "from the masses, and to the masses". To make sure that it does come "from the masses" and particularly that it does go "to the masses", close contact must be established not only between the Party and the masses outside the Party (the class and the people), but first of all between the leading bodies of the Party and the masses within the Party (the cadres and the membership); in other words, there must be a correct line of organisation. Thus, in each period of the Party's history, Comrade Mao Tse-tung, in laying down a political line that champions the interest of the people, laid down also an organisational line that is in the service of the political line of maintaining contact with the masses both inside and outside the Party. Important results were achieved in developing such a line during the Agrarian Revolutionary War and were crystallised in the resolution of the Ninth Party Conference of the Fourth Front Red Army in 1929.[39] On the one hand, this resolution raised the task of Party-building to the level of ideological and political principle, firmly upheld the leadership of proletarian ideology, correctly condemned the pure military approach, subjectivism, individualism, equalitarianism, the ideology of the roving insurgents and adventurism, and pointed out the sources and harmful consequences of these deviations and the methods to rectify them; on the other hand, it insisted on strict democratic centralism and opposed undue restrictions on either democracy or centralisation. In the interest of the unity of the whole Party, Comrade Mao Tse-tung also insisted on subordinating the part to the whole and, in accordance with the specific features of the Chinese revolution, defined the correct relation between new and old cadres, between native cadres and cadres coming from other places, between cadres working in the army and those working among civilians and between cadres of different departments or localities. Thus Comrade Mao Tse-tung has set us an example of combining the maintenance of truth as a matter of principle and submission to the organisation as a matter of discipline, an example of correctly conducting inner-Party struggles as well as correctly maintaining inner-Party unity. Conversely, every time an erroneous political line became dominant, an erroneous organisational line invariably appeared along with it, and the longer the former's dominance, the more damaging the latter's effect.

This is why during the Agrarian Revolutionary War the "Left" line of different periods opposed not only Comrade Mao Tse-tung's political line but also his organisational line, bringing about not only the kind of sectarianism which alienates the Party from the masses outside it (a sectarianism that does not regard the Party as the champion of the people's interests or the concentrated expression of the people's will), but also the kind of sectarianism which alienates the Party from the masses within it (a sectarianism that refuses to subordinate the partial interest of a section of the membership to the interest of the whole Party, or to regard the Party's leading body as the concentrated expression of the will of the whole Party). In particular, in order to carry their ideas thoroughly into effect, exponents of the "Left" line of the third period invariably attached, irrespective of the circumstances, damaging labels to all comrades in the Party who, finding the erroneous line impracticable, expressed doubts about it, disagreed with it, resented it, supported it only lukewarmly or executed it only half-heartedly—labels like "Right opportunism", "line of the rich peasants", "Lo Ming's line", "line of conciliation" and "double-dealing", waged "relentless struggles" against them, dealt them "merciless blows" or even waged "inner-Party struggles" against them as if they were criminals and enemies. Such erroneous inner-Party struggles became a regular means for a leader or follower of the "Left" line to heighten his own prestige, fulfil his *own* desire and intimidate the Communist cadres. Within the Party it violated the fundamental principal of democratic centralism, eliminated the democratic spirit of criticism and self-criticism, turned Party discipline into mechanical regulation, fostered tendencies towards blind obedience and parrotry and thus jeopardised and obstructed the development of vigorous and creative Marxism. In combination with such a mistaken inner-Party struggle was a sectarian cadres policy. Instead of regarding the veteran cadres as valuable assets of the Party, the sectarians persecuted, punished and deposed large numbers of these veterans in the central and local organisations, comrades experienced in work and closely connected with the masses but who proved uncongenial to them and were unwilling to follow them blindly or chime in with them. They did not give proper education to new cadres, nor did tl ey handle the promotion of such cadres seriously (especially cadres of working-class origin), but carelessly replaced veterans in the central and local organisations with new cadres or cadres coming from other places who either lacked experience in work or had no close contact with the masses, but who proved congenial to them and did nothing but follow them blindly and chime in with them. In this manner they not only disheartened the old cadres but also spoiled the new ones. In many places, where sectarianism in cadres policy was further complicated by an erroneous anti-espionage policy, large numbers of good comrades were wrongly indicted and unjustly punished; this led to the most lamentable losses inside the Party. Such sectarian errors weakened the Party to an immense extent by severing its higher bodies from the lower and occasioning many other anomalies.

This enlarged plenary session of the Central Committee hereby declares: Any penalty or any part of it that was wrongly inflicted upon comrades by the erroneous lines should be rescinded according to the merits of the case. Comrades who, upon investigation, are proved to have died as victims of a miscarriage of justice should be absolved from false accusations, reinstated as Party members and for ever remembered by all comrades.

4. Ideologically:

The correctness or incorrectness of a political, military or organisational line fundamentally depends on whether it starts ideologically from the Marxist-Leninist theory of dialectical materialism and historical materialism and from the objective realities of the Chinese revolution and the objective needs of the Chinese people. Ever since the day he joined the Chinese revolution, Comrade Mao Tse-tung has emphasised the application of the universal truth of Marxism-Leninism in the investigation and study of the actual conditions of Chinese society; especially during the Agrarian Revolutionary War, he stressed again and again the truth, "no investigation, no right to speak", and fought again and again the dangers of doctrinairism and subjectivism. The political, military and organisational lines he laid down in that period were nothing else than the brilliant conclusions which he, on the basis of the universal truth of Marxism-Leninism, of dialectical and historical

materialism, arrived at by concretely analysing the actual
situation inside and outside the nation and the Party and its
specific features, and by concretely summing up the historical
experiences of the Chinese revolution, especially of the revolution during 1924–7. When Communists who live and fight in
China study dialectical materialism and historical materialism,
they should do so for the purpose of applying them, as Comrade
Mao does, to investigate and solve the actual problems of the
Chinese revolution. But naturally, none of the comrades who
committed "Left" errors at that time could understand or
follow his approach, and the exponents of the "Left" line of the
third period even slandered him as a "narrow empiricist"
because their ideas were rooted in subjectivism and formalism,
which during the third reign of the "Left" line became so
pronounced as to take the form of doctrinairism. The characteristic of doctrinairism is to start not from actual conditions
but from certain words and phrases torn at random out of
books. A doctrinaire does not adopt the Marxist-Leninist
standpoint and method to study conscientiously the political,
military, economic and cultural aspects of China in the past
and at present and the actual experience of the Chinese
revolution, draw his conclusions therefrom for guiding our
actions in the Chinese revolution and test their validity through
the practice of the masses; on the contrary, he discards the
essence of Marxism-Leninism and imports certain words and
phrases in Marxist-Leninist literature as dogmas without ever
considering whether they are applicable under the actual
conditions in China today. Small wonder that his "theories"
are divorced from reality and his leadership from the masses,
and that he believes himself infallible instead of seeking truth
from facts, and swaggers and brags while afraid of just criticism
or self-criticism.

Empiricism, as the collaborator and accomplice of doctrinairism during its dominance, is also a manifestation of
subjectivism and formalism. Empiricism differs from doctrinairism in that it starts from narrow experience rather than
bookish knowledge. It should be emphatically pointed out that
all the useful experiences gained by the broad ranks of comrades
through practical work are very valuable assets. It is definitely
not empiricism but Marxism-Leninism to summarise such

experiences scientifically for guiding our actions in future, just as it is definitely not doctrinairism but Marxism-Leninism to regard Marxist-Leninist theories and principles as a guide to revolutionary action but not as dogmas. But if any comrade experienced in practical work rests content with, or still more, rests content solely with, his own limited experiences, as though they were dogmas applicable everywhere, if he does not understand or refuses to understand the truth that "without a revolutionary theory there can be no revolutionary practice"[40] and that "in order to lead, one must foresee",[41] and consequently belittles the study of Marxism-Leninism which is a summary of the world's revolutionary experiences, and if he is obsessed with narrow-minded and unprincipled "pragmatism" and routine activities which require no brain-work and lead nowhere, while sitting on the commander's platform and thoughtlessly styling himself a hero and veteran, and refusing to listen to comrades' criticism or to practise self-criticism—if he does all this, then he becomes an empiricist. Thus the empiricists and the doctrinaires, though starting from different directions, agree with each other essentially in their way of thinking. Both separate the actual practice of the Chinese revolution from the universal truth of Marxism-Leninism; both run counter to dialectical materialism and historical materialism and exaggerate relative and partial truth as universal and absolute truth; and none of their ideas corresponds to the objective, actual situation taken as a whole. Hence they have held in common many erroneous ideas on Chinese society and the Chinese revolution (such as their erroneous notion about the city as the centre of gravity, or about work in the White areas as the centre of gravity, or their notions about "regular" warfare, which have nothing to do with actual circumstances). These created an ideological common ground for the collaboration between comrades belonging to these two categories. With only limited and fragmentary experience, most empiricists often lacked independent, clear and comprehensive views on questions concerning a situation taken as a whole, and thus generally played second fiddle in their association with doctrinaires; but as the history of our Party proves, without the collaboration of empiricism there would have been little chance for doctrinairism "to spread the poison throughout the Party" and, after the defeat of doctrinairism, empiricism became more emphatically the main obstacle to the development of Marxism-Leninism in the Party. Hence we must overcome not only subjectivist doctrinairism but subjectivist empiricism as well. Only by thoroughly eliminating the ideology of doctrinairism and empiricism can the Marxist-Leninist ideology, line and style in work spread far and wide and strike root deep in the Party.

The above-mentioned mistakes in the political, military, organisational and ideological spheres were indeed the fundamental ones committed by the "Left" line at different times, especially the third time. And all the political, military and organisational mistakes stemmed invariably from the ideological violation of Marxist-Leninist dialectical materialism and historical materialism, from subjectivism, formalism, doctrinairism and empiricism.

This enlarged plenary session of the Central Committee points out that in repudiating the "Left" mistakes of different periods we must bear in mind and carry out Comrade Mao Tse-tung's instruction that "we should adopt an analytical attitude towards any problem, and must not negate everything".[42] It should be pointed out that the comrades who made such mistakes were not wrong in all their other views; some of their views on combating imperialism and feudalism, on the agrarian revolution and on the war against Chiang Kai-shek did agree with those of the comrades who stood for the correct line. It should be further noted that, despite the particularly long rule of the "Left" line of the third period and the particularly heavy losses it brought on the Party and the revolution, the Party, thanks to the active work and heroic struggle the broad ranks of cadres and Party members carried on together with the broad masses of the soldiers and the people, did make splendid achievements during this period in the practical work of many areas and departments (for instance, in battles, in army building, in war mobilisation, in building up political power, and in work in the White areas). It was precisely because of such achievements that we were able to keep up our war to repel the attacks of the enemy for several years and deal severe blows to him; and it was only because of the rule of the erroneous line that these achievements were finally nullified. All the leaders, directors and cadres inside and outisde the Party, all Party members and all non-Party people who have heroically given their lives for the people's cause during each of the reigns of the "Left" line, just as those who have sacrificed themselves in any other period in the Party's history, will be esteemed for ever by the Party and the people.

V

That the "Left" line committed mistakes in the above-mentioned four spheres was not accidental, but the result of deep-seated social causes.

While the correct line represented by Comrade Mao Tse-tung reflects the ideology of the vanguard of the Chinese proletariat, the "Left" line reflects the ideology of the Chinese petty-bourgeois democrats. Semi-colonial and semi-feudal China is a country with an enormous petty bourgeoisie. Our Party is not only externally surrounded by this enormous social stratum, but internally made up of a membership overwhelmingly petty-bourgeois in origin; this is because large numbers of petty-bourgeois revolutionary democrats turn to the ranks of the proletariat to find a way out, since the possibility of establishing a strong petty-bourgeois party in China was precluded by the great victory of Marxism-Leninism in the world after the October Revolution, by the existing social and political conditions in China and especially by the historical development of the Kuomintang and that of the Communist Party. Besides, the economic conditions in China being what they are, even the masses of workers and Party members of working-class origin are apt to be infected by the petty bourgeoisie. It is therefore inevitable and not surprising that petty-bourgeois ideology of various shades should often be reflected in our Party.

Among the petty-bourgeois masses outside the Party, apart from the peasants who form the main force in the Chinese bourgeoise-democratic revolution, the great majority of the urban petty bourgeoisie in China also constitute a basic motive force in the present stage of the revolution, because they, suffering also from all kinds of oppression and being driven constantly and rapidly into poverty, bankruptcy and unemployment in large numbers, urgently need economic and political democracy. But the petty bourgeoisie, as a transitory social class, has a dual nature; so far as its good and revolutionary aspect is concerned, a great majority of its ranks are receptive of the political, organisational and even ideological influence of the proletariat and demand at present a democratic revolution and can unite and fight for it, and may follow in future the path towards socialism along with the proletariat; but so far as its undesirable and backward aspect is concerned, the petty bourgeoisie not only possesses weaknesses which distinguish it from the proletariat, but it may, when severed from proletarian leadership, often be influenced by the liberal bourgeoisie or even the big bourgeoisie and become their captive. In the present stage, therefore, the proletariat and its vanguard, the Communist Party, should on the one hand be considerate towards the masses of the petty bourgeoisie outside the Party on the basis of a firm and broad alliance with them, and should tolerate their liberal ideas and behaviour in so far as this does not impede the struggle against the enemy or the common social life we lead with them, and on the other hand give them appropriate education so as to consolidate our alliance with them.

But the case is entirely different with those petty bourgeois who have voluntarily abandoned their original stand and joined the party of the proletariat. The Party should adopt towards them policies different in principle from those towards the petty-bourgeois masses outside the Party. Because they have long been in contact with the proletariat and have joined its party voluntarily, they can, through the Party's Marxist-Leninist education as well as the steeling in the practical revolutionary struggles of the masses, gradually become proletarianised in ideology and in turn can do much for the ranks of the proletariat; in fact most people of petty-bourgeois origin who have joined our Party have fought bravely and made sacrifices for the Party and the people and improved themselves ideologically, and many of them are already Marxist-Leninists. Yet it must be stressed that the revolutionary quality of a petty bourgeois who is not yet proletarianised is essentially different from that of the proletariat, a difference that may often develop into antagonism. Party members with petty-bourgeois revolutionary quality have joined the Party organisationally, but they have not joined it ideologically or have not done so in a full sense, and they are often liberals, reformists, anarchists, Blanquists,[43] etc., appearing as Marxist-Leninists and are therefore incapable of leading to victory not only China's Communist movement of the future but even her new-democratic movement of today. If advanced proletarians do not firmly maintain a clear line of demarcation between Marxism-Leninism and the old ideology of the Party members of petty-bourgeois origin, and if they do not educate them as well as struggle against them in a serious but appropriate and patient manner, then such members will not only keep their petty-bourgeois ideology but endeavour to mould the Party's features, the features of the vanguard of the proletariat, in their own image and to capture the Party, thus damaging the cause of the Party and the people. The greater the size of the petty bourgeoisie outside the Party and the more numerous the Party members of petty-bourgeois origin, the more strictly should the Party watch over its purity as the vanguard of the proletariat, for otherwise it will be subject to fiercer attacks by the petty-bourgeois ideology and suffer even greater losses. The struggle between the correct line and various erroneous lines in the history of our Party has essentially reflected the class struggle outside the Party, and the above-mentioned mistakes committed by the "Left" line in the political, military, organisational and ideological spheres precisely reflect such petty-bourgeois ideology in the Party. This problem can be analysed in three aspects.

First, the way of thinking. Basically speaking, the way of thinking of the petty bourgeois manifests itself in subjectivism and one-sidedness in approaching a problem, *i.e.* in starting not from an objective, complete picture of the relative strength of the classes, but taking one's subjective wishes, impressions and empty talk for real conditions, a single aspect for all the aspects, the part for the whole and the tree for the wood. The way of thinking of those petty-bourgeois intellectuals who are detached from the practical processes of production is apt to be doctrinaire as mentioned above, because these people have only bookish knowledge but no practical knowledge. The way of thinking of those petty bourgeois who are associated with production is liable to be empiricist, as also mentioned above. For though these people are not without practical knowledge, they suffer from the narrowness, undisciplinedness, isolation and conservatism characteristic of the small producer.

Secondly, political tendency. Politically the petty bourgeois generally tend to vacillate between the left and the right because of their way of life and the resultant subjectivism and one-sidedness in their way of thinking. Many typical petty-bourgeois revolutionaries long for a quick victory of the revolution, which will bring about a radical change in their present status; consequently, keenly interested in "Left" revolutionary phrases and slogans, they lack the patience for protracted revolutionary endeavour and are apt to become sectarian or adventurist in their feelings and actions. Such a petty-bourgeois political tendency, when reflected in the Party, gives rise to the above-mentioned mistakes of the "Left" line on the questions of revolutionary tasks, revolutionary bases, tactical direction and military line.

But under different circumstances, the same group or another section of petty-bourgeois revolutionaries may express pessimism and despair and be imbued with Rightist sentiments and viewpoints, tagging after the bourgeoisie. The Ch'en Tu-hsiu-ism of the latter period of the 1924–7 revolution, the Chang Kuo-t'ao-ism of the latter period of the Argarian Revolution and the flight-ism of the early period of the Long March, were all reflections of such petty-bourgeois Rightist ideas in the Party. And on one occasion capitulationist ideas appeared during the resistance to Japan. Generally speaking, "Left" mistakes are more likely to occur when there is a split between the bourgeoisie and the proletariat (e.g. the "Left" line dominated the leading body of the Party no less than three times during the Agrarian Revolution), and Rightist mistakes when there is an alliance between the two classes (such as in the latter period of the 1924–7 revolution and the early period of the Anti-Japanese War). And both "Left" and Right tendencies are detrimental to the revolution and favourable only to the counter-revolution. The undesirable aspect of the ideology of the petty-bourgeois is characterised, according to the vicissitudes of circumstances, by vacillation between the left and the right, proneness to go to the extreme, empty talk or an opportunist approach. All this reflects ideologically their economic instability.

Thirdly, organisation. Because of the limitations of their ways of life and thinking, and particularly because of China's backward and decentralised social environment of clan and guild organisations, the petty bourgeois are, in organisational matters, liable to tend towards individualism and sectarianism which separate them from the masses. Such tendencies, when reflected in the Party, take the form of the erroneous "Left" organisational line as previously mentioned... Such tendencies develop all the easier because the Party has been for a long time fighting a decentralised guerrilla war in the countryside. They are not tendencies towards working for the Party and the people in a spirit of self-sacrifice, but towards exploiting the power and undermining the interests of the Party and the people for personal or sectarian ends; they are therefore incompatible with the Party's principle of forging its links with the masses, the Party's democratic centralism or Party discipline. These tendencies, which undermine the Party's connections with the masses and its internal unity, take various forms, including bureaucracy, patriarchal despotism, misuse of disciplinary measures, authoritarianism, individualist heroism, semi-anarchism, liberalism, extreme democratisation, the assertion of independence, the guild spirit, the sentiment of the mountain-stronghold, favouritism towards townsmen and schoolmates, factional struggle and rascally tricks.

These are the three aspects of petty-bourgeois ideology. Subjectivism in ideology, "Left" and Right deviations in political orientation and factionalism in organisation, all of which have appeared repeatedly in our Party, are obviously anti-Marxist-Leninist and anti-proletarian manifestations of petty-bourgeois ideology, whether or not they develop into a line and dominate the Party leadership. In the interest of the Party and the people, it is fully necessary to analyse the petty-bourgeois ideology in the Party and overcome it through education, thus aiding its bearers to cross over and take up a proletarian stand.

VI

It can be seen from the above that the "Left" line that dominated the Party in different periods, especially in the third period, was no accident but the product of certain social and historical conditions. Hence neither careless nor hasty action can be of any help in overcoming erroneous "Left" or Rightist ideology; we must intensify Marxist-Leninist education, raise the ability of all Party members to distinguish proletarian from petty-bourgeois ideology, promote democracy in the Party, develop criticism and self-criticism, carry on persuasion and education with patience, make a concrete analysis of the features of the mistakes and point out their dangers, explain their historical and ideological source and the way to rectify them. This is the correct attitude that Marxist-Leninists should adopt in overcoming mistakes within the Party.

This enlarged plenary session of the Central Committee hereby points out that the course adopted by Comrade Mao Tse-tung in the present rectification campaign and the campaign for studying the Party's history, i.e. a course of "learn from past experience in order to avoid similar mistakes in the future, to treat the illness in order to save the man", and "clarify our ideas and unite our comrades",[44] exemplifies the correct attitude a Marxist-Leninist should adopt in overcoming mistakes within the Party. Thanks to this course, big successes have been achieved in the task of uplifting and consolidating the whole Party ideologically, politically and organisationally.

This enlarged plenary session points out that in the Party's history the struggles waged against Ch'en Tu-hsiu-ism and Li Li-san-ism were absolutely necessary. The defect in these struggles was that they were not consciously undertaken as a crucial step to rectify the petty-bourgeois ideas which existed in the Party to a serious extent and consequently failed to explain fully the ideological essence and source of these mistakes and to indicate the proper methods to rectify them, thus giving them a chance to crop up again; meanwhile there was an undue stress on personal responsibility, with the assumption that everything would be all right once attacks pure and simple were made on the wrongdoers. Having examined the mistakes committed both at and after the Central Committee's plenary session of January 1931, the Party considers that henceforth in any inner-Party ideological fight we should avoid such mistakes and firmly adhere to the course set by Comrade Mao Tse-tung. So long as a comrade who has committed mistakes in the past realises them and begins to rectify them, we should welcome him without prejudice and unite with him to work for the Party. Even in the case of those who have not fully realised their mistakes and are not yet correcting them in earnest, if they no longer persist in them we should be sincere and comradely in helping such comrades to realise their mistakes and correct them. The whole Party has now reached a unanimous understanding of the erroneous lines in the past and rallied round the Central Committee headed by Comrade Mao Tse-tung. Henceforward, therefore, the task of the Party is to strengthen its solidarity by clarifying our ideas and holding fast to principles in order, as stated in the second section of this Resolution, to unite the entire Party membership "like a family living in harmony and a solid piece of steel to fight for the final victory in the Anti-Japanese War and the complete liberation of the Chinese people". All the analyses, criticisms and debates of our Party regarding its historical problems should take solidarity as the starting point as well as the goal, and any violation of this principle is a mistake. But the entire membership should realise that it still requires a long and continuous struggle to overcome erroneous ideas before the Party can completely achieve its Marxist-Leninist ideological unity, in view of the existing social roots of petty-bourgeois ideology in the Party and the fact that the Party has been for a long time fighting a decentralised guerrilla war in the countryside, in view of the existing remnant of doctrinairism and empiricism and especially the scanty criticism levelled against the latter, and in view of the fact that the sectarian sentiment of the mountain-stronghold is quite widespread although the more serious kind of sectarianism in the Party has been basically eliminated. This enlarged plenary session therefore resolves: The whole Party must intensify its ideological education in Marxism-Leninism and lay stress on linking it with practice in the Chinese revolution, so as to cultivate a sound Party style in work and overcome thoroughly tendencies of doctrinairism, empiricism, sectarianism and the sentiment of the mountain-stronghold.

VII

This enlarged plenary session emphatically points out that the practice of the Chinese revolution has confirmed for the last twenty-four years and continues to confirm that the line of the struggle of our Party and of the broad masses of the whole nation, a line represented by Comrade Mao Tse-tung, is perfectly correct. The great successes achieved by our Party and the decisive role played by it in the present war against Japan testify most vividly to the correctness of this line. The errors of the "Left" and Right deviations committed by the Party during certain periods form but a minor part of the picture of the entire course of the Chinese revolution together with its magnificent development, tremendous achievements and abundant experience gained in the past twenty-four years under the leadership of our Party. These errors could hardly have been avoided when the Party was not yet well-experienced and fully conscious, and it is precisely through the struggle to overcome these mistakes that the Party has become more consolidated, so that today the whole Party recognises the correctness of Comrade Mao Tse-tung's line with unprecedented unanimity and rallies under his banner with unprecedented consciousness. When the Marxist-Leninist ideology as represented by Comrade Mao Tse-tung spreads extensively among and penetrates deeply into the ranks of the cadres and Party members and the masses of the people, the result will certainly be the tremendous progress and invincible power of the Party and the Chinese revolution.

This enlarged plenary session of the Central Committee firmly believes that the Chinese Communist Party, with such rich experiences as have been gained in the struggles of the Northern Expedition, the Agrarian Revolutionary War and the Anti-Japanese War, will assuredly lead the Chinese revolution to complete victory under the correct leadership of the Central Committee headed by Comrade Mao Tse-tung.

SERVE THE PEOPLE

A speech delivered at a memorial meeting for Comrade Chang Szu-teh, held by organisations directly subordinate to the Central Committee of the Chinese Communist Party.

Our Communist Party and the Eighth Route and New Fourth Armies under its leadership belong to the camp of revolution. This camp devotes itself to the liberation of the people and works entirely for their interests. Comrade Chang Szu-teh[1] belonged to our camp.

Death awaits all men but its significance varies with various persons. The ancient Chinese writer Szuma Ch'ien said: "Although death befalls all men alike, in significance it may be weightier than Mount Tai or lighter than a swan's down."[2] In significance, to die for the interests of the people is weightier than Mount Tai, but to work hard and die for the fascists, for those who exploit and oppress the people, is lighter than a swan's down. Comrade Chang Szu-teh died for the interests of the people, and his death is indeed weightier in significance than Mount Tai.

If we have shortcomings, we are not afraid to have them pointed out and subjected to criticism, because we are serving the people. Anyone may do this to us, no matter who he is. So long as he is right, we will correct ourselves immediately. If what he proposes will benefit the people, we will accept it. The idea of "picked troops and simplified administration", for example, was put forward by Mr. Li Ting-ming,[3] a non-Party man; since he made a good suggestion that would benefit the people, we have adopted it. If, in the interests of the people, we persist in doing what is good as well as rectifying what is wrong, our camp will surely thrive.

We come from all corners of the country, and have met together on the road leading to a common revolutionary goal. Along this road we shall yet march with the vast majority of the Chinese people. Today, we are already exercising leadership over a population of 91 million[4] in the base areas, but this is not enough, and to liberate the entire nation the number must be further increased. In times of difficulty our comrades must be able to see our achievements and the bright side of things and screw up their courage. Since the Chinese people are suffering and we have the duty to save them, we must exert ourselves in struggle. Struggle necessarily entails sacrifice, and death is a common occurrence. But if we keep in mind the interest of the people and the sufferings of the great majority, then we see that to die for the people's sake is to die a worthy death. Nevertheless, we ought to avoid as much as possible unnecessary sacrifices. Our cadres should be concerned about every soldier, and all people in the revolutionary ranks should care for each other and love and help each other.

From now on, if anyone in our ranks who has done some good work passes away, there should be a funeral procession and a memorial meeting to render him honour, whether he is a cook or a soldier. This should become a regular practice. And it should also be introduced among the common people. When someone dies in a village, hold a memorial meeting for him. This will serve to express our mourning for the deceased and to unite all the people.

September 8, 1944

ON CHIANG KAI-SHEK'S SPEECH ON THE DOUBLE TENTH FESTIVAL

This is an editorial written for the *Hsinhua News Agency*.

One of the peculiarities about Chiang Kai-shek's Double Tenth[1] speech is that it has absolutely no content and leaves unanswered all of the questions in which the people feel a deep concern. Chiang Kai-shek said that the enemy is not to be feared because there are still wide expanses of land in the big rear. Up to now the autocratic Kuomintang leaders have shown neither willingness nor ability to introduce political reforms and keep the enemy at bay, and the only wherewithal ready to hand for them to draw upon is "land". But it is obvious to everybody that, without a correct policy and human endeavour, this wherewithal does not suffice, for Japanese imperialism is daily menacing the remaining piece of land. In all probability Chiang Kai-shek has acutely felt the enemy's menace, and this is shown precisely by the fact that he has repeatedly assured the people that no such menace exists, and even said: "In the twenty years since I founded the army at the Whampoa Military Academy, the revolutionary situation has never been so stable as at present." He also says repeatedly that we should not "lose our self-confidence", and this precisely reflects the loss of confidence among many people within the ranks of the Kuomintang and in various circles in the Kuomintang-controlled areas. Chiang is now casting about for some means to revive that confidence. In looking for such means, however, he has not examined the policy or work in any field—political, military, economic or cultural; instead he has resorted to the stonewalling of criticism and the whitewashing of mistakes. He said that all "foreign observers" are "ignorant of the true inwardness of the matter" and that "the babel of foreign criticism of our military and political affairs" is entirely due to a credulity in "the rumours and tricks of the invaders and their Chinese collaborators". Curiously enough, such foreigners as Franklin D. Roosevelt, just like such Kuomintang members as Soong Ch'ing-ling, many members of the People's Political

Council and all Chinese who have a conscience, disbelieve the plausible explanation offered by Chiang Kai-shek and his confidents and raise a "babel of criticism of our military and political affairs". Chiang Kai-shek feels annoyed at this, but not until the Double Tenth Festival of this year did he discover an argument which, in his opinion, combines sound reasoning and compelling force *i.e.* the people's credulity in believing "the rumours and tricks of the invaders and their Chinese collaborators". Thus in his speech he vehemently denounced at great length "the rumours and tricks of the invaders and their Chinese collaborators". He fancies that his scurrilities will seal once and for all the lips of all foreigners and Chinese. Those who again raise "a babel of criticism" of his "military and political affairs" are simply demonstrating their credulity in believing "the rumours and tricks of the invaders and their Chinese collaborators".

We regard Chiang Kai-shek's recriminations as extremely ridiculous. For the invaders and their Chinese collaborators have never criticised the Kuomintang for its autocracy, its half-heartedness in the Resistance, its corruption and incompetence, or the Kuomintang government for its fascist decrees and defeatist military orders; on the contrary, they have warmly welcomed all these things. Chiang Kai-shek's *China's Destiny*, a book which has aroused general disapproval, has received bouquets of sincere praise from the Japanese imperialists. The invaders and their Chinese collaborators have never said half a word about reorganising the National Government and its supreme command, because it is their cherished wish to keep intact such a government and supreme command which daily oppress the people and lose battles. Is it not a fact that Chiang Kai-shek and his group have always been the object of the Japanese imperialists' baiting for capitulation? Is it not also a fact that, though the Japanese imperialists originally proposed the slogans of "Opposing the Communists" and "Annihilating the Kuomintang", they have long ago dropped the one about the Kuomintang and retained only the one about the Communists? Up to now they have not declared war on the Kuomintang government, saying that no state of war exists between it and Japan. Up to now the invaders and their Chinese collaborators have taken good care of the property of the Kuomintang magnates in Shanghai, Nanking, Ningpo or thereabouts. Hata Shunroku, an enemy chief, sent his representatives to Fenghwa to offer sacrifices at Chiang Kai-shek's ancestral tombs. The emissaries secretly dispatched by Chiang Kai-shek's confidents are maintaining almost uninterrupted contact and carrying on clandestine parleys with the Japanese invaders in Shanghai and elsewhere. Such contacts and parleys multiply especially whenever the Japanese offensive is intensified. Are not all these things true? Thus, are those people who raise "the babel of criticism" about the military and political affairs of Chiang Kai-shek and his group really "ignorant of the true inwardness of the matter", or are they, on the contrary, well aware of the "true inwardness"? Where does the "true inwardness" lie—in the "invaders and their Chinese collaborators" with their "rumours and tricks", or in Chiang Kai-shek himself and his group?

Another statement in Chiang Kai-shek's speech denies that civil war will break out in China. But he adds: "I am sure that no one dare again rebel against the Republic and undermine the Resistance, as Wang Ching-wei and his like have done." Chiang Kai-shek is here looking for an excuse for civil war and has indeed found one. Any Chinese gifted with memory will not forget that in 1941, when the betrayers of China were ordering the dissolution of the New Fourth Army and the Chinese people were rising to avert the crisis of civil war, Chiang Kai-shek said in a speech that there would never be any war for "annihilating the Communists" and that, should there be one, it would be a punitive war for suppressing rebels. People who have read *China's Destiny* will also remember his remark that in 1927, during the period of the Wuhan Government, the Chinese Communist Party was "in league with" Wang Ching-wei. In the resolutions of the Eleventh Plenary Session of the Kuomintang's Central Executive Committee in 1943, another label was attached to the Chinese Communist Party: "Undermining the Resistance and endangering the state." A perusal of Chiang Kai-shek's present speech makes one feel that the danger of a civil war not only exists but is growing. From now on the Chinese people should bear well in mind that one fine morning Chiang Kai-shek will order a punitive expedition against the "rebels" with the indictment that they "rebel against the Republic and undermine the Resistance", and do things which "Wang Ching-wei and his like have done". Chiang Kai-shek is good at playing this hand; he is not good at declaring rebels people like P'ang Ping-hsun, Sun Liang-ch'eng and Ch'en Hsiao-ch'iang,[2] or at launching punitive expeditions against them, but he is indeed very good at declaring the New Fourth Army in Central China and the Dare-to-Die Corps[3] in Shansi "rebels", and is especially so at launching punitive expeditions against them. The Chinese people must not forget that while proclaiming his intention not to fight a civil war, Chiang Kai-shek has been dispatching an army of 775,000 men exclusively to encircle or attack the Eighth Route Army, the New Fourth Army and the people's guerrillas in South China.

On the positive side, Chiang Kai-shek's speech has absolutely no content and has not answered in any way the eager wishes of the Chinese people for strengthening the anti-Japanese front. On the negative side, it is fraught with hints of danger. Chiang's attitude is getting more and more anomalous, as witness his stubborn opposition to the people's demands for political reform, his bitter hatred of the Chinese Communist Party and his hint at the pretext for the anti-Communist civil war he is preparing. However, Chiang Kai-shek will succeed in none of his schemes. Unless he is willing to mend his ways, he will be lifting a rock only to have his own toes squashed. We sincerely hope he will change his ways, because he is now following an absolutely blind alley. Since he has declared that "a greater latitude will be allowed to the voicing of opinions",[4] he should not resort to such calumnies as credulity in believing "the rumours and tricks of the invaders and their Chinese collaborators", in order to scare people into holding their tongues and refraining from a "babel of criticism". Since he has proclaimed that "the period of political tutelage will be shortened", he should not reject the people's demand for reorganising the government and the supreme command. Since he has proclaimed that "the Communist problem will be solved by political means", he should not again seek a pretext for preparing a civil war.

October 11, 1944

THE UNITED FRONT IN CULTURAL WORK

This is a speech at a conference of cultural and educational workers in the Shensi-Kansu-Ningsia border region.

All branches of our work aim at defeating Japanese imperialism. The Japanese imperialists, like Hitler, are heading for ruin. But we have to make further efforts to bring about their final annihilation. In our work the prosecution of war is of prime importance, production comes next, and then cultural work. An army without culture is an ignorant army, and an ignorant army cannot defeat the enemy.

There are two sides to the culture of the liberated areas, the progressive and the backward. In the liberated areas the people's new culture already exists, but a good many vestiges of feudalism still remain. Among the 1,500,000 population of the Shensi-Kansu-Ningsia border region, there are more than one million illiterates and two thousand practitioners of witchcraft, and the broad masses are still under the influence of superstitions. These are our enemies inside the minds of the masses. It is often more difficult to fight these enemies than to fight the Japanese imperialists. We must tell the masses that they should wage a struggle against their own illiteracy, superstitions and unhygienic habits. To carry out such a struggle there must be a broad united front. And such a united front has to be a particularly extensive one in a place like the Shensi-Kansu-Ningsia border region, which is thinly populated, poorly provided with communication facilities, culturally backward and, in addition, embroiled in war. Thus in our education there must be not only large, regular primary and middle schools but also small, irregular village schools, together with newspaper-reading groups and literacy classes. We must not only have schools of the modern style but also utilise and remould the old-style schools in the villages. In the arts, we must have not only modern drama, but also the Ch'in-operas[1] and yangko.[2] We must not only have new Ch'in-operas and new yangko, but also utilise and gradually remould the old dramatic troupes and the old *yangko* teams that comprise 90 per cent of the total of the existing *yangko* teams. In medicine this principle is even more important. In the Shensi-Kansu-Ningsia border region the mortality rate among men is very high, a great number of cattle die of disease and yet many people still pin their faith on witchcraft. In such circumstances, we cannot solve our problems by merely relying on the doctors of the new school. Of course, the doctors of the new school are superior to those of the old school; but if they do not concern themselves about the sufferings of the people, train more doctors like themselves to serve the people and unite with the thousand and odd doctors and veterinary surgeons of the old school in the border region in order to help them to make some improvement, then they will be actually helping the practitioners of witchcraft and showing indifference towards the high mortality rate of men and cattle. There are two principles of the united front: one is unity and the other is criticism, education and remoulding. In forming a united front, capitulationism is as erroneous as sectarian intolerance and arrogance. Our task is to unite with all the intellectuals, artists and doctors who come from the old society but are useful, and to help, educate and remould them. In order to remould them we must first unite with them. They will welcome our help if only we act properly.

Our culture is a culture of the people, hence our cultural workers must show the greatest devotion in serving the people, and must be linked with and not isolated from the masses. In order to link themselves with the masses they should meet the latter's needs and wishes. In working for the masses we must start from their needs, not from our wishes, however good. It sometimes happens that the masses objectively need some reform, but are not yet subjectively awakened to it and willing or determined to bring it into effect; in that case, we should wait patiently and introduce the reform only when, through our work, most of the masses have become awakened to the need and are willing and determined to start it, for otherwise we shall certainly isolate ourselves from the masses. Unless the masses are awakened and willing, any kind of work that needs their participation will turn out to be an empty formality and end in failure. The saying, "haste brings no success"[3] does not mean that we should not make haste, but that we should not take reckless action, which will inevitably lead to failure. This is true of any kind of work and particularly of cultural and educational work involving the ideological remoulding of the masses. Here we have two principles: first, what the masses actually need rather than what we fancy they need; and second, what the masses are willing and determined to do rather than what we are determined to do on their behalf.

October 30, 1944

WE MUST LEARN TO DO ECONOMIC WORK

This is a speech made at a conference of labour heroes and model workers of the Shensi-Kansu-Ningsia border region.

Dear Labour Heroes and Model Workers; you have attended this conference and summed up your experiences; we all welcome you and honour you. You possess three good qualities and play three roles. First, the role of the initiator. That is, you have made surpassing efforts and many innovations and your work has become an example for people in general, raised the standard of workmanship and inspired others to learn from you. Secondly, the role of the backbone. Most of you are not cadres yet, but you have formed the backbone, the nucleus of the masses; with you, it is easier to push forward our work. In the future you may become cadres; at present you are cadres in reserve. Thirdly, the role of a link. You are a link between the leadership above and the broad masses below, and it is through you that the opinions of the masses are transmitted upwards and those of the leadership downwards.

You have good qualities and have scored great achievements, but beware of arrogance. You deserve the respect of the public, but this is apt to foster arrogance. If, arrogant and self-complacent, you cease to exert yourselves any more and do not respect others, the cadres and the masses, then you will no longer be labour heroes and model workers. There have been such people in the past, and I hope you will not follow their example.

This conference has summed up your experiences. The summary was very well done and is applicable not only here but also everywhere; so I am not going to dwell upon that. I shall only say something about our economic work.

In recent years we have for the first time learnt to do economic work and have made great achievements in it, but this is only the beginning. We must see to it that in two or three years the Shensi-Kansu-Ningsia border region and the liberated areas in the enemy's rear become completely or largely self-sufficient in foodstuffs and manufactured goods, and even accumulate a surplus. We must strive to achieve even greater successes in agriculture, industry and trade than at present. Only then can we consider ourselves as having learnt more about economic work and learnt to do it better. If the living conditions of the army and the people in any locality are not improved, if the material foundation for the counter-offensive is not yet secure, and if agriculture, industry and trade, instead of making progress with each passing year, are stagnant or even declining, then evidently the personnel of the army, government and Party there have not learnt to do economic work and that locality will be beset with great difficulties.

I must once again remind you of one thing, namely, that our ideas should be adapted to our immediate circumstances. Nobody seems to have any doubt that our immediate circumstances are those of the countryside. Who does not know that we are living in the countryside? Actually, many people do not. Though many of our comrades lead their daily life in the countryside and pretend to know the countryside, they do not know it at all, at least not profoundly. Not starting from the fact that the countryside is founded on individual production, cut up by the enemy and embroiled in a guerrilla war, they often deal improperly, or not quite properly, with political, military, economic or cultural problems, or Party affairs, or the movements of workers, peasants, youth and women. They manage rural affairs from an urban viewpoint and often run their heads against a brick wall by subjectively formulating many inappropriate plans and forcing people to carry them out. In recent years our comrades have learnt much from the campaigns to rectify the style in work on the one hand and the failures they met with in their own work on the other. But we must further see to it that our ideas are fully adapted to our circumstances before we can make our work yield fruits in every field, and yield them quickly. If we truly understand that we are in the rural base areas founded as they are on individual production, cut up by the enemy and embroiled in a guerrilla war, and if we start every kind of work from this viewpoint, our progress may appear very slow and not spectacular enough; but how does the result compare with the work done from a different viewpoint; for example, from an urban viewpoint?

The progress is not slow but quick. For if we do things from the urban viewpoint disregarding the actual conditions of today, it will not then be a matter of efficiency, high or low, but of repeated failures with no results at all.

An obvious proof of this is the great results of the present form of production campaign that we have introduced among the army and the people.

We want to deal blows to the Japanese aggressors as well as make preparations to break into the cities and recover the lost territories. But since we are in the rural areas founded on individual production, cut up by the enemy and embroiled in a guerrilla war, how can we attain this aim? We cannot imitate the Kuomintang, which does nothing but relies entirely on foreigners even for such daily necessities as cotton cloth. We advocate regeneration through our own efforts. We hope that there will be foreign aid, but we cannot count on it; we rely on our own efforts, on the creative power of the army and the people. But what ways and means can we find? Our ways and means are to start campaigns for extensive production simultaneously in the army and among the people.

Since we are in the rural areas where manpower and material resources are scattered, we have adopted the policy of "centralised leadership and decentralised operation" for production and supply.

Since we are in the rural areas where the peasants are dispersed individual producers employing antiquated means of production and where most of the land still belongs to the landlords and the peasants are subject to feudal exploitation in the form of land rent, we have adopted two policies, the reduction of rent and interest and the organisation of mutual labour aid, to arouse the peasants' interest in production and increase the productivity of agricultural labour. The reduction of rent has aroused the peasants' enthusiasm in production and mutual aid in labour has increased the productivity of agricultural labour. I have obtained data from various places in North and Central China, all of which indicate that since the rent reduction the peasants have shown much greater interest in production, that they are willing to organise mutual-aid groups like the work-exchange teams we have here and that the productivity of three persons now equals that of four in the past. Such being the case,

90 million people would be equal to 120 million. There are also instances of two persons doing what used to require the effort of three. If instead of adopting a compulsory and authoritarian policy, which defeats its own purpose by seeking quick results, we pursue a policy of patient persuasion and examplary performance, then within a few years most of the peasants can be organised into mutual-aid groups for agricultural and handicraft production. Once the formation of such production groups becomes a usual practice, not only will the output be greatly increased, but all kinds of innovations will also be forthcoming, the people's political understanding will be increased, their cultural level raised, their sanitary conditions improved, the riff-raff remoulded and social customs changed and, before very long, the means of production will also be improved. When all this happens, our rural society will eventually grow up on a new basis.

If our personnel make a careful study of this task and devote the best part of their energy to helping the rural population to develop production campaigns, in a few years there will be a plentiful supply of foodstuffs and articles of daily necessity in the rural areas, so that we will not only be able to keep up the war and cope with crop failures, but also accumulate a large stock of these things for future use.

We should organise for production not only the peasants, but the troops and public agencies as well.

Since in the rural areas we are constantly ravaged by the enemy and embroiled in a protracted war, the troops and public agencies must engage in production. And since guerrilla fighting is sporadic, the troops and public agencies can engage in production. And, moreover, as the troops and public agencies constitute an unduly large proportion of the population of the Shensi-Kansu-Ningsia border region, they would starve if they did not engage in production; and, if they take too much from the people, the people would be unequal to the burden and would likewise starve. We have therefore resolved to launch campaigns of extensive production. Take the Shensi-Kansu-Ningsia border region, for instance. The annual demand of the troops and public agencies for high-grade staple foodstuff (millet) totals 260,000 piculs (300 catties making a picul), of which they get 160,000 piculs from the people and produce the rest themselves; if they produced nothing, it is certain that either they or the people would starve. Since the production campaigns have been got going, not only has starvation been averted, but both the troops and the people are quite well fed.

Apart from grain, clothes and bedding, the public agencies of the border region are self-sufficient in most necessities, and some units are self-sufficient in all of them. Many units can even supply part of their own grain, clothes and bedding.

The troops of the border region can claim an even greater achievement. Many armed units are entirely self-sufficient in grain, clothes, bedding and everything else, *i.e.* they are 100 per cent self-sufficient and demand nothing from the government. This is the highest standard, the first standard, which has been attained only gradually in the course of several years.

At the front, since fighting must be kept up, this standard cannot be adopted. There we may adopt a second or a third standard. The second standard means that, except in grain, clothes and bedding which are supplied by the government, self-sufficiency in all other needs should be achieved through production, *e.g.* cooking-oil (0·5 *liang* for each person a day), salt (0·5 *liang* for each person a day), vegetables (1–1·5 catties for each person a day), and meat (1–2 catties for each person a month); expenses for fuel, education, office supplies, miscellaneous items, health and materials for cleaning weapons; as well as tobacco, shoes, socks, gloves, towels, tooth-brushes, etc., totalling about 50 per cent of the entire expenditure—a standard which can be gradually attained in two or three years. And in some places it has been already attained. It may be adopted in the consolidated areas.

The third standard is to be adopted in areas along the borders and in the guerrilla zones, where the armed units cannot achieve a 50 per cent self-sufficiency, but can meet 15–25 per cent of their own needs. It is good enough if they can do so.

In short, with the exception of those under special conditions, all armed units and public agencies must engage in production during their spare time from battles, training or work. Apart from making use of such spare time to engage collectively in production, they should organise certain people to engage regularly in production, people who can start farms, vegetable gardens, pastures, workshops, small factories, transport teams and co-operatives, or raise grain and vegetables in partnership with the peasants. Under present conditions, in order to get over the difficulties, every public agency or armed unit ought to build its own economic base. Unwillingness to do so, characteristic of loafers, is disgraceful. In order to stimulate the development of production, we should also institute a system of individual bonuses, graded according to the quality of work, for all who take a direct part in it. Further, as the only way to push forward effectively the work of production, the head of an organisaton must assume responsibility and personally take part in it, applying the methods of linking the core of leadership with the broad masses and of linking a general directive with specific guidance.

Some people say that if the troops are engaged in production they will be unable to fight or undergo training, and that if the public agencies are engaged in production, they will be unable to perform their duty. This argument is incorrect. In recent years our troops in the border region have engaged in extensive production to provide themselves amply with clothing and food, and at the same time they have undergone training and taken up political and cultural studies, all much more successfully than before and, moreover, have achieved even greater solidarity both among themselves and with the people. At the front, while campaigns for extensive production went on throughout the last year, great successes were scored in fighting and a campaign for training was started everywhere. In consequence of their production, the personnel of the public agencies have improved their own living conditions and are performing their duties with greater devotion and efficiency, as is the case both in the border region and at the front.

Thus it can be seen that, if the public agencies and troops embroiled in a guerrilla war have started production campaigns for self-sufficiency, they will become even more energetic and active when they fight, undergo training or perform their duties, and their discipline as well as their solidarity, both among themselves and with the outside people, will be even further strengthened. This is the product of the long guerrilla war in our country, this is our glory. Once we have learnt this, no material difficulty can daunt us. We shall become more vigorous and energetic with every passing year and grow stronger with every battle; then the enemy will not be able to overcome us, but we shall certainly overcome him.

Here is yet another point which deserves the attention of our comrades at the front. Some of our recently opened areas are quite rich in material resources and the personnel there, counting upon this, do not want either to economise or to engage in production. This is very bad, for they are bound to suffer in future. Wherever we are, we must treasure our man-power and material resources and must not confine our view to the present and run to wastefulness and extravagance. Wherever we are, we must, from the first year of our work, take into account the many years to come, the long war to keep up, the counter-offensive and the reconstruction after the enemy is driven out. This means, on the one hand, the determination to avoid wastefulness and extravagance, and on the other, vigorous development of production. In the past people in some places incurred great losses because they failed to take a long-range view and neglected to spare manpower and material resources and to develop production. Having learnt such a lesson, we must be careful from now on.

Regarding manufactured goods, it has been decided in the Shensi-Kansu-Ningsia border region that within two years complete self-sufficiency is to be achieved in cotton, cotton yarn, cloth, iron, paper and many other daily necessities. We must now ourselves produce locally whatever is not produced here at all or is produced only in small quantities, and thus become completely independent of imports. This whole task is to be accomplished jointly by the public, private and co-operative enterprises. What we want is not only a large output but also good quality, i.e. the products should wear well. The Border Region Government, the Joint Defence Headquarters of the Eighth Route Army and the North-west Bureau of the Party's Central Committee are absolutely right in closely supervising all such work. I hope that the same will be done in various places at the front. People in many places are already doing this, and I wish them success.

In the border region and all the liberated areas, it will take another two or three years for us to learn every branch of economic work. The day when we raise all or most of our own grain, manufacture all or most of our own goods and are thus fully or largely self-sufficient and even have a surplus, is also the day when we will have learnt thoroughly how to do economic work in the rural areas. When in the future the enemy is driven out of the cities, we shall also be able to take up new kinds of economic work. China depends on us for her reconstruction; we must exert ourselves to learn.

January 10, 1945

PRODUCTION IS ALSO POSSIBLE IN THE GUERRILLA ZONES

This is an editorial written for the *Liberation Daily* published in Yenan.

Whether we can and should launch a production campaign among the army and the people in the relatively consolidated bases in the liberated sections of the enemy's rear, has ceased to be a problem because it was solved long ago. But whether we can do the same in the guerrilla zones and in the rear of the enemy-occupied areas is a point which in many people's minds, for want of proof, has not yet been settled.

But there is proof now. According to Comrade Chang P'ing-k'ai's report on the production campaign of the guerrilla units in the Shansi-Chahar-Hopeh border area, published in the *Liberation Daily* of January 28, production on a large scale has already been undertaken since 1944 in many guerrilla zones in that border area and, moreover, good results have been achieved. The districts and contingents listed in Comrade Chang's report are: in central Hopeh, the sixth sub-district, the fourth district contingent in the second sub-district, the eighth district contingent in the fourth sub-district, the Sushui-Tinghsien contingent, the Paoting-Mancheng contingent and the Yunpiao contingent; and in Shansi, the troops in the counties of Tai and Kuo. The conditions in those areas are very unfavourable:

> "The enemy and his puppet forces, with multitudes of strongholds and blockhouses plus networks of ditches, walls and highways, taking advantage of their military superiority and communication facilities, often launch surprise attacks, encirclement campaigns and 'mopping-up' actions against us; under such conditions the guerrillas frequently have to shift their positions."

Nevertheless, they can still set the production campaign going in the breathing space between operations. The result is as follows:

"Everybody has got better food—each person can now have 0·5 *liang*[1] of cooking oil and salt and one catty[2] of vegetable per day, and 1·5 catties of meat per month. Furthermore, tooth-brushes, tooth-powder and primers, which for years were unavailable, are now all provided."

Just look at that! Who can say that production is impossible in the guerrilla zones?

Many people complain that there is no spare land in the densely populated areas. Is there really no land? Please look at the example of the same border area:

"First, in accordance with the policy which makes agriculture the chief concern, they solved the land problem. They have nine ways in all: (1) razing the walls and filling the ditches used by the enemy for blockade purposes; (2) destroying the motor-roads of which the enemy may make use and planting crops along them; (3) making use of small pieces of waste land; (4) giving help and armed protection to the militia while they plant crops on the fields round the enemy's blockhouses on moonlit nights; (5) ploughing in co-operation with peasants short of working hands; (6) sending disguised soldiers to plough more or less openly the fields around the enemy's blockhouses or strongholds; (7) making use of river banks, by building dikes, improving sand-banks and moving away the sand so that fields may become available; (8) helping peasants to turn dry lands into paddy-fields; and (9) planting in company with the peasants in all the villages where we are active."

But though it is possible to develop agricultural production, perhaps it is impossible to develop handicraft or other production. Is this really impossible? Please again look at the example of the Shansi-Chahar-Hopeh border area:

"The troops beyond the trench-lines do not confine their production to agriculture; but, as in the consolidated areas, they have also developed handicraft and transport. The fourth district contingent has started a felt-hat workshop, an oil press and a flour mill, and in seven months it has netted a profit of 500,000 dollars in local currency. Not only have the difficulties confronting it been overcome but the needs of the masses in the guerrilla zones are being satisfied. The soldiers can now fully supply their own woollen clothes."

But with military operations taking place so frequently in the guerrilla zones, is not the fighting handicapped when the troops are engaged in production? Is that really so? Please look at the example of the same border area:

"Applying the principle of combining labour power with armed strength, they consider production as important a task as fighting.

"Take, for instance, the fourth district contingent in the second sub-district. When the spring ploughing started, a special detachment was sent to attack the enemy and a powerful political offensive was launched at the same time. Precisely because of this, military operations became active and the fighting capacity of the troops increased. From February to early September this small detachment fought 71 battles, took strongholds like Chutungsheh, Shangchwang, Yehchwang, Fengchiachai and Yaitou, inflicted 165 casualties on the Japanese and puppet troops, took 91 puppet soldiers prisoner and captured 3 light machine-guns and 101 rifles and pistols.

"Co-ordinating military action with agitational work in the campaign for extensive production, they immediately started a political offensive—'knock down anyone who attempts to wreck the campaign for extensive production'. The enemy forces in the country towns of Tai and Kuo asked the inhabitants: 'Why has the Eighth Route Army recently become so strong?' The inhabitants replied: 'Because you want to wreck the campaign for extensive production in the border area.' Men in the puppet forces said to one another: 'They are carrying out a campaign for extensive production; it is better for us to remain in our quarters.' "

Is it also possible for the masses of the people in the guerrilla zones to start a production campaign? In those places where there is still no rent reduction, or where rent reduction is not being thoroughly carried out, are the peasants interested in increasing production? This has been answered in the affirmative in the Shansi-Chahar-Hopeh border area:

"Furthermore, through the development of the production campaign of the troops beyond the trench-lines direct help is rendered to the local masses. On the one hand, the masses are given armed protection in their production and, on the other, they receive extensive reinforcements of labour power. With some armed units it is even a rule during the busy farming seasons to help the masses in their production without payment and with half their total strength. Thus the enthusiasm of the masses for production has been greatly heightened; the relations between the army and the people have become even more harmonious; and the masses are all able to earn their keep. Henceforth the masses in the guerrilla zones are feeling even more sympathy towards the Communist Party and the Eighth Route Army and are giving them even greater support."

It is beyond all doubt that the army and the people in the guerrilla zones can and must carry out a broad campaign for production. We urge that all the personnel in military, political and Party work in the liberated areas, especially the personnel in the guerrilla zones, be made to realise this point fully; once they realise the "possibility" and "necessity" of this, things can be started everywhere. People in the Shansi-Chahar-Hopeh border area also started from this point:

"In the production campaign of the troops beyond the trench-lines, because the cadres have re-oriented themselves ideologically, seriously attended to promoting production and gearing working ability to fighting capacity and thereby reared many labour heroes and model workers among the masses (the preliminary summing-up lists sixty-six labour heroes and model workers), our troops beyond the trench-lines have, in a period of only five months, not only fulfilled the production plan on time, but have also made many innovations based on actual conditions."

In 1945, a production campaign of the army and the people, more extensive in scope than any that has gone before, must be carried out in every liberated area through the united effort of all, and in the winter of this year we shall compare the achievements of all areas.

War is not only a military and political contest but also an economic contest. To defeat the Japanese aggressors we must, among other things, put great energy into economic work and master it within a period of two or three years; in this year, 1945, we must strive to achieve even greater results than before. This is what the Central Committee of the Chinese Communist Party eagerly expects of all the personnel and people throughout the liberated areas, and we hope that this objective will be attained.

January 31, 1945

CHINA'S TWO POSSIBLE DESTINIES

This is the opening speech at the Seventh National Congress of the Chinese Communist Party.

Comrades, the Seventh National Congress of the Chinese Communist Party is open today.

What is the significance of our Congress? This is a congress on which hangs the destiny of 450 million Chinese people. China has two possible destinies; someone has written a book on one of the two,[1] but this Congress stands for the other and we shall also write a book on it.[2] The aim of our Congress is to overthrow Japanese imperialism and liberate all the Chinese people. This is a congress for defeating the Japanese aggressors and building up a new China, for uniting all the Chinese people and the peoples of the whole world to win final victory.

The present situation is quite favourable to us. In Europe Hitler will soon be knocked down. One of the major theatres in the world-wide anti-fascist war is in the West where, thanks to the efforts of the Soviet Red Army, victory is coming soon. The Red Army's guns are already being heard in Berlin, which will probably fall before long. In the East the war to overthrow Japanese imperialism is also approaching the day of victory. Our Congress is being held on the eve of the final victory of the anti-fascist war.

Two roads lie before the Chinese people, the road to light and the road to darkness. Two possible destinies await China, a bright destiny and a gloomy destiny. At present Japanese imperialism is not yet defeated. But even when it is defeated, these two prospects will still confront us. Either a China independent, free, democratic, united and prosperous, *i.e.* a bright China, a new China with her people liberated, or a China semi-colonial, semi-feudal, divided, poor and weak, *i.e.* an old China. A new China or an old China: these two prospects lie before the Chinese people, the Chinese Communist Party and our Congress.

Since Japan is not yet defeated and, even when she is, these two prospects will remain, how shall we set about our work? What is our task? Our task is none other than boldly arousing the masses to action, expanding the people's forces and uniting all forces in the country that can be united so that, under our Party's leadership, they will fight to defeat the Japanese aggressors and build a bright new China, a China that is independent, free, democratic, united and prosperous. We should use all our energies to fight for this, the bright prospect, the bright destiny, and against the other, the gloomy prospect, the gloomy destiny. This is precisely our task! Indeed, this is the task of our Congress, of the whole Party, and of all the Chinese people.

Can our hope be realised? We think it can. Such a possibility does exist, because at present we have already secured the following conditions:

1. A powerful Chinese Communist Party with rich experiences and a membership of 1,210,000;

2. Strong and big liberated areas with a total population of 95,500,000, an army of 910,000 and a militia of 2,200,000;

3. The support of the broad masses throughout the country; and

4. The support of the peoples of the whole world, especially the people of the Soviet Union.

Under these conditions—a powerful Chinese Communist Party, strong and big liberated areas, the support of all the people in our country and the support of the peoples of the world—can our hope be realised? We think it can. All these conditions never existed in China before. True, for quite a number of years such conditions existed, but not so fully as they do now. The Chinese Communist Party has never been so strong; there have never been so huge a population and so large an army in the revolutionary base areas; the Chinese Communist Party's prestige among the people in both the Japanese-occupied and the Kuomintang-controlled areas has never been so high; and the revolutionary forces of the Soviet Union and the peoples of other countries have never been so strong. We should say that under these conditions it is entirely possible to defeat the aggressors and build up a new China.

We need a correct policy. And its basic point is boldly to arouse the masses to action and expand the forces of the people so that, under the leadership of our Party, they will defeat the aggressors and build a new China.

The Chinese Communist Party has gone through twenty-four years since its foundation in 1921, and has accumulated a rich store of experience in the three historical periods of heroic struggle—the Northern Expedition, the Agrarian Revolutionary War and the Anti-Japanese War. At present our Party has become the centre of gravity in the Chinese people's resistance to Japan and their endeavour to save the nation, in their struggle for liberation and in defeating the aggressors and building a new China. The centre of gravity in China does not lie anywhere else: it lies right here.

We must be modest and cautious, guard against arrogance and rashness and serve the Chinese people heart and soul in order to unite all the people in our country to defeat the Japanese aggressors at present and to build a new-democratic state in the future. Provided we can do so, provided we have a correct policy and make a unanimous effort, we can definitely fulfil our task.

Down with Japanese imperialism!

Long live the liberation of the Chinese people!

Long live the Chinese Communist Party!

Long live the Seventh National Congress of the Chinese Communist Party!

April 23, 1945

ON COALITION GOVERNMENT

This is a political report made at the Seventh National Congress of the Chinese Communist Party.

I. THE BASIC DEMANDS OF THE CHINESE PEOPLE

After nearly eight years of resolute, heroic and unyielding struggles waged by the Chinese people through untold difficulties and self-sacrifices against the Japanese aggressors, a new situation has emerged in which the world-wide sacred and just war against the fascist aggressors has gained decisive victory and the defeat of the Japanese aggressors by the Chinese people in co-ordination with the Allied countries is imminent; it is under such circumstances that our Congress is being held. But China remains disunited and is still confronted with a grave crisis. Under such circumstances, what are we going to do? In China, an urgent need exists beyond all doubt for representatives of all political parties and groups and of people without party affiliation to unite and establish a provisional democratic coalition government so as to carry out democratic reforms, surmount the present crisis, mobilise and unify all the anti-Japanese forces of the country and co-ordinate effectively with the Allies in military operations, thereby defeating the Japanese aggressors and liberating the Chinese people from their clutches. After that, we should, on a broad democratic basis, convene a national assembly and form a permanent democratic government, which will also be a coalition and include on an even larger scale representatives of all parties and groups and of people without party affiliation, and which will lead the liberated people throughout the country to build up a new China, independent and free, democratic and united, prosperous and powerful. In short, we must follow a line of unity and democracy in order to defeat the aggressors and build up a new China.

We believe that only so doing represents what the Chinese people basically demand. Thus my report will chiefly deal with such demands. To form or not to form a democratic coalition government in China has become the deep concern of the Chinese people and the democratic section of public opinion in the Allied countries. Therefore the elucidation of this problem will receive the main stress in my report.

During the eight years' War of Resistance the Chinese Communist Party has overcome numerous difficulties and scored great achievements, but in the present circumstances serious difficulties still confront our Party and the people. The present situation demands that our Party should work still better to carry out the most urgent tasks in a more practical spirit, continue to overcome difficulties and strive for the fulfilment of the basic demands of the Chinese people.

II. THE INTERNATIONAL AND DOMESTIC SITUATION

Can the Chinese people fulfil the basic demands we put forward above? This depends on how far the Chinese people are awakened and united and are prepared to exert themselves. The present international and domestic situation, however, provides the Chinese people with extremely favourable conditions. If they can make good use of these conditions and continue to struggle actively, resolutely and with ever-renewed efforts, they will undoubtedly defeat the aggressors and build up a new China. The Chinese people should redouble their efforts in the struggle for the fulfilment of their sacred tasks.

What is the present international situation?

The military situation at present is that the Soviet Army has begun its attack on Berlin, and in concerted action with it the allied forces of Great Britain, the United States and France are attacking the remnant forces of Hitler, while the Italian people have started uprisings. All these things will finally bring about Hitler's end. When Hitler meets his end, the defeat of the Japanese aggressors will not be far distant. Contrary to the prediction of the reactionaries at home and abroad, the fascist forces of aggression will certainly be overthrown and the people's democratic forces will certainly be victorious. The world will take the path of progress and not the road of reaction. Of course, we must be fully vigilant and realise that certain temporary and even serious setbacks may occur in the course of history; in many countries reactionary forces are still quite strong which grudge the people at home and abroad their unity, progress and liberation. Whoever overlooks this is bound to commit political blunders. The general trend of history, however, is clearly defined and unalterable. This situation is only unfavourable to the fascists and their virtual accomplices, the reactionaries in various countries, but augurs well for the people of all countries and their organised democratic forces. It is the people, and the people alone, that are the motivating force in making the history of the world. The Soviet people have built up their great strength and have become the main force in defeating fascism. The efforts of the Soviet people plus those of the other anti-fascist Allies have made the defeat of the fascists possible. The war has educated the people and they will win the war as well as peace and progress.

This new situation differs considerably from the First World War. At that time there was still no Soviet Union, nor were the peoples of various countries so awakened as they are now. The two world wars represent two entirely different epochs.

The defeat of the fascist aggressors, the end of the Second World War and the establishment of international peace do not mean that struggles will cease. The remnant fascist forces strewn all over the world will certainly continue to make trouble, and the forces opposing democracy and oppressing other nations, which are found in the very camp opposing the fascist war of aggression, will continue to oppress the people of various countries, the colonies and semi-colonies. Therefore, after the establishment of international peace, a good part of the world will still be full of struggles between the masses of the anti-fascist people and the remnant fascist forces, between democracy and anti-democracy, between national liberation and national oppression. Only through prolonged efforts to overcome the remnant fascist forces and all the anti-democratic and imperialist forces can victory come to the broadest masses of the people. To be sure, that day will not arrive quickly or easily, but arrive it certainly will. Victory in the anti-fascist Second World War will pave the way for victory of the people's post-war struggles. A consolidated and lasting peace can be ensured only after victory in such struggles.

What is the domestic situation at present?

China's protracted war has been and will still be carried on at the cost of enormous sacrifices on the part of her people; but at the same time it is this very war that has steeled them. This war has enhanced the awakening and unity of the Chinese people to a degree unequalled in all their great struggles in the last hundred years. On the one hand, the Chinese people are confronted with both a formidable national enemy and powerful domestic reactionary forces which are actually assisting the enemy. On the other, they have not only been more awakened than ever before but have also created the powerful Chinese liberated areas and developed a nation-wide democratic movement that is daily growing. All these are the favourable domestic conditions. If all the Chinese people's struggles in the last hundred years met with failure or setbacks because certain necessary conditions, international as well as domestic, were lacking, then it is quite different now, and all the necessary conditions are present. There is every possibility of avoiding defeat and winning victory. We shall win victory if we can unite the people of the whole country to carry on vigorous struggles and can give them proper guidance.

The Chinese people are now much more confident than before that they can unite themselves to defeat the aggressors and build up a new China. It is time for the Chinese people to overcome all difficulties and fulfil their basic demands of great historical significance. Can there be any doubt about this? I think there is none.

Such is the general international and domestic situation at present.

III. TWO LINES IN THE ANTI-JAPANESE WAR

The Key to China's Problems

Speaking of the domestic situation, we have yet to make a specific analysis of China's Anti-Japanese War.

China is one of the five biggest countries taking part in the world-wide anti-fascist war and the main force in fighting the Japanese aggressors on the continent of Asia. The Chinese people have not only played a great role in the Anti-Japanese War, but will also play a great role in safeguarding peace in the post-war world and a decisive role in safeguarding peace in the

East. During the eight years of the Anti-Japanese War, China has made enormous efforts to liberate herself and help the Allied countries. Such efforts have been made chiefly by the people of China. Large numbers of officers and men in the Chinese armies have fought and shed their blood at the front; the Chinese workers, peasants, intellectuals and industrialists have worked hard in the rear; the oversea Chinese have rendered financial support to the war; and all the anti-Japanese political parties, except such members as are opposed to the people, have done their bit in the war. In short, for eight long years, by blood and sweat the Chinese people have heroically fought the Japanese aggressors. But for many years the Chinese reaction-aries have spread rumours and misled public opinion in order to keep the world from knowing what role the Chinese people have really played in the Anti-Japanese War. At the same time no one has yet made a comprehensive summing-up of the various kinds of experiences China has gained during her eight years' war against Japan. Therefore, this Congress ought to make a proper summing-up of all such experiences in order to educate the people and to provide a basis for the Party to formulate its policy.

In summing up experiences, everybody can see clearly that there are two different guiding lines in China. One enables us to defeat the Japanese aggressors and the other, instead of this, actually helps one way or another the Japanese aggressors and hampers us from carrying on the Anti-Japanese War.

The Kuomintang government's policy of passive resistance to Japan and its reactionary policy of active repression of the people at home have resulted in military setbacks, enormous territorial losses, financial and economic crisis, oppression and hardship for the people and disruption of national unity. Such a reactionary policy has hindered the mobilisation and unifica-tion of all the anti-Japanese forces of the Chinese people for the effective prosecution of the war, and hindered the people from awakening and getting united. But the movement of the Chinese people to become awakened and united has never ceased and has developed along a tortuous route under the twofold repression of the Japanese aggressors and the Kuomintang government. Clearly two lines have co-existed in China for a long time: the Kuomintang government's line of oppressing the Chinese people and carrying on a passive resistance, and the Chinese people's line of becoming awakened and united to wage a people's war. Herein lies the key to all China's problems.

A History that Follows a Tortuous Route

In order to know why the problem of these two lines is the key to all other problems of China, it is necessary to trace the history of our Anti-Japanese War.

The Chinese people's Anti-Japanese War has developed along a tortuous route. It began far back in 1931. On September 18 of that year the Japanese aggressors occupied Mukden, and in a few months took the whole of the three north-eastern provinces. The Kuomintang government adopted a policy of non-resistance. But led or assisted by the Chinese Communist Party, the people and a section of the patriotic troops of these provinces organised, in defiance of the Kuomintang government, the Anti-Japanese Volunteers and the Anti-Japanese Amalgamated Armies to wage a heroic guerrilla war. This heroic guerrilla war for a time developed to great dimensions and, though it met with many difficulties and setbacks in the course of its operations, the enemy has never been able to put an end to it. When the Japanese aggressors attacked Shanghai in 1932, the Kuomintang government was again defied by a group of patriots in the Kuomintang, who led the Nineteenth Route Army to repel the attacks of the Japanese aggressors. When the Japanese aggressors invaded Jehol and Chahar in 1933, the Kuomintang government was defied for the third time by another group of patriots in the Kuomintang who entered into co-operation with the Communist Party and organised the Anti-Japanese Allied Army to put up resistance. To all these military actions against Japan, however, only the Chinese people, the Chinese Communist Party and other democratic groups and the oversea Chinese gave their assistance, while the Kuomintang government, pursuing a policy of non-resistance, contributed nothing. Moreover, the anti-Japanese activities in Shanghai and Chahar were even disrupted by the Kuomintang government. In 1933 the people's government established by the Nineteenth Route Army in Fukien was also destroyed by the Kuomintang government.

Why did the Kuomintang government adopt a policy of non-resistance at that time? The main reason lies in the fact that it had in 1927 broken up the Kuomintang-Communist co-operation and disrupted the unity of the Chinese people.

In 1924 Dr. Sun Yat-sen accepted the proposal of the Chinese Communist Party, called the First National Congress of the Kuomintang with the Communists taking part, adopted the three cardinal policies of alliance with Russia, co-operation with the Communists and assistance to the peasants and workers, established the Whampoa Military Academy and formed the national united front of the Kuomintang, the Communist Party and all sections of the people; consequently the reactionary forces in Kwangtung were wiped out in 1924–5, the victorious Northern Expedition was carried out during 1926–7, a large part of the areas along the Yangtze and Yellow rivers was taken over, the forces of the Northern warlord government were defeated and the people's struggle for liberation on a scale unprecedented in Chinese history was set afoot. But during the late spring and early summer of 1927, when the Northern Expedition was taking a critical turn, the Kuomintang authorities, by means of their treacherous, anti-popular policies of "party purge" and massacre, disrupted the national united front of the Kuomintang, the Communist Party and all sections of the people which stood for the cause of the Chinese people's liberation, and nullified all its revolutionary policies. In their eyes, the allies of yesterday, the Chinese Communist Party and the Chinese people, became enemies, and the enemies of yesterday, imperialism and feudalism, became allies. As a result, they launched a perfidious, sudden attack on the Chinese Communist Party and the Chinese people, and the great revolution in China, full of life and vigour, was crushed. Since then civil war has replaced solidarity, dictatorship has replaced democracy, and a dark China has superseded a bright China. But the Chinese Communists and the people of China were not intimidated, conquered or exterminated. They rose to their feet again, wiped off the blood-stains on their way, buried their fallen comrades and carried on the fight. They held high the great standard of revolution and put up armed resistance; over a vast territory of China they set up a people's government, carried out agrarian reform, built up a people's army—the Chinese Red Army—and preserved and expanded the revolutionary forces of the Chinese people. Dr. Sun Yat-sen's revolutionary Three People's Principles, abandoned by the Kuomintang reactionaries, were upheld by the Chinese people, the Chinese Communists and other democrats.

After the Japanese aggressors penetrated into the three north-eastern provinces, the Chinese Communist Party proposed in 1933, on the condition of stopping attacks, granting democratic rights to the people and arming them so as to facilitate a united resistance to Japan, to conclude a truce agreement with any of the Kuomintang troops then attacking the revolutionary base areas and the Red Army. But the Kuomintang leadership rejected this proposal.

Thenceforth, on the one hand, the Kuomintang government became even more rampant in carrying out its civil war policy; and on the other, the voice of the Chinese people grew ever more powerful in demanding cessation of civil war and united resistance to Japan. Popular patriotic organisations of all sorts were formed in Shanghai and many other places. Between 1934 and 1936 the main forces of the Red Army on both sides of the Yangtze river, under the leadership of the Central Committee of our Party, underwent untold hardships and moved to the north-west to join forces with the Red Army units there. It was in these two years that the Chinese Communist Party, adapting itself to the new situation, decided on and carried out a new, well-integrated political line—the line of the Anti-Japanese United Front—aimed at achieving united resistance to Japan and establishing a new-democratic republic. On December 9, 1935, under our Party's leadership, the masses of students in Peiping started a courageous patriotic movement and formed the "Vanguard of China's National Liberation",[1] and spread this patriotic movement to all the big cities in the country. On December 12, 1936, two groups of patriotic members of the Kuomintang which stood for resistance to Japan, i.e. the North-eastern Army and the Seventeenth Route Army, jointly staged the famous Sian Incident to oppose militantly the Kuomintang authorities' reactionary policies of compromising with Japan and massacring the people at home. At the same time other patriots in the Kuomintang were likewise dissatisfied with the policies of the Kuomintang authorities. Under these circumstances the Kuomintang authorities were forced to abandon their civil war policy and yield to the demands of the people. With the peaceful settlement of the Sian Incident as the turning-point, an internal co-operation under new circumstances took shape and a nation-wide war against Japan was started. In May 1937, shortly before the Lukouchiao Incident, our Party called a national conference of historical significance which ratified the new political line followed by the Central Committee of the Party since 1935.

From the Lukouchiao Incident of July 7, 1937, up to the fall of Wuhan in October 1938, the Kuomintang government made comparatively great efforts in the war against Japan. During this period the large-scale onslaught of the Japanese aggressors and the ever-mounting righteous, patriotic indignation of the whole people compelled the Kuomintang government to make resisting the Japanese aggressors the centre of gravity of its policy, to bring about an upsurge of armed struggle of the army and the whole people, creating for a time a new atmosphere of hopefulness. All the people, with the Communists and other democrats, then pinned great hopes on the Kuomintang government; they hoped that it would earnestly introduce democratic reforms and put into practice Dr. Sun Yat-sen's revolutionary Three People's Principles at a moment when the nation was in peril and the people's spirits were high. But such hopes came to nothing. For even in those two years, while a comparatively active resistance was going on, the Kuomintang authorities continued to refuse to mobilise the broad masses of the people to take part in the people's war and to restrict the people's voluntary efforts to unite themselves for activities that helped the resistance to the Japanese and furthered the cause of democracy. Although the Kuomintang government had changed somewhat its old attitude towards the Chinese Communist Party and other anti-Japanese groups, it continued to deny equal status to them and to restrict their activities in all sorts of ways. Many patriotic political prisoners were still in jail. What mattered most was that the Kuomintang government still preserved the oligarchy it had established since the outbreak of the civil war in 1927, and as a result it proved impossible to create a democratic coalition government with nation-wide support.

At the very beginning of this period we Communists pointed out that there were two guiding lines in China's Anti-Japanese War: a people's total war which leads to victory, and a partial war, with the people under oppression, which leads to defeat. We also pointed out that the war would be protracted and would inevitably meet with numerous hardships and difficulties but that, through their own efforts, the Chinese people would definitely win the final victory.

The People's War

During this period the main force of the Chinese Red Army under the Chinese Communist Party's leadership, which had moved to the north-west, was reorganised as the Eighth Route Army of the Chinese National Revolutionary Army, and the guerrilla units of the Chinese Red Army, which had remained in the areas on both sides of the Yangtze river, were reorganised as the New Fourth Army of the Chinese National Revolutionary Army; they were sent one after the other to North and Central China respectively to fight the Japanese invaders. During the civil war period, the Chinese Red Army preserved as well as developed the democratic tradition of the Whampoa Military Academy and the National Revolutionary Army in the Northern Expedition, and for a time it went on expanding up to several hundred thousand strong. But, among other things, the Kuomintang government's ruthless destruction of our southern base areas and the losses incurred during the Long March combined to reduce it to a few tens of thousands at the outbreak of the Anti-Japanese War. Some, therefore, belittled this army and thought that in the resistance to Japan reliance should chiefly be placed on the Kuomintang. The people, however, were the best judges; they knew that the Eighth Route and New Fourth Armies, though small in number at that time, were superb in quality, that they alone could prosecute a real people's war and that once they were dispatched to the anti-Japanese front and united themselves with the broad masses there, what they would accomplish would be beyond the most generous estimate. The people were right, because up to the moment when I am making this report, our army has already expanded to 910,000 men, and the number of militiamen who are not detached from their civilian occupations has grown to more than 2,200,000. Despite the fact that our regular army is at present still numerically much smaller than the Kuomintang army (including the Central army and local forces), it has already become the main force in China's Anti-Japanese War in view of the strength of the Japanese and puppet forces it now engages, the extensiveness of its war zone, its fighting capacity, the broad masses fighting in co-ordination with it, its political integrity, its internal unity and solidarity, etc.

This army is powerful because all who have joined it are self-disciplined; they have united themselves and fought together not for the private interests of a few individuals or a small clique, but for the interests of the broad masses of the people and the interests of the whole nation. To stand firmly on the side of the Chinese people and to serve them whole-heartedly —that is the sole aim of this army.

Fighting for this aim, this army marches forward unchallenged, vanquishes all enemies and never yields to them. No matter what the difficulties and tribulations, so long as one man remains, he will fight on.

Fighting for this aim, this army has achieved a high degree of solidarity both internally and externally. Internally, between officers and men, between upper and lower ranks and between commanders, political workers and workers in the auxiliary services of the rear, and externally, between the army and the people, between the army and organs of government and between our army and friendly armies—all are united. It is an imperative duty to remove anything that impairs this solidarity.

Fighting for this aim, this army adopts a correct policy in winning over enemy officers and men and in treating war prisoners. It welcomes all enemy soldiers who surrender, come over to us or, after laying down their arms, are willing to join in the fight against the common foe, and gives them necessary education. No war prisoner is to be killed, ill-treated or insulted.

Fighting for this aim, this army has built up a system of strategy and tactics necessary for a people's war. It is versed in carrying on flexible guerrilla war according to the ever-changing concrete conditions and it is equally good at mobile warfare.

Fighting for this aim, this army has developed a system of political work which is necessary for a people's war and aims at promoting its own unity as well as that of its friendly armies and of the people, disintegrating enemy forces and ensuring victory in combat.

Fighting for this aim, the whole of this army, under the conditions of guerrilla warfare, is able to do and has in fact already done the following: to utilise the intervals between battles and training to produce foodstuffs and other daily necessities so that the army may be wholly, or half or just partly self-supporting, thereby overcoming economic difficulties, improving its own living conditions and lightening the people's burden. In various military bases we have tried our best to establish a number of small-scale war industries.

Furthermore, this army is powerful because it has such a host of organised armed forces of the masses as the people's self-defence corps and the militia fighting in co-ordination with it. In the liberated areas of China all young and middle-aged men and women are organised in the anti-Japanese people's self-defence corps on a voluntary and democratic basis and on the principle that they do not quit their civilian occupations. The crack members of the corps, except those who have joined the army or the guerrilla units, are organised into the ranks of the militia. Without the co-ordination of such armed forces of the masses we shall not be able to win victory over the enemy.

Moreover, this army is powerful because it is divided into main forces and regional forces; the former may be sent to operate in any region at any time, while the latter make it their specific task to defend their own regions or attack the enemy in their neighbourhood in co-ordination with the militia and the self-defence corps. Such a division of labour has won the whole-hearted support of the people. Were it not for such appropriate division, e.g. were attention paid only to the role of the main forces but not to that of the regional forces, it would be impossible to win victory over the enemy under the conditions of the Chinese liberated areas. Regional forces have formed numerous armed units—groups of people, well trained and prepared for military and political work and for work among the people—which have already achieved considerable results in penetrating deep into the rear of the enemy-occupied area, attacking the enemy and arousing the masses to take part in the struggle against the Japanese invaders in order to support military operations on the fronts of the various liberated areas.

In the liberated areas of China the whole population taking part, under the leadership of the democratic government, in the struggle against the Japanese invaders are called upon to join the workers', peasants', youths', women's and cultural organisations as well as professional and other social organisations, and are enthusiastically fulfilling all kinds of tasks in support of the army. Such activities include not only mobilising the people to join the army, transporting the army's food supplies, taking good care of the families of anti-Japanese fighters and helping the troops to overcome their material difficulties, but also stepping up the activities of guerrilla units, the militia and the self-defence corps, broadening the movement of raiding and mining the enemy, making reconnaissance, cleaning up traitors and spies, transporting and protecting the wounded and giving direct help to the army in its operations. At the same time all the people in the liberated areas are enthusiastically taking up various kinds of political, economic, cultural and sanitary and medical construction work. In this respect the most important thing is to mobilise all the people for production of foodstuffs and other daily necessities and make all government bodies and schools, with special cases excepted, utilise their spare time from work or study to engage in production for self-support, so as to co-ordinate with the production campaign waged for the same purpose by the army and the people, thereby creating a great fervour for production to sustain the long War of Resistance. The enemy has wrought great havoc in China's liberated areas, and floods, droughts and locusts have also visited these areas frequently. However, the people there, under the leadership of the democratic government, have overcome or are overcoming these difficulties in an organised way, and the great mass campaigns for locust-extermination, flood control and relief for victims of natural calamities have achieved results unprecedented in history, so that the Anti-Japanese War can be kept up for a long time. In a word, everything is for the front, for the defeat of the Japanese aggressors and for the liberation of the Chinese people—this is the general slogan and the general directive for all the armed forces and the people in China's liberated areas.

Such is a real people's war. Only by waging such a peoples' war can we defeat our national enemy. The Kuomintang has failed precisely because it frantically opposed the people's war.

Once equipped with modern weapons, the armies of China's liberated areas will become even more powerful and will bring about the final defeat of the Japanese aggressors.

Two Battle Fronts

From the very beginning there have been two battle fronts in China's Anti-Japanese War: the Kuomintang front and the front of the liberated areas.

After the fall of Wuhan in October 1938, the Japanese aggressors stopped their strategic offensive on the Kuomintang front and gradually shifted their main force to the front of the liberated areas; at the same time, keeping their eyes on the defeatism prevailing in the Kuomintang government, they declared that they were willing to conclude peace by making a compromise; moreover, they lured the traitor Wang Ching-wei to leave Chungking and establish a puppet government in Nanking to carry out a policy of deceiving the nation. Thereafter the Kuomintang government began to change its policy, gradually shifting its emphasis from resisting Japan to opposing the Communists and the people. This was manifested first of all in military affairs. The Kuomintang government adopted a policy of passive resistance to Japan so as to conserve its own military strength, leaving the heavy burden of fighting to the front of the liberated areas; thus it enabled the Japanese invaders to direct their large-scale onslaught against the liberated areas, while it "sat atop a mountain to watch the tigers fight".

In 1939, the Kuomintang government adopted the re-actionary "Measures to Restrict the Activities of Alien Parties" and completely deprived the people and the anti-Japanese parties of whatever rights they had won during the early period of the War of Resistance. Since then all the democratic parties in the Kuomintang-controlled areas, first and foremost the Chinese Communist Party, have been driven underground by the Kuomintang government. The prisons and concentration camps in every province in the Kuomintang-controlled areas have been packed with Communists, patriotic youths and other fighters for democracy. In five years, from 1939 to the autumn of 1943, the Kuomintang government has started three large-scale "anti-Communist upsurges",[2] breaking up internal solidarity and creating a serious danger of civil war. It was in this period that there occurred the world-shaking incident of "disbanding" the New Fourth Army and annihilating more than nine thousand of its troops in southern Anhwei. Up to now the Kuomintang troops have not stopped attacking the armies of the liberated areas and there is no indication that they will stop. Under such circumstances, the Kuomintang reactionaries have been spouting slander and calumny of all sorts. Names and accusations like "the traitor's party", "the traitor's army", "the traitor's district", and "undermining the resistance and endangering the state", etc.—all hurled libellously at the Communist Party, the Eighth Route and New Fourth Armies and the liberated areas—are the coinage of those reactionaries. To meet the crisis, the Central Committee of the Chinese Communist Party issued on July 7, 1939, a manifesto setting forth the following slogans: "Uphold resistance and oppose capitulation; uphold solidarity and oppose split; uphold progress and oppose retrogression." In accordance with these timely slogans our Party had in five years vigorously repulsed the three reactionary, anti-popular "anti-Communist up-surges" and overcome the crisis.

During these years there was actually no serious fighting on the Kuomintang front. The bayonet of the Japanese aggressors was mainly pointed at the liberated areas. By 1943, the army and the people of the liberated areas engaged 64 per cent of the Japanese forces invading China and 95 per cent of the puppet forces, while the Kuomintang front sustained the charge of only 36 per cent of the Japanese troops and 5 per cent of the puppet forces.

In 1944 the Japanese aggressors launched operations to capture the trans-continental communication lines,[3] and the Kuomintang forces, panic-stricken, were absolutely unable to resist. Within a few months an extensive area covering the provinces of Honan, Hunan, Kwangsi and Kwangtung fell into the enemy's hands. It was only then that some change took place in the percentage of the enemy forces engaged on each of the two fronts. At the very moment I am making this report, however, out of the forty divisions or 580,000 men of the Japanese forces invading China (not including those in Manchuria), twenty-two divisions and a half, numbering 320,000 or 56 per cent of the enemy troops, are engaged on the front of the liberated areas, while no more than seventeen divisions and a half, numbering 260,000 or only 44 per cent of the enemy troops, are engaged on the Kuomintang front. There has been no change whatsoever as to the ratio of the puppet forces engaged on the two fronts.

Furthermore, it should be pointed out that the puppet forces numbering more than 800,000 men (including the regular and local puppet forces) are chiefly composed of either troops which surrendered to the enemy under their Kuomintang commanders or troops which the surrendered Kuomintang officers have organised. The Kuomintang reactionaries first equipped these puppet forces with the absurd treasonable theory of "national salvation along a curvilinear line", and then supported them both morally and organisationally, directing them to conspire with the Japanese aggressors against the liberated areas of the Chinese people. In addition, these reactionaries have mobilised large forces amounting to 797,000 men to blockade and attack the Shensi-Kansu-Ningsia border region and other liberated areas. Because of the Kuomintang government's policy of news blockade, many Chinese and foreigners are kept in the dark about this grave situation.

China's Liberated Areas

China's liberated areas under the leadership of the Chinese Communist Party have now a population of 95,500,000. They cover a region from Inner Mongolia in the north to Hainan Island in the south; almost wherever the enemy goes, there he finds the Eighth Route Army, the New Fourth Army or some other people's forces operating. This vast liberated portion of China consists of nineteen major liberated areas, covering the greater or lesser parts of the provinces of Liaoning, Jehol, Chahar, Suiyuan, Shensi, Kansu, Ningsia, Shansi, Hopeh, Honan, Shantung, Kiangsu, Chekiang, Anhwei, Kiangsi, Hupeh, Hunan, Kwangtung and Fukien. Yenan is the guiding centre of all these liberated areas. In this vast liberated portion of China the Shensi-Kansu-Ningsia border region west of the Yellow river, with a population of only 1,500,000, is but one of the nineteen liberated areas; and except for two liberated areas, one in eastern Chekiang and the other on Hainan Island, it is the smallest in population. Some people, unaware of this fact, think that China's liberated areas consist mainly of the Shensi-Kansu-Ningsia border region. This is a misconception resulting from the Kuomintang government's news blockade. In all the liberated areas, the essential policies of the Anti-Japanese National United Front have been wholly put into practice, and governments based on co-operation between the Communists and representatives of other anti-Japanese parties as well as people without party affiliation, *i.e.* local coalition governments, have been or are being elected by the people. In the liberated areas all the people have been mobilised. It is owing to all these factors that, despite the pressure of a formidable enemy, the blockade and attacks of the Kuomintang troops and the complete absence of outside help, China's liberated areas have been able to stand unshaken, to develop daily by reducing the enemy-occupied areas and expanding themselves, and become the model of a democratic China and a main force in co-ordinated action with the Allied countries to drive out the Japanese aggressors and liberate the Chinese people. The armed forces of the liberated areas—the Eighth Route Army, the New Fourth Army and other armed forces of the people— have played not only a heroic, exemplary role in fighting the Japanese but also an exemplary role in carrying our various democratic measures of the Anti-Japanese National United Front. On September 22, 1937, the Central Committee of the Chinese Communist Party made the declaration that "Since the Three People's Principles of Dr. Sun Yat-sen are what China needs today, our Party pledges itself to fight for their complete realisation", a declaration which has been completely translated into deeds in China's liberated areas.

The Kuomintang-controlled Areas

The chief ruling clique in the Kuomintang has persisted in its dictatorial rule and pursued a policy of passive resistance to

Japan as well as an anti-popular domestic policy. As a result, the Kuomintang's armed forces have shrunk to less than half their original size, with most of them nearly deprived of fighting capacity; a deep rift has developed between the Kuomintang and the broad masses of the people and a grave crisis has been brought about, causing the people to suffer from wretched poverty, seethe with discontent and rise in revolt everywhere; and finally this has led to the chief ruling clique of the Kuomintang not only playing a sharply reduced role in the war against the Japanese invaders but also becoming an obstacle to the mobilisation and unification of all anti-Japanese forces of the Chinese people.

Why has such a grave situation arisen under the leadership of the Kuomintang's chief ruling clique? Because that clique represents the interests of China's big landlords, big bankers and big compradors. This reactionary stratum composed of a handful of people monopolises all the important military, political, economic and cultural organisations under the control of the Kuomintang government. These people place the safeguarding of their own interests above the Anti-Japanese War. They also say that "the nation is above all", but their actions never conform to the demands of the majority of the nation. They also say that "the state is above all", but what they mean is the feudal and fascist dictatorial state of the big landlords, big bankers and big compradors, not a democratic state of the masses of the people. Therefore they are afraid of the rise of the people, of democratic movements and of an Anti-Japanese War in which the whole nation is thoroughly mobilised. Herein lies the root cause of their policy of passive resistance to Japan and their reactionary anti-popular, anti-democratic and anti-Communist policy at home. They have adopted in every field a dual policy. For instance, they resist Japan on the one hand and adopt a passive war policy on the other and, more often than not, they are chosen by the Japanese aggressor as the object for his blandishments to surrender. They declare that they will develop China's economy but in fact they amass great wealth to build up their own bureaucratic capital, *i.e.* the capital of the big landlords, big bankers and big compradors, and monopolise the life-lines of China's economy, ruthlessly oppressing the peasants, the workers, the petty bourgeoisie and the national bourgeoisie. They declare that they will realise "democracy" and "return the state power to the people", but in fact they ruthlessly suppress the people's democratic movements and refuse to introduce the slightest democratic reform. On the one hand they declare that "the Communist problem is a political one and should be solved by political means", but on the other hand they ruthlessly repress the Chinese Communist Party militarily, politically and economically, regarding the Communist Party as their "enemy No. 1", and the Japanese aggressors as only "enemy No. 2"; and day in and day out they are actively preparing a civil war and concocting schemes for annihilating the Communists. They declare that they will establish a "modern state", but in fact they are trying hard to maintain the feudal and fascist dictatorial rule of the big landlords, big bankers and big compradors. In appearance they maintain diplomatic relations with the Soviet Union but in reality they are hostile towards it. On the one hand they chime in with the American isolationists that "Asia comes before Europe" in order to prolong the life of fascist Germany, indeed the life of all fascists and of their own fascist rule over the Chinese people, but on the other they gamble and try to pull a diplomatic coup, while masquerading as anti-fascist heroes. If you want to know the source of such self-contradictory dual policies, the answer is that they all stem from one root—the social stratum of the big landlords, big bankers and big compradors.

But the Kuomintang is not a homogeneous political party. Though controlled and led by the reactionary clique representing the stratum of the big landlords, big bankers and big compradors, it must not be identified as a whole with this reactionary bloc. Some leading figures of the Kuomintang do not belong to this bloc but are even attacked, excluded or despised by it. A large number of the Kuomintang cadres and many among the rank and file of both that party and the Three People's Principles Youth Corps are dissatisfied with the leadership of that clique, and some of them are even opposed to it. Such a situation obtains in all the Kuomintang armies, government bodies and economic and cultural institutions under the control of this reactionary clique. In all of them there lurk large numbers of democratic people. Far from being a close-knit body, this reactionary clique is divided into several factions fighting against one another. It is undoubtedly wrong to regard the Kuomintang as a homogenous body of reactionaries.

A Contrast

The Chinese people can see a striking contrast between the liberated areas and the Kuomintang-controlled areas.

Is not the situation clear enough? Here are two lines, the line of a people's war and the line of passive resistance opposed to it; as a result, one triumphs even though the conditions are adverse and foreign aid is lacking, as in the Chinese liberated areas, and the other fails even though conditions are extremely favourable and foreign aid can be obtained, as in the Kuomintang-controlled areas.

The Kuomintang government attributes its defeat to lack of armament. Yet one may ask: who lacks armament, the Kuomintang troops or the troops of the liberated areas? Of all Chinese troops, those of the liberated areas suffer most acutely from the lack of armament; they can only capture arms from the enemy and manufacture their own under the most adverse conditions.

Is not the armament of the Kuomintang Central Army far better than that of the provincial troops? Yet in fighting capacity the Central Army is mostly inferior to the provincial troops.

The Kuomintang commands vast resources of manpower, but owing to its erroneous policy of conscription, replenishment of manpower becomes extremely difficult. Though cut off from each other by the enemy and busy waging a ceaseless struggle, China's liberated areas have secured for themselves an inexhaustible supply of manpower by adopting extensively a system of militia and self-defence corps well adapted to the need of the people, and by eliminating waste and abuse of manpower.

The Kuomintang rules over vast areas abounding in grain and is supplied annually by the people with 70,000,000 to 100,000,000 market piculs[4] of grain, the greater part of which, however, is embezzled by those in charge, so that the Kuomintang army faces a constant food shortage and its soldiers are lean and pale starvelings. A major portion of China's liberated areas is situated in the enemy rear and is devastated by the enemy through his policy of triple atrocity of burning all, killing all and looting all, and in some districts, like northern Shensi, land is poor for cultivation; yet we have with our own hands successfully solved the food problem by developing agricultural production.

The Kuomintang-controlled areas are facing an extremely grave economic crisis; most of the industrial enterprises there have gone bankrupt and even such daily necessities as cloth have to be imported from the United States. China's liberated areas, however, are able to produce their own cloth and other daily necessities through the development of industry.

In the Kuomintang-controlled areas, workers, peasants, shop assistants, government workers, intellectuals and cultural workers live in extreme misery. In China's liberated areas all the people have food and clothes, and all are employed.

A characteristic of the Kuomintang-controlled areas is that government officials are concurrently engaged in business, profiteering out of the Anti-Japanese War and making graft a fashion, and are utterly lost to shame and honour. On the other hand a characteristic of China's liberated areas is that the cadres play an exemplary role in hard struggles, engaging in production besides performing their regular duties, and honesty is promoted and graft completely prohibited.

The people in the Kuomintang-controlled areas are deprived of all freedoms. But the people in China's liberated areas are given full freedoms.

Such is the abnormal situation confronting the Kuomintang rulers. Who is to blame? They themselves or others? The foreign countries for not giving them sufficient aid, or the Kuomintang government for its dictatorial rule, its corruption and incompetence? Is the answer not obvious enough?

Who "Undermines the Resistance and Endangers the State"?

Is it not precisely the Kuomintang government that has, on indisputable evidence, undermined the Chinese people's resistance and endangered their state? That government devoted itself wholeheartedly to civil war for fully ten years, pointing its bayonet at the people while utterly neglecting national defence and, through its policy of non-resistance, giving away the four north-eastern provinces. When the Japanese aggressors broke their way inside the Shanhai pass, it put up resistance in a flurry and then retreated from Lukouchiao all the way to the province of Kweichow. Yet the Kuomintang people allege that "the Communist Party undermines the Resistance and endangers the state" (see Resolution of the Eleventh Plenary Session of the Central Executive Committee of the Kuomintang, held in September 1943). The only evidence they can adduce is the fact that the Communist Party, uniting with all sections of the people, has created the liberated areas of China which are fighting the Japanese heroically. Since the logic of such Kuomintang members is so different from that of the Chinese people, small wonder that no common understanding can be reached on many problems.

Here are two questions:

First, what exactly has made the Kuomintang government abandon so vast a territory stretching from Heilungkiang to Lukouchiao and again from Lukouchiao to the province of Kweichow, and so huge a population in all those areas? Can it be anything else than the policy of non-resistance, the policy of passive resistance to Japan and the domestic policy of opposing the people that the Kuomintang government has adopted?

Secondly, what exactly has enabled China's liberated areas to repulse successfully the ruthless attacks of the Japanese and puppet forces over a long period, to recover such vast territories and liberate such an immense population from the grip of the national enemy? Can it be anything else than the correct line of a people's war?

So-called "Disobedience to Government Decrees and Military Orders"

The Kuomintang government constantly accuses the Chinese Communist Party of "disobedience to government decrees and military orders". But we can only answer that fortunately the Chinese Communists share the common sense of the Chinese people and have not obeyed "government decrees and military orders" which actually mean handing over to the Japanese aggressors China's liberated areas, areas recovered by the

Chinese people from the Japanese through difficulties and hard-ships, as witness the "Measures to Restrict the Activities of Alien Parties" (1939), the orders to "disband the New Fourth Army" and "have it withdrawn to the north of the old course of the Yellow river" (both 1941), the demand that "the Chinese Communist Party be dissolved" (1943), the demand that all our troops "except ten divisions be disbanded within a time limit" (1944), the "concession" made by the Kuomintang government in its recent talks with us requesting that we hand over to them our armed forces and local governments in exchange not for a coalition government but for a few posts for the Communists in the Kuomintang dictatorial government, etc. Fortunately we have not obeyed these decrees and orders and have thus been able to preserve for the Chinese people a stretch of unsullied soil and a brave anti-Japanese army. Should not the Chinese people congratulate themselves on such "disobedience"? Does the Kuomintang still feel dissatisfied after giving over to the Japanese aggressors, through its own fascist government decrees and defeatist military orders, the land and people of the vast area from Heilungkiang to Kwei-chow? Outside the Japanese aggressors and the reactionaries, could there be any patriotic and conscientious Chinese who would welcome such "government decrees and military orders"? Without a coalition government, a coalition govern-ment not merely in form but in essence, which is democratic and not fascist-dictatorial, is it conceivable that the Chinese people would permit the Chinese Communists to hand over on its own to the defeatist, fascist and dictatorial Kuomintang government the Chinese liberated areas where the people have won freedom together with their army which has accomp-lished meritorious deeds in the War of Resistance? Were it not for the Chinese liberated areas and their armies, could the anti-Japanese cause of the Chinese people be continued as it is today? And is it conceivable what would become of the future of the nation?

The Danger of Civil War

The chief ruling clique of the Kuomintang has thus far adhered to its reactionary policy of dictatorship and civil war.

There are many indications that it has long prepared, and is preparing particularly at this moment, to start a civil war as soon as the forces of a certain Allied country have driven the Japanese aggressors out of a good portion of the Chinese mainland. It also expects the generals of certain Allied countries to perform the same duties in China as the British general Scobie is performing in Greece. It cheers the massacres perpetrated by Scobie and the reactionary Greek government. It attempts to plunge China again into the maelstrom of civil war of 1927–37. Under the smoke-screen of "convening the National Assembly" and "political settlement", the chief ruling clique of the Kuomintang is now making clandestine preparations for a civil war. If our fellow conntrymen fail to notice and expose this dirty scheme and stop such preparations, then one fine morning they will be aroused by the cannonade of civil war.

Parley

In order to defeat the Japanese aggressors, build up a new China and prevent civil war, the Chinese Communist Party, after consulting other democratic parties, demanded in September 1944 at the People's Political Council that the Kuomintang one-party dictatorship be abolished immediately and a democratic coalition government be formed. This demand was undoubtedly a timely one, and within a few months it won responses from the broad masses of the people.

On the questions of abolishing the one-party dictatorship, forming a coalition government and carrying out necessary democratic reforms, we have held many parleys with the Kuomintang government, but all our proposals have been rejected. The Kuomintang is neither willing to abolish its one-party dictatorship and form a coalition government, nor willing to carry out any urgently needed democratic reforms, such as abolition of the secret service, annulment of reactionary laws and decrees for suppressing the freedoms of the people, release of political prisoners, recognition of the legal status of the various political parties and of the liberated areas and withdrawal of the armies encircling and attacking these areas. Thus political relations in China have become very strained.

Two Prospects

Considering the whole situation and the above analysis of the actual conditions, both international and domestic, I request everyone here not to expect that all will go smooth and fine with our cause. No, that is not the case; in fact, we are faced with two possibilities or two prospects, good as well as bad. One possibility or one prospect is the continuance of the dictatorial fascist rule which permits no democratic reforms and stresses opposition to the people rather than to the Japanese aggressors; a civil war may break out even after the defeat of the Japanese aggressors, dragging China back into untold sufferings, into her old status of being dependent and unfree, undemocratic and disunited, poverty-stricken and weak. This possibility or prospect remains, and does not cease to exist or disappear by itself merely because the international situation is favourable, or the people at home have become more awakened and their organised strength has grown. Those who hope that this possibility or prospect will become a reality in China are the anti-popular clique in the Kuomintang at home and foreign reactionaries cherishing imperialist notions. This is one aspect of the matter that we must pay heed to.

But on the other hand, considering the whole situation, the international and domestic conditions analysed above, we have more confidence and courage in striving for the second possibility, the second prospect. That means overcoming all difficulties, uniting the people of the whole country, abolishing the fascist dictatorial rule of the Kuomintang, carrying out democratic reforms, consolidating and expanding the anti-Japanese forces, defeating the Japanese aggressors thoroughly and building up a new China that is independent and free, democratic and united, prosperous and powerful. Those who hope that this possibility or prospect will become a reality in China are the broad masses of the people, the Communist Party and other political parties at home, and all nations who treat us as equals and the progressives and the broad masses of the people abroad.

We are fully aware that the Chinese people and we Communists are still facing great difficulties and numerous obstacles and that we still have a long and tortuous route to traverse.

But we are equally aware that we, together with the Chinese people, will certainly overcome whatever difficulties or obstacles lie before us and fulfil our historical tasks in China. The great task for ourselves and the Chinese people is to make every exertion to avert the first possibility and realise the second, to avert the first prospect and realise the second. The international and domestic situation is in the main favourable to us and the Chinese people. This I have clearly explained above. We hope that in view of the general trend of world events and the aspirations of the Chinese people, the Kuomintang authorities will resolutely change their present erroneous policies so as to win the Anti-Japanese War, mitigate the suffering of the Chinese people and hasten the advent of a new China. It must be understood that, however tortuous the route may be, the Chinese people will fulfil their tasks of achieving independence and liberation and the time for them to do so has already arrived. The great aspirations of countless martyrs of the past hundred-odd years must be fulfilled by our generation; whoever attempts to deter us will certainly fail in the end.

IV. THE POLICY OF THE CHINESE COMMUNIST PARTY

The above is my analysis of the two lines in China's Anti-Japanese War. Such an analysis is absolutely necessary. For up to this moment many among the broad masses of Chinese people still do not know the actual situation of China's Anti-Japanese War. Because of the Kuomintang's policy of news blockade, many people in the Kuomintang-controlled areas and in foreign countries are blindfolded. Before the visit in 1944 of a group of Chinese and foreign correspondents, many people outside knew practically nothing about China's liberated areas. As the Kuomintang government was very much afraid that the actual conditions of the liberated areas might be known to the world, no sooner had this group of correspondents left in that year than the Kuomintang government bolted the door, permitting no more visits to the liberated areas by any correspondent. In the same manner it drew a veil over the actual conditions in its own areas. I therefore feel that we are in duty bound to reveal to the public as clearly as possible the true picture of the "two different areas". Only with a clear grasp of the whole situation in China can the people understand why there are such differences in policy between the two major political parties in China, the Chinese Communist Party and the Kuomintang, and why there is such a struggle between the two lines. Only then can we make people understand that the dispute between the two parties is not unnecessary or unimportant, and decidedly not wilful as some people have alleged, but one of principle and a matter of life and death for hundreds of millions of people.

In the present grave situation in which China finds herself, all the Chinese people, all democratic parties and individuals, all the people of foreign countries who are concerned about the Chinese situation cherish the hope that disunity will be replaced by unity and that democratic reforms will be introduced; and all desire to learn about the policies adopted by the Chinese Communist Party for solving many vital problems of today. Our Party members, of course, feel even greater concern about these matters.

Our policies of an Anti-Japanese National United Front have always been unequivocal and have been tested in the eight years of war. This Congress should sum all of them up in order to guide our future struggles.

I shall give below a number of definite conclusions which our Party has reached on the important policies for the solution of China's problems.

Our General Programme

In order to mobilise and unify all the anti-Japanese forces of the Chinese people, to annihilate thoroughly the Japanese aggressors and to build up a new China which is independent and free, democratic and united, prosperous and powerful, the Chinese people, the Chinese Communist Party and all the anti-Japanese democratic parties are in urgent need of a common programme to which they all agree.

Such a common programme may be divided into two parts, the general and the specific. Let us first take up the general programme and then the specific one.

At the present stage of China's development we Communists, upon the major premise of annihilating completely the

Japanese aggressors and building up a new China, are at one with the overwhelming majority of the Chinese population on certain basic points. They are: first, China's state system should not be a feudal, fascist and anti-popular one under the dictatorship of the big landlord class and the big bourgeoisie, because this anti-popular system has proved completely bankrupt in the eighteen years in which the Kuomintang's chief ruling clique has been in power. Secondly, it is impossible and therefore inadvisable for China to establish a democratic state of the old type under the sole dictatorship of the national bourgeoisie, because in China, on the one hand the national bourgeoisie has shown itself very flabby both economically and politically and, on the other, a new factor has already emerged, namely, the Chinese proletariat (together with its leader, the Chinese Communist Party) which has awakened politically, demonstrated its great ability on the Chinese political stage and assumed leadership over the broad masses of the peasantry, the urban petty bourgeoisie, the intelligentsia and other democratic people. And thirdly, it is impossible for the Chinese people to put a socialist state system into practice at the present stage when it is still their task to overthrow foreign and feudal oppression and the requisite social and economic conditions for socialism are still lacking.

What then do we propose? We propose to establish, after the complete defeat of the Japanese aggressors, a new-democratic state system, as we call it, namely, a state of the united front or democratic alliance based on the overwhelming majority of the people under the leadership of the working class.

This is a state system which truly meets the demands of the overwhelming majority of the Chinese population, because it has won and can win: first, the approval of millions of industrial workers and tens of millions of handicraftsmen and farm labourers; secondly, the approval of 80 per cent of the Chinese population, i.e. 360 million peasants out of a population of 450 million; and thirdly, the approval of the broad masses of the urban petty bourgeoisie, the national bourgeoisie, the enlightened gentry and other sections of patriotic people.

There are, of course, still contradictions among these classes, notably the contradiction between labour and capital; consequently each class puts forward certain special demands. It would be dishonest and erroneous to ignore these contradictions and different demands. But throughout the stage of New Democracy, these contradictions or differences in demands will not grow and should not be allowed to grow beyond the limits set by the common demands. An adjustment can be made between all these contradictions and differences. And through such an adjustment the classes can jointly carry out the political, economic and cultural construction of the new-democratic state.

The new-democratic politics we advocate consists in the over-throw of foreign oppression and feudal and fascist oppression within the country and the setting up of a political system, not of the democracy of the old type but of the united front of all democratic classes. These views of ours are completely in accord with Dr. Sun Yat-sen's views on revolution. Dr. Sun says in the Manifesto of the First National Congress of the Kuomintang drawn up by himself:

> "The so-called democratic system in modern nations is usually monopolised by the bourgeoisie and has simply become an instrument for oppressing the common people. As to the Principle of Democracy of the Kuomintang, it stands for something to be shared by all the common people and not to be monopolised by a few."

This is a great political dictum of Dr. Sun Yat-sen. The Chinese people, the Chinese Communist Party and all other democratic people must respect this dictum, resolutely put it into practice and must, in order to defend and develop this perfectly correct political principle of New Democracy, wage relentless struggles against any person or group of people who violate or oppose it.

The state structure of New Democracy should be based on democratic centralism, with the people's congresses at various levels determining the major policies and electing the government. It is at once democratic and centralised, i.e. centralised on the basis of democracy and democratic under centralised guidance. Only this sytem can, on the one hand, give full expression to democracy by investing with full powers the people's congresses at all levels and, on the other, guarantee the centralised administration of state affairs by enabling the

governments at various levels to effect centralised administration of all affairs entrusted to them by the people's congresses
at their corresponding levels and protect all the indispensable
democratic activities of the people.

Troops and other armed forces constitute an important part
of the apparatus of the new-democratic state power; without
them the state cannot be defended. All armed forces of the new-
democratic state, like all the organs of power, belong to the
people and protect the people; they have nothing in common
with the troops and police of the old type which belong to a few
persons and oppress the people.

The new-democratic economy we advocate also conforms to
Dr. Sun's principles. On the agrarian problem, Dr. Sun stood
for "land to the tillers". On the problem of industry and commerce, Dr. Sun stated in the Manifesto quoted above:

"Enterprises, whether Chinese-owned or foreign-owned,
which are either monopolistic in character or of a very large
scale and cannot be managed by private interests such as
banks, railways, air communications, etc., shall be operated
and managed by the state, so that private capital cannot
hold in its grasp the livelihood of the people: this is the main
principle of the control of capital."

In the present stage we fully agree with these views of Dr. Sun
on the economic problem.

Those people are mistaken who think that the Chinese Communists are against the development of individual initiative, the
development of private capital and the protection of private
property. Foreign and feudal oppression cruelly fetters the
development of the Chinese people's individual initiative,
hinders the development of private capital and destroys the
property of the broad masses of the people. The task of the
New Democracy we advocate is precisely to remove such fetters
and stop such destruction; to assure the broad masses of the
Chinese people the possibility of freely developing personal
initiative in society, freely developing a private capitalist
economy which, however, must not "hold in its grasp the
livelihood of the people" but must bring them benefits, and also
secure the protection of all private property legitimately
acquired.

In accordance with Dr. Sun's principles and the experience of the Chinese revolution, China's national economy at the present stage should be composed of state, private-capitalist and co-operative sectors. But the state referred to here must certainly not be one "monopolised by a few", but a new-democratic state "shared by all the common people" under the leadership of the proletariat.

The new-democratic culture must likewise be one "shared by all the common people", that is to say, a national, scientific and popular culture; it must not be a culture "monopolised by a few".

Such is the general or basic programme which we Communists advocate for the present stage and for the entire course of the bourgeois-democratic revolution. In comparison with our future or maximum programme of socialism and communism, this is our minimum programme. The realisation of this programme will enable China to advance a step from her present status as a country or society, *i.e.* to develop from a colonial, semi-colonial and semi-feudal country or society into a new-democratic country or society.

The political leadership of the proletariat and the state enterprises and co-operatives directed by the proletariat, as stipulated in this programme, are factors of socialism. However, the realisation of this programme cannot yet turn China into a socialist society.

We Communists never conceal our political stand. It is definite and beyond any doubt that our future or maximum programme is to head China for socialism and communism. Both the name of our Party and our Marxist world-view unequivocally point to this ultimate ideal of the future, a future of incomparable brightness and beauty. Upon joining the Party, every Communist bears in his mind the struggle for two clearly defined objectives, namely, the new-democratic revolution at present and socialism and communism in the future, and this despite the animosity, calumny, vituperation and ridicule which, out of their ignorance and baseness, the enemies of communism level against us and which we must resolutely combat. As to the well-meaning sceptics, we should not attack them but explain things to them with goodwill and patience. All this is very clear, definite and unequivocal.

But all Chinese Communists and all who sympathise with the ideas of Communism must struggle to achieve the objective of the present stage; they must struggle against foreign and feudal oppression and for the deliverance of the Chinese people from their tragic fate of colonialism, semi-colonialism and semi-feudalism, and for the establishment of a new-democratic China under proletarian leadership and with the liberation of the peasantry as its main task, *i.e.* a China of the revolutionary Three People's Principles of Dr. Sun Yat-sen, a China independent and free, democratic and united, prosperous and powerful. We have actually been doing so: we Communists, together with the broad masses of the Chinese people, have heroically fought for this end for the past twenty-four years.

If any Communist or person sympathising with the Communist Party refuses to strive for this objective, looks down upon this bourgeois-democratic revolution, slackens ever so slightly his effort or neglects his work in this revolution and shows the least bit of disloyalty, luke-warmness or reluctance to shed his blood or give his life for it, while prattling about socialism and communism, he is more or less, wittingly or unwittingly, betraying socialism and communism and is certainly not a conscious, faithful believer in communism. It is only through democracy that socialism can be attained—this is the fundamental truth of Marxism. In China the fight for democracy will be a protracted one. It would be a sheer illusion to try to build socialism on the ruins of the colonial, semi-colonial and semi-feudal order, without a united new-democratic state, without the development of a new-democratic state, without the development of private capitalist and co-operative enterprises, without the development of a national, scientific and popular culture that is a new-democratic culture, or without the liberation and development of the individual initiative of hundreds of millions of people—in short, without pushing to the end the democratic revolution which is bourgeois in character, a democratic revolution of a new type led by the Communist Party.

Some people fail to understand why the Communists should advocate the development of capitalism under given conditions instead of fearing it. Our answer is simple: to replace the oppression of foreign imperialism and native feudalism with capitalism developed to a certain degree is not only an advance but also an unavoidable process. Such development is beneficial not only to the bourgeoisie but also, or even more, to the proletariat. Foreign imperialism and native feudalism are things unneeded in China today but native capitalism is not; on the contrary, there is too little of it. Strangely enough, some spokesmen of the Chinese bourgeoisie dare not openly advocate the development of capitalism, but refer to it in a roundabout way. There are others who flatly deny that capitalism in China should be given a chance to develop to a necessary extent and talk about turning China straight away into a socialist society and "accomplishing at one stroke" the tasks of the Three People's Principles and socialism. Obviously these opinions are either a reflection of the weakness of the Chinese national bourgeoisie or a trick of the big landlords and the big bourgeoisie to mislead the people. Basing ourselves on the Marxist understanding of the laws of social development, we Communists clearly realise that under the conditions of a China with a new-democratic state system, we can facilitate the further progress of society only when we, together with the state's own enterprises and the individual and co-operative enterprises of the toiling masses, assist the development of private capitalist enterprises in so far as they are not permitted to hold the livelihood of the people in their grasp. As for us Chinese Communists, we shall not allow any empty talk or deceitful tricks to confuse our clear heads.

Some people wonder whether we Communists are quite sincere in stating that "the Three People's Principles being what China needs today, our Party pledges itself to fight for their complete realisation". This is because they do not understand that the basic tenets of the Three People's Principles enunciated by Dr. Sun Yat-sen in the Manifesto of the First National Congress of the Kuomintang of 1924, which we accept, agree with certain basic tenets of our Party's programme for the present stage, *i.e.* our minimum programme. It should be pointed out, however, that the Three People's Principles of Dr. Sun Yat-sen concur with our Party's programme for the present stage only in certain basic tenets and not in everything. The new-democratic programme of our Party is, of course, much more comprehensive than Dr. Sun's principles; particularly in the twenty years since Dr. Sun's death, the development of the Chinese revolution has led to a great development in our Party's theory, programme and practice of New Democracy, and there will be an even greater development from now on. In essence, however, Dr. Sun's Three People's Principles are the programme of New Democracy as distinguished from the old Three People's principles; naturally they are "what China needs today" and "our Party pledges itself to fight for their complete realisation". To us Chinese Communists the struggle to implement the minimum programme of our Party and the struggle to implement Dr. Sun's revolutionary or new Three People's Principles are basically (though not in every respect) one and the same thing. Therefore it will be proved, as it has always been, that the Chinese Communists are the most sincere and thoroughgoing in implementing the revolutionary Three People's Principles.

Some people wonder whether the Chinese Communists, once in power, would follow the example of the Russian Communists and establish a proletarian dictatorship and a one-party government. Our answer is that a new-democratic state based on an alliance of several democratic classes is different in principle from a socialist state under proletarian dictatorship. Beyond doubt, our system of New Democracy will be built under the leadership of the proletariat, of the Communist Party, but throughout the stage of New Democracy there cannot and therefore should not be in China a system of one-class dictatorship and one-party government. We have no reason to refuse co-operation with any political party, social group or individual, so long as their attitude towards the Communist Party is co-operative and not hostile. Russian history has shaped the Russian system—in Russia the social system of man's exploitation of man has been abolished; the political, economic and cultural system of the newest type of democracy, socialism, has been realised; the people have discarded all anti-socialist political parties and support only the Bolsheviks; all these things, perfectly necessary and reasonable for the Russians, have made Russia what it is. But even in Russia, where the Bolshevik Party is the only political party, the system adopted in the organs of political power is still one of the alliance of

workers, peasants and intellectuals, or one of the alliance of
Party members and non-Party people, and not a system which
allows the participation of the working class alone or of the
Bolsheviks alone. Similarly, Chinese history of the present stage
will shape a Chinese system for the present stage, and for a long
time to come there will exist in China a particular form of
state and political power, *i.e.* New Democracy based on the
alliance of several democratic classes, a system which is distinguished from the Russian system and which is perfectly
necessary and reasonable for us.

Our Specific Programme

On the basis of the general programme outlined above our
Party should have a specific programme for each particular
stage. Throughout the course of the bourgeois-democratic
revolution, which may last for several decades, our general
programme of New Democracy will remain unchanged. But
in different stages, as conditions change and differ, it is only
natural that our specific programmes should change accord-
ingly. For example, in the periods of the Northern Expedition,
the Agrarian Revolutionary War and the War of Resistance,
owing to the changes that took place in the camps of our
enemies and of our allies, changes had to be made in our
specific programmes, while our general programme of New
Democracy remained the same.

At present the Chinese people find themselves under the
following circumstances: (1) the Japanese aggressors have not
yet been defeated; (2) the Chinese people urgently need to
unite themselves and carry out democratic reforms in order to
achieve national unity, speedily mobilise and unite all forces
fighting the Japanese invaders, and defeat the invaders in
co-ordination with the Allies; and (3) the Kuomintang government is disrupting national unity and obstructing democratic
reforms. Under such circumstances, what is our specific
programme or, in other words, what are the Chinese people's
immediate demands?

We consider the following to be their proper and minimum
demands:

Mobilise all forces and co-ordinate with the Allies to

defeat thoroughly the Japanese aggressors and establish international peace:

Abolish the Kuomintang's one-party dictatorship and form a democratic coalition government and a joint supreme command;

Punish the pro-Japanese elements, fascists and defeatists who are disrupting national unity and opposing the people, so as to achieve national unity;

Punish the reactionaries who are creating a threat of civil war, so as to ensure internal peace;

Punish the collaborators, take punitive action against officers who have gone over to the enemy, and punish Japanese spies;

Liquidate the secret police as a reactionary weapon and its activities for the suppression of the people, and abolish the concentration camps;

Revoke all reactionary laws and decrees aimed at suppressing the people's freedoms of speech, of the press, of assembly, of association, of political convictions, of religious belief and of person, and secure full civil rights to the people;

Recognise the legal status of all democratic parties;

Release all patriotic political prisoners;

Withdraw all troops encircling and attacking the Chinese liberated areas and dispatch them to the front of the Anti-Japanese War;

Recognise the legal status of all the forces in the liberated areas fighting the Japanese invaders and of governments there elected by the people;

Consolidate and expand the liberated areas and their armed forces and recover all lost territories;

Help the people in the enemy-occupied areas to organise underground forces and prepare armed uprisings;

Allow the people to arm themselves and defend their homes and their country;

Reform politically and militarily the armies directly under the Kuomintang supreme command, which constantly lose battles, oppress the people and discriminate against "alien" armies, and punish the commanders responsible for disastrous defeats;

Reform the conscription system and improve the living conditions of officers and men;

Take good care of the families of soldiers serving in the war against the Japanese invaders, so that they will fight at the front with their minds at ease;

Take good care of disabled veterans and the families of the soldiers who have died for the country, and help the demobilised veterans to find jobs or a means of making a living;

Develop war industry to facilitate the prosecution of the war;

Distribute impartially the military and financial aid of the Allies to all armies fighting the Japanese invaders;

Punish corrupt officials and institute a clean government;

Improve the material conditions of government workers of the middle and lower grades;

Secure democratic rights to all citizens of the country;

Abolish the *pao-chia*[5] system that oppresses the people;

Extend relief to war refugees and people suffering from the effects of natural calamities;

Appropriate substantial funds for the extensive relief of war victims in the enemy-occupied areas after the recovery of these areas;

Abolish exorbitant taxes and miscellaneous assessments and establish a system of consolidated progressive taxation;

Carry out rural reforms, reduce rent and interest, give proper protection to tenant rights, grant low-interest loans to poor peasants and get the peasants organised in order to facilitate the development of agricultural production;

Outlaw bureaucrat-capital;

Abolish the present policy of economic control;

Stop the unrestricted inflation and rise in prices;

Give assistance to various privately owned industrial enterprises by giving them facilities for obtaining loans, purchasing raw material and marketing their products;

Improve the living conditions of the workers, extend relief to the unemployed and get the workers organised, in order to facilitate the development of industrial production;

Abolish the education of the Kuomintang indoctrination[6] and promote culture and education that is national, scientific and popular;

Guarantee the means of livelihood of the teaching and administrative staff members of educational institutions and guarantee academic freedom;

Protect the interests of youth, women and children, and extend aid to youths who cannot afford to attend school;

Get youth and women organised in order to participate on an equal footing with the other people in all kinds of work contributing to the war effort and promoting social progress;

Bring about freedom of marriage and equality between men and women and provide young people and children with a useful education;

Give better treatment to the national minorities in the country and grant them the right of self-government;

Protect the interests of oversea Chinese and give assistance to those who have returned to the motherland;

Protect foreigners who have fled to China from the oppression of the Japanese aggressors and support their struggle against the latter; and

Improve Sino-Soviet relations;

Etc., etc.

To do all this, it is of the utmost importance that the Kuomintang's one-party dictatorship be immediately abolished and a provisional central coalition government, a national democratic government be established, including the representatives of all parties and people without party affiliations fighting against the Japanese invaders. Without this prerequisite it is impossible to carry out any serious reform throughout the country, that is to say, in the Kuomintang-controlled areas.

All these demands are the voice of the broad masses of the Chinese people as well as the voice of the broad democratic press circles in the Allied countries.

A minimum specific programme unanimously agreed upon by all democratic parties fighting against the Japanese invaders is absolutely indispensable, and we are prepared to consult with them on the basis of the programme outlined above. Different parties may have different demands, but they should agree upon a common programme.

In the Kuomintang-controlled areas at present this programme is only a demand; in the enemy-occupied areas, except for the call to organise underground forces for armed uprisings, no part of it can be put into practice before these areas are recovered; but in the liberated areas it is already being put into practice and should be carried on.

In the above-mentioned immediate demands or specific programme of the Chinese people, many vital war-time and post-war problems are involved and require further explanation. In explaining them we shall both criticise some of the erroneous views of the Kuomintang's chief ruling clique and answer some questions raised by other people.

1. Thoroughly Annihilate the Japanese Aggressors and Make No Compromise

The Cairo conference[7] decided that the Japanese aggressors should be forced to surrender unconditionally. This is correct. But the Japanese aggressors are now working stealthily for a negotiated peace, while the pro-Japanese elements in the Kuomintang government are flirting unrestrainedly with Japanese emissaries through the puppet government of Nanking. Hence the danger of compromise is not yet entirely over. The Cairo conference made another good decision, namely, that the four north-eastern provinces, Taiwan and the Penhu Islands should be returned to China. But judging from its present policies we cannot rely upon the Kuomintang government to fight all the way to the Yalu river and recover all the lost territories. Under such circumstances, what should the Chinese people do? The Chinese people should demand that the Kuomintang government shall annihilate thoroughly the Japanese aggressors and make no compromise. They should demand that intrigues for compromise be immediately stopped. They should demand that the Kuomintang government changes its present policy of passive resistance and employs all its military strength to fight Japan actively. The Chinese people, instead of relying solely on the Kuomintang, should expand their own armies—the Eighth Route Army, the New Fourth Army and the other armed forces of the people—and develop extensively and on their own initiative anti-Japanese armed forces in all places where the enemy has reached in order to fight in direct co-ordination with the Allies and recover all lost territories. To defeat the Japanese aggressors is the sacred right of the Chinese people. If the reactionaries want to deprive them of this sacred right, to suppress their anti-Japanese activities or undermine their anti-Japanese forces, the Chinese people should, if reasoning proves useless, take up self-defence and resolutely repulse their attacks. For such reactionary deeds, which betray the interests of the nation, only aid and abet the Japanese aggressors.

2. Abolish the Kuomintang One-Party Dictatorship and Establish a Democratic Coalition Government

To wipe out the Japanese aggressors it is necessary to carry out democratic reforms throughout the country. Yet this is impossible unless the Kuomintang's one-party dictatorship is abolished and a democratic coalition government established.

The so-called one-party dictatorship of the Kuomintang is in reality a dictatorship of its anti-popular clique which disrupts China's national unity, which is to blame for the defeats on the Kuomintang front in the Anti-Japanese War and which forms the main obstacle to the mobilisation and unification of the forces of the Chinese people fighting against the invaders. Through their bitter experience in the eight years' war against Japan, the Chinese people have fully realised the evils of this dictatorship and naturally demand its immediate abolition. This anti-popular dictatorship is also the root of civil war; unless it is abolished immediately, the calamity of civil war will befall us again.

How unpopular and unrespected is "political tutelage" or "one-party dictatorship" can be seen from the fact that the appeal of the Chinese people for abolishing this anti-popular dictatorship has spread so wide and become so resounding that the Kuomintang authorities themselves cannot but openly recognise the need to "terminate political tutelage at an earlier date". No one dare say again that "political tutelage" or "one-party dictatorship" can do any good and should not be abolished or terminated—this is a great change in the present situation.

It is definite and beyond any doubt that it should be "terminated". But opinions differ as to how to terminate it. Some say: terminate it immediately and establish a provisional democratic coalition government. Others say: wait a bit, let's convene a "national assembly" and "return the state power to the people", but not to a coalition government.

What do all these things indicate?

They indicate two ways of doing things: the honest way and the dishonest way.

First, the honest way. This is, in line with the immediate demands of the Chinese people we have already mentioned, to proclaim immediately the abolition of the Kuomintang's one-party dictatorship, to establish a provisional Central government composed of representatives of the Kuomintang, the Communist Party, the Democratic League and people without party affiliations, and to promulgate a democratic political programme in order to regain national unity and defeat the Japanese aggressors. The representatives of the various parties and of people without party affiliation should hold a round-table conference to discuss and reach agreement upon these matters and then take action. This is the line of unity, supported resolutely by the Chinese people.

Secondly, the dishonest way. Arbitrarily convoking a "national assembly" entirely of its own creation in utter disregard of the demands of the broad masses and all democratic parties, the Kuomintang's anti-popular clique adopts an anti-democratic "constitution" for the practical purpose of maintaining its dictatorship, so that the cloak of "constitutionalism" is draped around the illegal "National Government"—a government which is privately appointed by a few dozen Kuomintang members, is devoid of any popular basis whatsoever and is imposed on the people—thereby pretending ostentatiously to "return the state power to the people" while actually "returning the state power" to the Kuomintang's anti-popular clique itself. Whoever objects to this will at once be accused of undermining "democracy" and "unity", and "reasons" will be found for ordering a punitive expedition against him. This is the line of disunity, opposed resolutely by the Chinese people.

The measures following from the line of disunity, which our anti-popular heroes are going to adopt, will expose them to the danger of ruin. They are putting a halter on their own necks, never to be loosened, and this halter is called the "national assembly". They planned to use the so-called "national assembly" as a magic wand, first, to counter the proposal for a coalition government, second, to maintain the dictatorship, and third, to find some justification for a civil war. History, however, will by its own logic take a course contrary to their wishes, and they are "lifting a rock only to have their own toes squashed". For it is now obvious to everybody that in the Kuomintang-controlled areas the people have no freedom, that in the Japanese-occupied areas the people cannot take part in the elections, and that in the liberated areas the people do enjoy freedom, but the Kuomintang government rejects them. Where, then, are the delegates of the national assembly to come from? How, then, can there be a "national assembly"? What the anti-popular heroes are clamouring for is the convention of something like the national assembly which the Kuomintang dictatorial government concocted single-handed eight years ago in the civil war period. If such an assembly is convened, the whole people will inevitably rise in opposition, and how can our anti-popular heroes get out of this predicament? All in all, the convention of such a concocted national assembly will only land them in an impasse.

We Communists propose to terminate the Kuomintang's one-party dictatorship by taking the following two steps: first, at the present stage, to form a provisional coalition government by common agreement of the representatives of all parties and people without party affiliation; secondly, at the next stage, through free and unrestricted elections, to convene a national assembly which will form a proper coalition government. In short, in both periods we shall establish coalition governments and unite with the representatives of all classes and political parties willing to join us in order to fight on a democratic common programme for the victory of the war against the Japanese invaders now and the building of a new China in the future.

No matter what the Kuomintang members or other parties and groups or individuals think about it, whether they are willing to follow it or not, aware of it or not, this is the only course China can take. This is a law of history, a necessary and inevitable trend which no force can alter.

On this problem and all others concerning democratic

reforms we Communists declare that, no matter how the Kuomintang authorities persist in their erroneous policies at present and how they may have resorted to negotiations as a means only to play for time and conciliate public opinion, we are ready to reopen negotiations with them as soon as they show willingness to renounce their erroneous policies and agree to carry out democratic reforms. But negotiations must be based on the general principle of resistance, unity and democracy, and we will not agree to any measures, plans or words, however attractive, that deviate from this general principle.

3. Freedoms for the People

At present the Chinese people's struggle for freedom is first and foremost directed against the Japanese aggressors. But the Kuomintang government has hindered them from fighting the Japanese aggressors by depriving them of their freedom and binding them hand and foot. Unless this problem is solved, the forces fighting the invaders cannot be mobilised and unified on a nation-wide scale. It is precisely to remove the cords binding the people and give them freedom to fight Japan, achieve unity and win democracy that we have put forward in the above-mentioned programme such demands as abolition of one-party dictatorship; establishment of a coalition government; abolition of the secret service; revocation of laws and decrees suppressing the people's freedom; punishment of collaborators, spies, pro-Japanese elements, fascists and corrupt officials; release of political prisoners; recognition of the legal status of all democratic parties; withdrawal of troops encircling and attacking the liberated areas; recognition of the liberated areas; abolition of the *pao-chia* system; and many other demands relating to economic and cultural problems and to the mass movement.

Freedom must be fought for by the people and cannot be bestowed by anyone. The people in China's liberated areas have won their freedom, and the people in other areas can win theirs and should fight for it. The greater the freedom the Chinese people win and the greater the organised democratic forces grow, the greater will be the possibility for establishing a unified provisional coalition government. This coalition government, once formed, will in turn grant the people all their freedoms and thereby consolidate its own foundation. Only then can we effect, after defeating the Japanese aggressors, free and unrestricted elections throughout the country, convene a democratic national assembly and establish a permanent coalition government for a united nation. Without freedom for the people there can be no national assembly or government really elected by the people. Is not this clear enough?

The freedoms of speech, of the press, of assembly, of association, of political convictions, of religious belief and of person are the most important freedoms for the people. In China it is only in the liberated areas that these freedoms are fully enjoyed.

In 1925 Dr. Sun Yat-sen stated in his Testament:

"For forty years I have devoted myself to the cause of the national revolution with the aim of winning freedom and equality for China. My experiences during these forty years have firmly convinced me that to achieve this aim we must arouse the masses of the people and unite in a common fight with those nations of the world who treat us on the basis of equality."

Dr. Sun's unworthy successors have betrayed him; they oppress the masses of the people instead of arousing them, and strip the masses of their freedom of speech, of the press, of assembly, of association, of political convictions, of religious belief and of person, and attach the labels "traitors' party", "traitors' armies", and "traitors' areas", to the Communist Party, the Eighth Route and New Fourth Armies and the liberated areas, which are really arousing the people and protecting their freedoms and rights. We hope that the time of calling white black will soon pass. Should this be allowed to go on, the Chinese people will come to the end of their forbearance.

4.   Unity of the People

In order to annihilate the Japanese aggressors, prevent civil war and build up a new China, divided China must become a unified China, and this is a historical task for the Chinese people.

But in what way will it be unified? To be unified autocratically by a dictator or to be unified democratically by the people? From the time of Yuan Shih-k'ai, the warlords of the Northern clique stressed autocratic unification. But what was the result? Contrary to their wishes, what they got was not unification but discord, and in the end they tumbled down from their pedestals. The Kuomintang's anti-popular clique, following in Yuan Shih-k'ai's footsteps, has pursued autocratic unification and prosecuted a civil war for fully ten years, only to usher in the Japanese aggressors and retreat to the summit of the Omei mountain[8] by themselves. And now they are yelling from the summit of the mountain about autocratic unification. Who will give ear to them? Can there be any patriotic and conscientious Chinese who will listen to them? Having lived for sixteen years under the rule of the Northern clique of warlords and for eighteen years under the Kuomintang's dictatorial rule, the Chinese people have acquired ample experience and discerning eyes. They demand a democratic unification by the masses of the people, not an autocratic unification by a dictator. As early as 1935, we Communists proposed the line of the Anti-Japanese National United Front, and since then not a day has passed but we have struggled for it. In 1939, when the Kuomintang carried out its reactionary "Measures to Restrict the Activities of Alien Parties", bringing about the threat of capitulation, split and retrogression, and the Kuomintang members were clamouring for autocratic unification, we again declared: It must not be unification for capitulation but unification for the resistance, not unification for split but unification for solidarity, and not unification for retrogression but unification for progress. Only the latter kind of unification is genuine unification and any other kind is bogus.[9] Six years have now elapsed, but the problem remains the same.

Without freedom for the people and the people's democratic system, can there be unification? No. But as soon as they come into being, there will be immediate unification. The Chinese people's movement for freedom, democracy and a coalition government is at the same time a movement for unification. It is for this reason that we have made in our specific programme a series of demands for freedom and democracy as well as for a coalition government. It is common knowledge to many people that unless the dictatorship of the Kuomintang's anti-popular clique is abolished and a democratic coalition government established, not only is it impossible to carry out any democratic reform in the Kuomintang-controlled areas or mobilise all the armies and the people there to defeat the Japanese aggressors, but the horrors of a civil war will inevitably follow. Why do so many democrats with and without party affiliation, including those within the Kuomintang, unanimously demand the establishment of a coalition government? Because they clearly see the present crisis and realise that without a coalition government it would be impossible to overcome the crisis and achieve unity against the enemy or unity for national construction.

5. The People's Army

Without an army that takes the stand of the people, the Chinese people cannot achieve freedom and unity, establish a coalition government, thoroughly defeat the Japanese aggressors or build up a new China. At present the armies that take a thoroughly popular stand are only the Eighth Route and the New Fourth Armies of the liberated areas, which are of no big size; that is far from enough. Yet the Kuomintang's anti-popular clique is deliberately seeking to undermine and annihilate the troops of the liberated areas. In 1944 the Kuomintang government made a "proposal" asking the Communist Party to "disband within a time limit" four-fifths of the troops of the liberated areas. During the latest negotiations in 1945 it again asked the Communist Party to hand over all the troops of the liberated areas or it would not grant the Communist Party a "legal status".

The Kuomintang's anti-popular clique told the Communists: "Hand over your troops and we'll grant you freedom." According to this proposition, the political parties without armed forces must have enjoyed freedom. But during 1924-7 when the Chinese Communist Party had but a small armed force, it completely lost its freedom as soon as the Kuomintang government carried out its policies of "party purge" and massacre. At present the Chinese Democratic League and the democrats within the Kuomintang have neither armed forces nor freedom. Under the rule of the Kuomintang government in the last eighteen years, the workers, peasants, students and people from the cultural, educational and industrial circles who seek progress—all have no armed forces, and also no freedom. Have they been denied freedom simply because they have organised an army, formed a "feudal independent regime", created a "traitor's area" or violated any "government decree or military order"? No, not at all. Just the opposite, it is precisely because they have done none of these things.

"The army belongs to the state"—this is quite right, and there is not a single army in the world that does not belong to a state. But to what kind of state? To a state under the feudal and fascist dictatorship of the big landlords, big bankers and big compradors, or to a new-democratic state of the masses of the people? In China only a new-democratic state should be established and, on the basis of it, a new-democratic coalition government; and all the armed forces of China must belong to such a government of such a state so that they may safeguard the people's freedom and effectively fight foreign aggressors. As soon as a new-democratic coalition government appears in China, the armed forces of the Chinese liberated areas will be immediately handed over to it. And all the Kuomintang troops should be handed over to it at the same time.

In 1924 Dr. Sun Yat-sen said: "This day should mark the beginning of a new epoch in the national revolution. . . . The first step is to unite the armed forces with the people, and the next step is to turn them into the armed forces of the people."[10] It is because they have followed this direction that the Eighth Route and the New Fourth Armies have become "the armed forces of the people", i.e. the armies of the people, and have been able to score victories. During the earlier period of the Northern Expedition the Kuomintang troops took what Dr. Sun called the "first step" and scored victories. From the latter period of the Northern Expedition up to the present they have even abandoned the "first step", taken the anti-popular stand, and therefore become more and more corrupt and degenerate; well versed in making civil war, they cannot but be incompetent in fighting foreign foes. All patriotic and conscientious officers in the Kuomintang army should rise to revive Dr. Sun's spirit and reform their troops.

In the reform of the old troops, proper education and assistance should be given to all officers who are not incorrigible, so that they can acquire correct viewpoints, clean up their antiquated ones and continue to serve in the people's army.

To struggle for the creation of an army of the Chinese people is the task of the whole nation. Without an army of the people there will be nothing for the people. We must not indulge in mere empty talk on this problem.

We Communists are willing to support the reform of the Chinese troops. All those that are willing to unite with the people and to oppose the Japanese aggressors rather than the Chinese liberated areas should be regarded by the Eighth Route Army and the New Fourth Army as friendly troops and be given proper assistance.

6. *The Agrarian Problem*

To annihilate the Japanese aggressors and build up a new China it is necessary to carry out agrarian reforms and liberate the peasants. Dr. Sun Yat-sen's proposition of "land to the tillers" is a correct one for China's bourgeois-democratic revolution at the present stage.

Why should we call China's revolution at the present stage a "bourgeois-democratic revolution"? Because the target of this revolution is not the bourgeoisie in general, but foreign and feudal oppression; because its general measure is not to abolish private property but to protect it; and because, though the working class will ultimately be able to accumulate enough strength to lead China towards socialism, there will be a long period for the regulated development of capitalism. "Land to the tillers" means to transfer the land from the hands of the feudal exploiters to those of the peasants, to turn the private property of the feudal landlords into that of the peasants and to free the peasants from feudal agrarian relations, thereby making it possible to transform an agricultural country into an industrial one. The proposition of "land to the tillers" is therefore a bourgeois-democratic and not a proletarian-socialist one; it is a proposition of all revolutionary democrats, and not of us Communists alone. What distinguishes us from the others is the fact that, under China's present conditions, we Communists alone take this proposition with special seriousness; we are not only talking about it but also putting it into practice. Who are the revolutionary democrats? Apart from the proletarians who are the most thoroughgoing revolutionary democrats, the peasants form by far the largest group of them. The overwhelming majority of the peasants, *i.e.* all except the rich ones who retain the tail of feudalism, positively demand "land to the tillers". The urban petty bourgeois are also a revolutionary democratic force and the policy of "land to the tillers" will also prove to their advantage, for it helps to develop the agricultural productive forces. The national bourgeoisie are a vacillating class—they approve of the policy of "land to the tillers" because they need markets, but many of them are frightened because they are mostly connected with landed interests. Sun Yat-sen was the first revolutionary democrat in China; representing the revolutionary group of the national bourgeoisie, the urban petty bourgeoisie and the peasants in the countryside, he carried out an armed revolution and put forward his proposition of "equalisation of land ownership" and "land to the tillers". But it is a pity that, when he held political power, he did not on his own initiative carry out agrarian reforms. The Kuomintang's anti-popular clique turned against his proposition completely as soon as it came to power. At the present moment it is precisely this anti-popular clique that is resolutely opposed to "land to the tillers", because it represents the stratum of the big landlords, big bankers and big compradores. In China, as no political party represents the peasantry exclusively, and as the political parties of the national bourgeoisie have no thoroughgoing agrarian programme, the Chinese Communist Party alone, which has formulated and carried out a resolute agrarian policy, fought earnestly for the peasants' interests and won the broadest masses of the peasantry as its great ally, has become the leader of the peasants and all revolutionary democratic forces.

During 1927–36 the Chinese Communist Party took measures to reform thoroughly the agrarian system and put into practice Dr. Sun's proposition of "land to the tillers". It was precisely the Kuomintang's anti-popular clique, a ring formed by all the unworthy followers of Sun Yat-sen, that fought the people tooth and nail for ten years in a civil war, a war against "land to the tillers".

In the period of the Anti-Japanese War the Chinese Communist Party has made a substantial concession by changing the policy of "land to the tillers" to one of reducing rent and interest. This concession is correct, for it has induced the Kuomintang to participate in the War of Resistance and the landlords of the liberated areas to mitigate their opposition to the mobilisation of the peasants for resisting Japan. If no particular obstacles turn up, we are ready to continue this policy after the war; we shall first enforce reduction of rent and interest throughout the country and then adopt proper measures to attain gradually the aim of "land to the tillers".

However, Dr. Sun's apostates are opposed not only to "land to the tillers" but also to reduction of rent and interest. The Kuomintang government promulgated such decrees as providing for a "25 per cent reduction of rent" but did not carry them out; the liberated areas alone have enforced these decrees and this is their "crime" for which they have won the label of the "traitors' areas".

During the Anti-Japanese War a theory appeared which divides the revolution into two stages: the stage of national revolution and the stage of revolution for democracy and the people's welfare; that is an erroneous theory.

"Confronted with a formidable enemy, we should not talk about democracy or the people's welfare; we had better wait until the Japanese are gone." This absurd theory has been put forward by the Kuomintang's anti-popular clique to prevent the Anti-Japanese War from achieving complete victory. Yet there are people who echo this absurd theory and become its servile adherents.

"Confronted with a formidable enemy, we cannot build up anti-Japanese bases to resist Japanese attacks unless we settle the issues of democracy and the people's welfare." This is what the Chinese Communist Party has advocated and, moreover, has carried out with remarkable success.

During the Anti-Japanese War, reduction of rent and interest and all other democratic reforms are carried out for the sake of the war. In order to mitigate the landlords' opposition to the war we have enforced only reduction of rent and interest without depriving the landlords of their ownership of land; besides, we have encouraged them to transfer their capital to industry and induced the enlightened gentry to take part in anti-Japanese social activities and government work together with all other representatives of the people. As to the rich peasants, we have encouraged them to develop production. All these things are absolutely necessary and are integrated in the line of resolutely carrying out democratic reforms in the rural areas.

There are two lines: to oppose resolutely the Chinese peasants' endeavour to settle the issues of democracy and welfare, thereby rendering oneself corrupt, impotent and utterly incapable of fighting Japan; or to support resolutely the Chinese peasants in their endeavour, thereby winning for oneself the greatest ally which constitutes 80 per cent of the whole population and building up tremendous fighting capacity. The former is the line of the Kuomintang government and the latter the line of the Chinese liberated areas.

It is an opportunist line to vacillate between the two, to profess to support the peasantry without the determination of carrying out reduction of rent and interest, arming the peasants or establishing democratic political power in the rural areas.

Rallying all the forces at its command, the Kuomintang's anti-popular clique has aimed at the Chinese Communist Party all kinds of poisoned darts, open darts as well as secret, military as well as political, those that cause bloodshed as well as those that do not. Viewed from its social implications, the point of controversy between the two parties really hinges on the issue of agrarian relationships. After all, on what score have we offended the Kuomintang's anti-popular clique? Is it not precisely on this score? Is it not precisely because the Kuomintang's anti-popular clique has on this score rendered great service to the Japanese aggressors that it has received welcome and encouragement from them? Is it not precisely because the Chinese Communist Party has on this score done conscientious work in the interest of the nation that it has been accused of "undermining the resistance and endangering the state", of being a "traitors' party", of maintaining a "traitors' army", of holding a "traitors' area", and of "disobeying government decrees and military orders"?

The peasants—the source of China's industrial workers. In future, tens of millions of peasants will go to the cities, to factories. In order to build up powerful industries of her own and a large number of modernised big cities, China will have to undergo a continuous process of transforming the rural inhabitants into urban inhabitants.

The peasants—the mainstay of the market for China's industry. Only the peasants can supply the largest amount of foodstuffs and raw materials and consume the largest amount of manufactured goods.

The peasants—the source of the Chinese army. The soldiers are peasants in military uniform, the mortal enemies of the Japanese aggressors.

The peasants—the main force fighting for a democratic order in China at the present stage. Chinese democrats can achieve nothing if they fail to rely on the support of peasant masses numbering 360 million.

The peasants—the chief concern of China's cultural movement at the present stage. Would not illiteracy-elimination, universal education, mass literature and art and public hygiene become largely empty talk if the 360 million peasants were left out of account?

In saying this, of course, I am not overlooking the importance of the remaining ninety million people in political, economic and cultural spheres, particularly not overlooking the working class, which is politically the most awakened and therefore the best qualified for leading the whole revolutionary movement; there should be no misunderstanding on the point.

An understanding of all this is absolutely necessary not only for the Chinese Communists but for all democrats.

Once reform is introduced into the agrarian system—even such an elementary reform as reduction of rent and interest— the peasants' enthusiasm for production will increase. Then the productive forces will develop as the peasants are helped to organise gradually and voluntarily agricultural producer's or other co-operatives. Although at present the agricultural producer's co-operatives can only be such collective and mutual-aid labour organisations based on individual farming (*i.e.* based on the private ownership of the peasants) as work-exchange teams, mutual-aid groups and work shifts, yet the increase in the rate of production and in output is already astonishing. This system of co-operatives has been widely adopted in China's liberated areas and should from now on be promoted as extensively as possible.

It must be pointed out here that such co-operative organisations as the work-exchange teams existed long ago among the peasants, but they were only a means by which the peasants tried to relieve their wretched living conditions. The present work-exchange teams in China's liberated areas are different in both form and content; they are now a means for the peasant masses to develop their productive forces and secure better living conditions.

The effect, good or bad, great or small, which the policy or practice of any Chinese political party produces on the Chinese people depends in the last analysis on whether it fetters or liberates their productive forces, or whether and how much it helps to develop their productive forces. China's social productive forces can be liberated and the Chinese people's approbation won only by annihilating the Japanese aggressors, carrying out the agrarian reform, liberating the peasantry, developing modern industry and building up a new China that is independent and free, democratic and united, prosperous and powerful.

It should be further pointed out that the intellectuals who have come from the cities to work in the countryside find it hard to understand the characteristics of the countryside, *i.e.* the countryside is at present still based on scattered, backward, individual peasant farms, and, in the case of the liberated areas, it is furthermore cut up for the moment by the enemy and embroiled in a guerrilla war. Because they do not understand these characteristics, they have often inappropriately approached rural problems and planned rural work from the viewpoint of city life and city work; consequently they fail to grasp the actual conditions of the countryside and to become one of the peasants. To change this situation these intellectuals must be given proper education.

China's vast numbers of revolutionary intellectuals must realise that it is necessary to unite with the peasants. The peasants need them, expecting their help. They should gladly go to the countryside, take off their school uniforms, put on coarse clothes and willingly take up any work, however trivial; they should go there to learn what the peasants demand, help to arouse and organise them and struggle for the accomplishment of one of the most important tasks in China's democratic revolution—the democratic revolution in the countryside.

After the Japanese aggressors are annihilated, their land and the land of the leading collaborators will be confiscated and distributed among those peasants who have little or no land.

7. Industrial Problems

In order to defeat the Japanese aggressors and build a new China, it is necessary to develop industry. But under the reign of the Kuomintang government, it is the rule to depend on foreign countries for everything, and this financial and economic policy is ruining all aspects of the people's economic life. In the Kuomintang-controlled areas the few surviving small industrial establishments are mostly bankrupt. Unless political reforms are forthcoming, all productive forces will be doomed to destruction, and this is true of both agriculture and industry.

Taken as a whole, China's industry cannot be developed unless the country is independent, free, democratic and united. To annihilate the Japanese aggressors is to achieve independence. To abolish the Kuomintang's one-party dictatorship, to form a democratic coalition government of national unity, to transform the troops of the whole country into the armed forces of the people, to carry out the agrarian reform and to liberate the peasantry is to achieve freedom, democracy and unity. Without independence, freedom, democracy and unity it is impossible to build up large-scale industries. Without industry there can be no solid national defence, no people's welfare and no national prosperity and power. The history of the 105 years since the Opium War of 1840, especially of the eighteen years since the Kuomintang's reign, has brought this important point home to the Chinese people. A China that is not poor and weak but prosperous and powerful is inseparable from a China that is not colonial and semi-colonial but independent, not semi-feudal but free and democratic, not divided but united. In a divided, semi-colonial and semi-feudal China, many people have for years cherished the dream of developing industry, building up national defence, promoting the people's welfare and bringing prosperity and power to the nation; but they have all become disillusioned. Believing that they could serve their country with their knowledge, many well-intentioned educators, scientists and students have buried themselves in work or study and stayed away from politics; but this turned out to be a dream and they have all become disillusioned too. This indeed is a good sign, since the shattering of such a childish dream is the first step leading to China's prosperity and power. The Chinese people have learnt a great deal during the Anti-Japanese War; they have come to understand that, after the defeat of the Japanese aggressors, it is necessary to build up a new-democratic China which enjoys independence and freedom, democracy and unity, prosperity and power, and that all these are interrelated and none can be dispensed with. If China achieves this, then a bright future lies before her. Once released, the Chinese people's productive forces can develop fully when the political conditions of New Democracy obtain in all parts of China. This is being realised by more and more people.

After the realisation of the political conditions of New Democracy, the Chinese people and their government must take effective measures to build up gradually light and heavy industries within a prescribed period, thereby turning China from an agricultural into an industrial country. A new-democratic state cannot be consolidated if it is not based on a solid economy, an advanced agriculture that is much more developed than at present, large-scale industries that occupy an absolutely predominant position in national economy and that have as their basis a proportionate development in communications, trade, finance, etc.

We Communists are willing to fight for the achievement of the above-mentioned objective in co-operation with various democratic parties and various sections of industrialists throughout the country. The Chinese working class will play a great role in accomplishing this task.

Since World War I, the Chinese working class has consciously struggled for China's independence and liberation. Since its vanguard, the Chinese Communist Party came into being in 1921, China's struggle for liberation has entered a new stage. During the three periods of the Northern Expedition, the Agrarian Revolutionary War and the Anti-Japanese War, the Chinese working class and the Chinese Communist Party have made great efforts and important contributions to the liberation of the Chinese people. The Chinese working class will play an important role in the struggle for finally defeating the Japanese aggressors, especially in the struggle for recovering the big cities and the important communication lines. It can be predicted that after the Anti-Japanese War the Chinese working class will make even greater efforts and contributions. The task of the Chinese working class is to struggle not only for the establishment of a new-democratic state but also for the industrialisation of China and the modernisation of her agriculture.

Under the new-democratic state system, measures will be adopted to adjust the interests of labour and capital. On the one hand, the interests of labour will be protected by instituting, according to actual circumstances, a workday of from eight to ten hours and appropriate unemployment relief and social insurance and by safeguarding the rights of trade unions while, on the other, reasonable profit will be guaranteed to properly managed state, private and co-operative enterprises so that both the state and the private individuals, both labour and capital, will work jointly for the development of industrial production.

When the Japanese aggressors are defeated, their enterprises and property in China and those of the leading collaborators will be confiscated and placed at the disposal of the government.

8. Problems of Culture, Education and the Intellectuals

The calamities which foreign and feudal oppression have brought on the Chinese people also affect our national culture. The progressive cultural and educational institutions and progressive cultural workers and educators have particularly suffered. The eradication of foreign and feudal oppression and the building up of a new-democratic China demands the efforts of a large number of people's educators, teachers, scientists, engineers, technicians, physicians, journalists, writers, artists and ordinary cultural workers. They must have the spirit of serving the people and work hard. All intellectuals who have performed meritorious service to the people should be esteemed as valuable assets of the nation and society. As China is a culturally backward country in consequence of foreign and feudal oppression and as the Chinese people's struggle for liberation urgently needs the participation of the intellectuals, the problem of the intelligentsia becomes particularly important. In the Chinese people's struggle for liberation during the past half-century, especially in the struggle since the May 4 Movement of 1919 and during the eight years of the Anti-Japanese War, large numbers of revolutionary intellectuals have played an important role. They will play an even more important role in the forthcoming struggles. The people's government should therefore systematically bring up from among the broad masses various catagories of intellectuals to serve as cadres and take care to unite and re-educate all the useful intellectuals we have at present.

To eliminate illiteracy among 80 per cent of the population is an important task for new China.

Proper and firm steps should be taken to eliminate all slavish, feudal, and fascist culture and education.

Positive measures should be taken to prevent and combat epidemics and diseases among the people and to promote public sanitation and medical services.

As to the old type of cultural and educational workers and physicians, we should take appropriate measures to educate them so that they may acquire new viewpoints and new methods to serve the people.

The Chinese people's culture and education should be new-democratic in aim, *i.e.* China should build up her own new culture and education that are national, scientific and popular.

It is wrong to adopt a policy of excluding foreign culture, and we must fully absorb progressive foreign culture as an aid to the development of China's new culture; but it is also wrong to import indiscriminately foreign culture into China, for we must proceed from the actual needs of the Chinese people and assimilate it critically. We should take the new culture created by the Soviet Union as our model in building the people's culture. Similarly, we must neither totally exclude nor blindly accept China's ancient culture; we must accept it critically so as to help the development of China's new culture.

9. The Problem of National Minorities

The Kuomintang's anti-popular clique denies the fact that there are numerous nationalities in China, and labels all national minorities besides the Hans as "clans".[11] Following entirely the reactionary policy of the Manchu régime and the Northern warlord régime, it has brutally oppressed and exploited the national minorities in every possible way. Witness the massacre of the Mongols of the Ikcho League in 1943, the armed suppression of the national minorities in Sinkiang province from 1944 up to the present and the massacre of the Hui people in Kansu province in recent years. These are manifestations of the erroneous pan-Hanist ideology and policy towards the national minorities.

In 1924, in his personally drafted Manifesto of the First National Congress of the Kuomintang, Dr. Sun Yat-sen stated:

"The Principle of Nationalism of the Kuomintang has a twofold meaning: the self-liberation of the Chinese nation and the equality of all nationalities in China. . . . The Kuomintang solemnly declares that it recognises the right to self-determination of all nationalities in China and that, when the anti-imperialist and anti-warlord revolution triumphs, a free and united republic of China (or a republic of China based on the free union of all nationalities) will be established."

The Chinese Communist Party fully agrees with Dr. Sun's policy towards the national minorities. Communists should actively assist the broad masses of all national minorities to struggle for the realisation of this policy and help them, including all their leaders who keep in close contact with them, to fight for their political, economic and cultural liberation and development and to build up their own armies to safeguard the interests of the masses. Their languages, written as well as spoken, their customs, traditions and religious beliefs should be respected.

The Shensi-Kansu-Ningsia border region and the liberated areas in North China have for all these years adopted a correct attitude towards the Mongols and Hui people, and the work among them has been fruitful.

10. The Problems of Foreign Policy

The Chinese Communist Party approves of the Atlantic Charter and the decisions of the international conferences of Moscow, Cairo, Teheran and Crimea,[12] because they all contribute to the defeat of the fascist aggressors and the maintenance of world peace.

The basic principle underlying the foreign policy of the Chinese Communist Party consists in establishing and developing diplomatic relations with all countries and in solving all problems of mutual concern, such as military co-ordination, peace conferences, international trade and foreign investments —all these on the basis of complete defeat of the Japanese aggressors, maintenance of world peace, mutual respect of national independence, mutual treatment as equals and mutual help in promoting national and popular interests and in advancing the friendship between nations and peoples.

As to the establishment of an organisation for safeguarding post-war international peace and security, the Chinese Communist Party fully agrees to the Dumbarton Oaks proposals and the decisions of the Crimea conference. The Chinese Communist Party welcomes the conference of the United Nations in San Francisco. It has sent its own representative to join the Chinese delegation to this conference in order to express the will of the Chinese people.[13]

We hold that the Kuomintang government must end its hostility towards the Soviet Union and immediately improve Sino-Soviet relations. The Soviet Union was the first country to renounce unequal treaties and sign new, equal treaties with China. During the period of the Kuomintang's First National Congress called by Dr. Sun Yat-sen in 1924 and the subsequent Northern Expedition, the Soviet Union was the only country that gave aid to China's war of liberation. When the Anti-Japanese War broke out in 1937, the Soviet Union was again the first to give aid to our country in its struggle against the Japanese aggressor. For such aid the Chinese people are grateful to the Soviet government and the Soviet people. We believe that without the participation of the Soviet Union, the problems of the Pacific cannot be settled finally and thoroughly.

We request all Allied governments, first of all the governments of Britain and the United States, to pay serious attention to the voice of the great majority of the Chinese people and take care that their foreign policy does not run counter to the wishes of the Chinese people and impair the friendship between the Chinese people and themselves. We believe that a foreign government will commit a grievous error if it supports the Chinese reactionaries and opposes the democratic cause of the Chinese people.

The Chinese people welcome the fact that many foreign governments have renounced the unequal treaties and concluded new, equal treaties with China. We believe, however, that the conclusion of equal treaties does not mean that China has actually won genuine equality. The Chinese people can never depend solely on the favour of foreign governments for such actual and genuine equality, but should win it chiefly through their own efforts—efforts aimed at building China into a new-democratic state politically, economically and culturally; otherwise independence and equality will be only apparent and not real. That is to say, given a policy like the one now pursued by the Kuomintang government, China can never achieve genuine independence and equality.

We hold that after the defeat and unconditional surrender of the Japanese aggressors, we must assist all democratic forces of the Japanese people to establish their own democracy so that Japanese fascism and militarism, together with the political, economic and social causes that gave birth to them, can be thoroughly eliminated. Unless the Japanese people establish a democratic system for themselves it is impossible to eliminate thoroughly Japanese fascism and militarism or guarantee peace in the Pacific.

We hold that the decision of the Cairo Conference regarding the independence of Korea is correct, and the Chinese people should help the Korean people to achieve liberation.

We hope that India will be independent. The reason is that an independent and democratic India is not only the demand of the Indian people but also a necessity of world peace.

As regards countries in South-east Asia—Burma, Malaya, Indonesia, Viet-Nam and the Philippines—we hope that after the defeat of the Japanese aggressors the peoples of these countries will win the right to form their respective independent and democratic states. Thailand must be treated in the same way as the fascist satellites in Europe.

.   .   .   .   .

So much for the explanation of the main points of the specific programme.

To repeat, without a democratic coalition government supported by the whole nation this specific programme cannot be successfully carried out in China on a nation-wide scale.

Through twenty-four years' struggle for the cause of the Chinese people's liberation, the Chinese Communist Party has attained such a position that it will be a grievous error and will lead to a foredoomed failure for any political party or social group, any Chinese or foreigner, to disregard the opinions of the Chinese Communist Party on questions of China. There have been people who insist on having their own way and disregard our opinions, but they have landed in an impasse. Why? Simply because all our opinions conform to the interests of the overwhelming majority of the Chinese people. The Chinese Communist Party is the most faithful spokesman of the Chinese people; whoever disregards its opinions in fact disregards the opinions of the overwhelming majority of the Chinese people and is doomed to failure.

Tasks in the Kuomintang-Controlled Areas

Now I have fully explained our Party's general and specific programmes. These programmes will undoubtedly be realised throughout China, and the international and domestic situation as a whole has opened up to the Chinese people the prospect for their realisation. However, since circumstances are at present different in the Kuomintang-controlled areas, the enemy-occupied areas and the liberated areas, we cannot but make distinctions between these areas when putting the programmes into practice. Different conditions give rise to different tasks. I have already mentioned some of these tasks, and I have to say something about the others.

In the Kuomintang-controlled areas, though the people are allowed no freedom for patriotic activities and democratic movements are outlawed, a vigorous movement embracing various social strata and democratic parties and individuals is gaining ground. The Chinese Democratic League issued in January 1945 a manifesto demanding the termination of the Kuomintang's one-party dictatorship and the establishment of a coalition government. Numerous sections of the people have made similar declarations. Even within the Kuomintang many people have become increasingly sceptical about and dissatisfied with the policies of their own leading body; they have become increasingly aware of the danger of their party's isolation from the broad masses of the people and are therefore demanding timely democratic reforms. In Chungking and other places a democratic movement is spreading among the workers, peasants, cultural workers, students, educational workers, women, industrialists and businessmen, government employees and even a section of the army. These facts indicate that all the democratic movements of the oppressed strata are gradually converging on a common objective. The whole movement, however, suffers from the defect that the basic section of society has not yet joined it on a broad scale and that the peasants, workers, soldiers and the low-ranking government employees and school teachers, who form an extremely important force and are suffering untold hardships, are as yet unorganised. The other defect of the movement is that many of the democrats taking part in it are still confused and hesitant about the basic policy of changing the state of affairs through a struggle waged according to democratic principles. However, the actual situation is compelling all oppressed classes, parties and social groupings to gradually awake and unite ever more closely. No matter how hard it tries to suppress the movement, the Kuomintang government can never check its development.

The democratic movement of all the oppressed classes, parties and groups in the Kuomintang-controlled areas should develop extensively, mustering gradually the scattered forces to fight for the realisation of national solidarity, the formation of a coalition government, the defeat of the Japanese aggressors and the building of a new China. The Chinese Communist Party and the people of the liberated areas should give them every possible help.

In the Kuomintang-controlled areas the Communists should

continue to pursue the policy of a broad Anti-Japanese National United Front. To fight for the common cause we should co-operate with anybody who is not opposing us today, even though he did so only yesterday.

Tasks in the Enemy-Occupied Areas

In the enemy-occupied areas Communists should call upon all people fighting the Japanese invaders to imitate the French and Italian people and organise themselves into various bodies, establish underground forces and make preparations for armed uprisings, so that when the time is ripe they can wipe out the Japanese aggressors by co-ordinating from the inside with the armies attacking from the outside. The persecution, plunder, rape and insult perpetrated by the Japanese aggressors and their servile jackals against our brothers and sisters in the enemy-occupied areas have roused the burning wrath of all Chinese, and the hour for revenge is fast approaching. The victories on the European front and those of the Eighth Route and New Fourth Armies in China have aroused the people in the enemy-occupied areas and greatly enhanced their fervour in fighting Japan. It is an urgent need that these people should be organised so as to be able to achieve liberation at the earliest possible date. We must therefore attach the same importance to our work in the enemy-occupied areas as to that in the liberated areas. Large numbers of personnel must be sent to the enemy-occupied areas. Large numbers of active people among the population there must be trained and placed in charge of local work. We should strengthen the underground activities in the four North-eastern provinces which have been occupied by the enemy longer than any other area and which form an industrial centre and important military base of the Japanese aggressors. We should increase our efforts to unite with refugees from those provinces and get ready to recover these lost territories.

In all the enemy-occupied areas Communists should pursue the policy of the broadest Anti-Japanese National United Front. All who are opposed to the Japanese aggressors and their servile jackals must unite to defeat the common enemy.

Let the puppet armies, the puppet police and other people

who are helping the enemy and opposing their countrymen be warned that they should immediately realise their crime, repent it in time and atone for it by helping their countrymen to fight the enemy. Otherwise the law of the nation will show them no leniency on the day of the enemy's collapse.

Communists should try, through persuasion, to win over all puppet organisations with a mass following, so that the masses who have been led astray will come over to our front to fight the national enemy. At the same time, we must collect information about those outright traitors who have committed the most heinous crimes and who refuse to repent, so that they can be brought to justice when the lost territories are recovered.

As regards the reactionaries within the Kuomintang who have betrayed the nation and organised the collaborators to oppose the Chinese people, the Chinese Communist Party, the Eighth Route Army, the New Fourth Army and other armed forces of the people, they must be warned to repent in time. Otherwise they, together with the collaborators, will be punished without leniency when the lost territories are recovered.

Tasks in the Liberated Areas

In the liberated areas we have carried out our Party's whole programme of New Democracy and achieved remarkable results, and in resisting the Japanese invaders we have rallied tremendous forces which should be further developed and consolidated by every means.

Under the present conditions the troops of the liberated areas should launch extensive attacks on all vulnerable positions occupied by the enemy and puppet troops in order to expand the liberated areas and reduce the enemy-occupied areas.

Meanwhile it should be borne in mind that the enemy is still strong and may launch further attacks on the liberated areas. The army and the people of the liberated areas must be ever ready to smash his attacks and must do all kinds of work to consolidate these areas.

We should expand the armies, guerrilla units, militia and self-defence corps of the liberated areas, intensify their reorganisation and training and raise their fighting capacity in order to muster sufficient strength for the final defeat of the aggressors.

In the liberated areas, the army should support the governments and care for the people, while the democratic governments should lead the people to support the army and take good care of the families of soldiers fighting Japan, so that relations between the army and the people will be further improved.

In local coalition governments and social organisations, Communists should continue to co-operate closely on the basis of the programme of New Democracy with all democrats standing in opposition to the Japanese invaders.

Similarly, in military work Communists should co-operate well, both inside and outside the army of the liberated areas, with all democrats fighting the Japanese invaders, who are willing to co-operate.

The policy of reducing rent and interest and of improving the living conditions of the workers and government personnel must be fully carried out in order to arouse the enthusiasm of the workers, peasants and all working people in the resistance and production. The personnel in the liberated areas must learn to do economic work. All available forces must be mobilised to develop on a large scale the agriculture, industry and trade of the liberated areas and improve the living conditions of the army and the people. For this purpose labour emulation competitions must be held and labour heroes and model workers be rewarded. And when the Japanese aggressors are driven out of the cities our personnel must speedily learn to do urban economic work.

In the liberated areas we must promote culture and education in order to raise the level of political consciousness among the masses of the people, above all among the broad masses of the workers, peasants and soldiers, and bring up a large number of cadres. In carrying on their work, the cultural and educational workers of the liberated areas should select proper materials and adopt proper ways of presenting such materials according to the specific conditions in the present-day countryside and the needs and wishes of the people there.

When carrying on various kinds of work in any liberated area, we must use sparingly its manpower and material resources; we must always take a long-term view and avoid misuse and waste. This is not only for the sake of defeating the Japanese aggressors but for the sake of building up a new China.

When carrying on various kinds of work in the liberated areas, we must take great care to assist the native people of a district to administer their own affairs and to bring up from among their promising members large numbers of cadres to do the work in their district. The great task of rural democratic revolution cannot be accomplished unless people coming in from the outside are at one with the native people, unless they render to the native cadres whole-hearted and unremitting assistance which fits in with actual conditions, and unless they take care of them like their own brothers and sisters.

On arriving at any place, the Eighth Route Army, the New Fourth Army and the other armed forces of the people should immediately assist the native people to organise not only militia and self-defence corps but local armed units and army corps headed by local cadres. Then they can organise main forces—armed units and army corps—under the leadership of the natives. This is an extremely important task. Without accomplishing this we cannot build strong anti-Japanese bases and expand the people's army.

Of course all native people should extend a warm welcome and help to the revolutionary workers and the people's army coming from other areas.

Attention must be called to the problem of dealing with hidden saboteurs of the national cause. The reason is that, although the enemies and saboteurs of the national cause in the open can be easily identified and therefore easily dealt with, they are hard to identify when under cover and are therefore hard to deal with. We should, consequently, adopt a stern attitude towards the latter and yet deal with them cautiously.

On the principle of freedom of religious belief, all religions are tolerated in the Chinese liberated areas. Protestantism, Catholicism, Mohemmedanism, Buddhism and all other religions will be protected by the people's government so long as the believers abide by the laws of the government. Everybody is free to believe or not to believe in a religion; neither compulsion nor discrimination is allowed.

Our Congress should propose to the people of the liberated areas that a people's congress of the Chinese liberated areas[14] be convened in Yenan at the earliest possible date in order to discuss such problems as the co-ordination of the activities of all these areas, the intensification of the anti-Japanese activities there, the assistance to be given to the people's anti-Japanese democratic movement in the Kuomintang-controlled areas and to the movement for the creation of people's underground forces in the enemy-occupied areas and the promotion of national solidarity and of the establishment of a coalition government. Now that the Chinese liberated areas have become the centre of gravity in the national cause of fighting Japan and saving the country, and the broad masses of the people have pinned their hope on us, we are duty-bound not to disappoint them. The convocation of a people's congress of the Chinese liberated areas will give a great impetus to the cause of national liberation of the Chinese people.

V. LET THE WHOLE PARTY UNITE TO FIGHT FOR THE ACCOMPLISHMENT OF ITS TASKS!

Comrades, we have now grasped our tasks and the policies for accomplishing them. What attitude should we adopt in carrying out these policies and accomplishing these tasks?

It is evident and beyond any doubt that, for us and the Chinese people, the present international and domestic situation opens up a bright prospect and provides such favourable conditions as never existed before. But at the same time serious difficulties still confront us. Anyone who sees only the bright side of the situation and not these difficulties cannot fight effectively for the accomplishment of the Party's tasks.

In the twenty-four years of the Party's history and in the eight years of the Anti-Japanese War, our Party has, together with the Chinese people, created a gigantic force for the Chinese people, and our achievements are remarkable and indisputable. Yet at the same time defects are still found in our work. Anyone who sees only the achievements and not the defects will likewise be unable to fight effectively for the accomplishment of the Party's tasks.

Since its birth in 1921, the Chinese Communist Party has in twenty-four years waged three great struggles, namely, the Northern Expedition, the Agrarian Revolutionary War and the Anti-Japanese War that is still going on. From its very beginning our Party has been a party based on the theory of Marxism-Leninism, for Marxism-Leninism is the crystallisation of the most correct and most revolutionary scientific thought of the world proletariat. Once the universal truth of Marxism-Leninism is integrated with the concrete practice of the Chinese revolution, the Chinese revolution assumes a new physiognomy and the whole historical stage of New Democracy emerges. Armed with Marxist-Leninist theory, the Chinese Communist Party has brought about among the Chinese people a new style of work mainly characterised by the integration of theory with practice, close contact with the masses of the people and the practice of self-criticism.

Once integrated with the concrete practice of the revolutionary struggles of China's proletariat and broad masses of people, the universal truth of Marxism-Leninism, which reflects the practice of the world proletariat in its struggles, becomes the Chinese people's all-conquering weapon. This the Chinese Communist Party has achieved. Our Party has grown and advanced in resolute struggles against all kinds of doctrinairism and empiricism which run counter to the truth of Marxism-Leninism. Doctrinairism departs from concrete practice while empiricism mistakes fragmentary experiences for universal truth, and both are opportunism running counter to Marxism. In its twenty-four years' struggle our Party has overcome and is overcoming these erroneous ideas, and has thus greatly consolidated itself ideologically. Our Party now has a membership of 1,210,000. The overwhelming majority of them have joined the Party during the Anti-Japanese War; they have retained incorrect ideas of all shades. This is also true of some of those who joined the Party before the Anti-Japanese War. In the last few years, however, the campaigns to correct styles of work have produced striking results and helped considerably in eradicating such incorrect notions. Such campaigns should be continued and ideological education within the Party more extensively developed in the spirit of "learning from past experience in order to avoid similar mistakes in the future" and "treating the illness in order to save the man". It should be made clear to the Party's core of leadership at all levels that a close unity of theory and practice is one of the outstanding features that distinguish the Communist Party from all other political parties. Therefore ideological education is the pivotal link in uniting the whole Party for great political struggles. Without accomplishing this task, no other political task of the Party can be accomplished.

Another outstanding feature that distinguishes us Communists from members of all other political parties is that we keep the closest contact with the broadest masses of the people. This is our point of departure: to serve the people whole-heartedly without isolating ourselves from them even for a moment, to start from the interests of the people and not from personal or cliquish interests and to harmonise our responsibility towards the people with our responsibiity towards the leading bodies of the Party. Communists must be ever ready to uphold truth, because truth always conforms to the people's interests; they must be ever ready to correct mistakes, for all mistakes run counter to the people's interests. The experience of the past twenty-four years shows that tasks, policies and styles of work are correct and proper whenever they are in keeping with the desire of the masses at a given time and place and linked with the masses, and they are incorrect and improper whenever they are at variance with the demands of the masses at a given time and place and are out of touch with the masses. Defects like doctrinairism, empiricism, authoritarianism, tailism, sectarianism, bureaucracy and arrogant styles of work are definitely undesirable and must be removed, and anyone who shows such defects must be rectified precisely because they separate us from the masses. Our Congress should call upon the whole Party to be vigilant and see to it that no comrade placed at any link in our work is isolated from the masses. Every comrade must be taught to love the masses of the people ardently and listen to their voice attentively; wherever he goes, he should become one with the masses, go into the midst of them and not lord it over them; he should try to induce the masses to awake and heighten their political consciousness from the level it has already attained; he should help the masses to organise themselves step by step and on a voluntary basis to unfold gradually struggles that are necessary and permissible under the external and internal conditions obtaining at a particular time and place. Whatever we do, authoritarianism is always erroneous because, as a result of our impetuosity, it makes us go beyond the degree of the masses' awakening and violate the principle of voluntary action on the part of the masses. Our comrades must not think that the broad masses understand what we ourselves already understand. To know whether the masses understand it or whether they are willing to take action about it, we must go into the midst of the masses and make investigations. If we do so, we can avoid authoritarianism. Whatever we do, tailism is also erroneous because, as a result of our inertia, it makes us lag behind the awakening of the masses and violate the principle that we must always lead the masses forward. Our comrades should not assume that the masses do not understand at all what we ourselves do not understand as yet. It often happens that while the broad masses have outstripped us and are anxious to go further, our comrades fail to lead them, and even become the tail of the backward section of the people, by championing their ideas and mistaking them for the ideas of the broad masses. In a word, we must make every comrade understand that the highest criterion for judging the words and deeds of the Communists is whether they conform with the best interests and win the support of the broadest masses of the people. It should also be made clear to every comrade that no enemy can crush us but we can crush any enemy and overcome any difficulty so long as we rely on the people, firmly believe in their inexhaustible creative power and consequently trust them and become one with them.

A conscientious practice of self-criticism is another outstanding feature that distinguishes us from other political parties. We have said that a room must be regularly cleaned or dust will accumulate in it, and that our faces must be regularly washed or they will be smeared with dirt. The same is true of our comrades' minds and our Party's work. The proverb: "running water does not go stale and door-hinges do not become worm-eaten", indicates how these things can by ceaseless motion be immune from the harmful effects of microbes or other organisms. To check up our work regularly, to promote the democratic style of work in the course of checking-up, to fear no criticism or self-criticism, to put into practice such good maxims of the Chinese people as "say all that you know and say it without reserve", "blame not him who speaks but heed what you hear" and "correct the mistakes if you have committed them and guard against them though you have not"—all these are the only effective methods for us to prevent various kinds of political dust and microbes from producing harmful effects on the minds of our comrades and the physique of our Party. The campaign to rectify the style in work, aimed at "learning from past experience, in order to avoid similar mistakes in the future" and "treating the illness in order to save the man", has been so effective because we have in this campaign unfolded criticism and self-criticism that are judicious and not biased, strict and not perfunctory. Since we Chinese Communists, starting from the best interests of the broadest masses of the Chinese people, are convinced that our cause is a perfectly righteous one and never hesitate to sacrifice anything we have, even our own lives, for the cause, how *can* we still be reluctant to discard some of the ideas, viewpoints, opinions or ways and means which do not suit the needs of the people? How *can* we still welcome any political dust and microbes to defile our clean faces or our fine physique? Since we as the survivors are saddened by the very thought of the numerous revolutionary martyrs sacrificing their lives for the people, how *can* there still be any personal interest that we cannot sacrifice or error that we cannot part with?

Comrades, after this Congress we shall, with the Congress resolutions as our guide, go to the front to fight for the final defeat of the Japanese aggressors and the building of a new China. To attain this aim, we must unite with the people of the whole country. Let me repeat: We must unite with any class, political party, social group or individual so long as he agrees to fight for the defeat of the Japanese aggressors and the building of a new China. To attain this aim, we must unite closely all the forces of our Party on the organisational and disciplinary principles based on democratic centralism. We must unite with any comrade so long as he is willing to abide by the Party's Programme, Constitution and decisions. In the period of the Northern Expedition our Party had a membership of less than 60,000, most of whom were dispersed later by the enemy of that time; in the period of the Agrarian Revolutionary War we had a membership of no more than 300,000, most of whom were likewise dispersed by the enemy then confronting us. Now we have a membership of more than 1,200,000 and under no circumstances must we allow ourselves to be dispersed by the enemy again. If we can profit by the experience of the three periods, be modest and guard against self-conceit and strengthen solidarity among all comrades within the Party and solidarity with the whole people, we can rest assured that we shall not be dispersed by the enemy but, on the contrary, shall annihilate the Japanese aggressors and their servile jackals resolutely, thoroughly, utterly and completely and build up a new-democratic China afterwards.

The experience of the three periods of the revolution, especially that of the Anti-Japanese War, has convinced us and the Chinese people that without the effort of the Chinese Communist Party, without the Chinese Communists as the mainstay of the Chinese people, China can neither achieve independence or liberation, nor carry out industrialisation and the modernisation of agriculture.

Comrades, I firmly believe that with such a party as the Communist Party of China, with the experience of the three revolutions, we can accomplish the great political tasks that confront us.

Thousands upon thousands of martyrs have heroically laid down their lives for the interests of the people; let us hold their banners high and march along the path crimson with their blood!

A new-democratic China will soon be born; let us hail that great day!

April 24, 1945

HOW YU KUNG REMOVED THE MOUNTAINS

This is the concluding speech at the Seventh National Congress of the Chinese Communist Party.

We have had a very successful congress. We have done three things. First, we have decided on the line of our Party, which is to boldly arouse the masses to action and strengthen the people's forces in order to defeat the Japanese aggressors, liberate the whole people and build up a new-democratic China under the leadership of our Party. Secondly, we have adopted a new Constitution of the Party. Thirdly, we have elected the leading body of the Party—the Central Committee. Henceforth our task is to lead the whole Party to carry out its line. Our Congress is a congress of victory, a congress of solidarity. Many delegates have made excellent comments on the three reports[1] submitted at the Congress. Many comrades have made self-criticism with solidarity as the aim and, through self-criticism, this has been attained. This Congress sets us an example of solidarity, of self-criticism and of inner-Party democracy.

When the Congress is over, many of you will go back to your respective posts, to various war fronts. Wherever you go, you should propagate the line of the Congress and, through the comrades of the Party, explain it to the people extensively.

To propagate the line of the Congress means to inspire the whole Party and the whole people with confidence that the revolution will certainly be victorious. First of all, we must awaken the vanguard so that they, determined and fearless of sacrifice, will overcome all sorts of difficulties and strive for victory. This, however, is not enough; we must also awaken the broad masses of the people throughout the country so that they may willingly and gladly join us in the common struggle for victory. We must instil into the people throughout the country the faith that China belongs to the Chinese people and not to the reactionaries. In ancient China there was the fable: "How Yu Kung Removed the Mountains."[2] It is the story of an old man in North China in ancient times, by the name of Yu Kung[3] of the North Mountain. His house faced south and its doorway was obstructed by two big mountains, Taihang and Wangwu. With great determination, he led his sons to dig up the mountains with pickaxes. Another old man, Chih Sho[4] witnessed their attempts and laughed, saying: "What fools you are to attempt this! To dig up the two huge mountains is utterly beyond your capacity." Yu Kung replied: "When I die, there are my sons; when they die, there will be their own sons, and so on to infinity. As to these two mountains, high as they are, they cannot become higher but, on the contrary, with every bit dug away, they will become lower and lower. Why can't we dig them away?" Mr. Yu Kung refuted Mr. Chih Sho's erroneous view and went on digging at the mountains day after day without interruption. God's heart was touched by such perseverance and he sent two celestial beings down to earth to carry away the mountains on their backs. Now there are also two big mountains lying like dead weight on the Chinese people: imperialism and feudalism. The Chinese Communist Party long made up its mind to remove them. We must work persistently, work ceaselessly, and we too may be able to touch God's heart. This God is no other than the masses of the people throughout China. And if they rise and dig together with us, why can't we dig these two mountains up?

Yesterday in a talk with two Americans who were leaving for the United States, I said that the U.S. Government was attempting to undermine us—a thing which will not be tolerated. We object to the U.S. Government's policy of opposing Communism and supporting Chiang Kai-shek. But we must first distinguish the U.S. people from their government and, secondly, the policy-makers in the U.S. Government from the ordinary personnel under them. I told the two Americans: "Tell the policy-makers in your government that we forbid you Americans to enter the liberated areas because your policy is to support Chiang Kai-shek in the struggle against the Communist Party and this cannot but put us on our guard. You can come to the liberated areas, if your errand has to do with the anti-Japanese war, but there must be an agreement about this. If you want to prowl about, that won't be allowed. Since Patrick J. Hurley has openly declared that there will be no more co-operation with the Chinese Communist Party,[5] why should you still want to prowl about in our liberated areas?"

The U.S. Government's policy of supporting Chiang Kai-shek in the struggle against the Communist Party shows the rampancy of the American reactionaries. But all schemes on the part of reactionaries, domestic or foreign, to prevent the Chinese people from achieving victory are doomed to failure. In the world today democracy is the main stream and reaction against democracy is only a counter-current. At present the counter-current of reaction attempts to overwhelm the main stream of national independence and people's democracy, but this counter-current can never become the main stream. Today in the old world there are still three major contradictions, as J. V. Stalin pointed out long ago: the contradiction between the proletariat and the bourgeoisie in the imperialist countries, the contradiction between various imperialist powers, and the contradiction between colonial and semi-colonial countries on the one hand and imperialist metropolitan countries on the other.[6] These three contradictions not only exist as before but are sharpening and growing. Thanks to the existence and development of these contradictions, although there exists the anti-Soviet, anti-Communist and anti-democratic counter-current, a counter-current of reaction, it will finally be overcome.

Now two great meetings are being held in China, the Kuomintang's Sixth National Congress and the Communist Party's Seventh National Congress. The two Congresses have completely different aims: one is to liquidate the Communist Party as well as other democratic forces in China, leading China to darkness; the other is to overthrow Japanese imperialism and its jackal, China's feudal forces, and to build up a new-democratic China, leading China to light. The two lines are at grips with each other. We firmly believe that the Chinese people, under the leadership of the Chinese Communist Party and the guidance of the line of its Seventh National Congress, will achieve complete victory, while the Kuomintang's counter-revolutionary line will end in failure.

June 11, 1945

ON THE ARMY'S PRODUCTION FOR SELF-SUPPORT AND ON THE IMPORTANCE OF THE GREAT CAMPAIGNS FOR INCREASING PRODUCTION AND RECTIFYING STYLE IN WORK

This is an editorial written for the *Liberation Daily* published in Yenan.

As our army faces extremely great material difficulties and is engaged in dispersed fighting, the leading bodies should in no way assume the full responsibility of supply, for that will hamper the freedom of action of the broad sections of the rank and file while failing to meet their needs. We should say: Comrades, let's all go into action and overcome our difficulties! If only the leadership at the higher level sets tasks properly and gives those subordinate to them a free rein to overcome the difficulties through their own efforts, then the problem of supply will be solved and solved in a more satisfactory manner. If the top levels fail to do this but try to shoulder all the burdens which are in fact beyond their capacity, if they dare not give the rank and file free rein to carry out their work and do not arouse the activity of the broad masses to overcome difficulties through their own effort, the result will be that, for all the efforts on the part of the top levels, both the top levels and the rank and file will find themselves in difficulties, and they will not be able to solve the problem of supply under present conditions. The experience of the last few years has amply proved this. The principle of "centralised leadership and decentralised operation" has proved a correct one for organising under present conditions all the economic activities in our liberated areas.

The troops of the liberated areas have increased to upwards of 900,000 men. But we must increase them several times more if we are to defeat the Japanese aggressors. However, we have yet received no support from the outside. Even if in the future we do receive support from the outside, we still have to provision ourselves; and there must be no deluding ourselves on this score. In the near future in order to carry out offensives against given objectives, the forces should leave the areas where they are now carrying on military operations with dispersed units and be concentrated into army groups. Not only can such big army groups for centralised action no longer engage in production for self-support, but they need ample supply from the rear; only the local armed units and the local army groups (which will be left behind in large numbers) can continue to engage at once in fighting and in production. Is there any doubt then that, in so far as fighting and training are not affected, all the troops should without any exception take the present opportunity to learn to fufil the task of production for partial self-support?

The army's production for self-support, under present conditions, may appear backward or retrogressive, but it is in essence progressive and of great historical significance. On the face of things, it runs counter to the principle of division of labour. But under present conditions—a country that is impoverished and divided (the result of the misdeeds of the chief ruling bloc of the Kuomintang), and also the protracted guerrilla operations of the people which are being waged in dispersed areas—it is progressive. You can see that the Kuomintang soldiers are pale and thin, while the soldiers in our liberated areas are healthy and strong. Just consider how difficult our situation was before we started production for self-support, and how free from discomfort we have been after that. Let us ask two armed units, say two companies, to choose one of the two ways, i.e. either the top level gives them all their provisions or it gives them little or nothing but lets them engage in production to supply themselves with the whole, or the greater part, or a half, or even a tiny fraction of what they need. Which way will yield better results? Which way would they like to follow? After a year's serious experiment in production for self-support, they would definitely answer that they chose to follow the second way, which in their opinion yielded better results, and that they rejected the first which yielded bad results. This is because by the second way the living conditions of all men in the army can be improved, whereas by the first way, under the present difficult material conditions, the men's wants will never be satisfied, no matter how hard the top levels may try. Through the adoption of what appears to be a "back-ward", "retrogressive" measure, the material difficulties of our troops are overcome, their living conditions improved and every soldier becomes healthy and strong; the burden of taxes on the people who are in the same predicament as the soldiers is lightened and hence their support is won, the protracted war can be kept up, our armed force increased, and hence the liberated areas can be expanded while the enemy-occupied areas are reduced until the final aim of defeating the aggressors and liberating the whole of China is achieved. Isn't this of historic significance?

Through production for self-support, not only have we improved the army's living conditions, lightened the people's burden and consequently made it possible to expand the army, but also gained many by-products. They are: (1) Relation-ships have improved between officers and men. As officers and men all take part in production, they become affectionate to one another like brothers. (2) The love of labour has been enhanced. What we have now is neither the old mercenary system nor conscription but a third system, the mobilisation of an army of volunteers. It is better than the mercenary system in that it does not produce so many loafers, but it is not so good as conscription. Nevertheless present conditions allow us only to adopt this system of mobilisation, and not that of con-scription. Soldiers recruited on such a system may easily lose their love of labour in a long course of army life and thus become loafers and acquire certain bad habits of the armies of the warlords. But since they have started production for self-support, their love of labour has been enhanced and lazy habits removed. (3) Discipline has been strengthened. Labour discipline enforced in the course of production tends not to weaken but to strengthen the men's discipline in action and in daily life. (4) The relationship between the army and the people has improved. Once the armed units have secured their own means of livelihood, encroachments upon the people's property rarely or never occur. As the army and the people exchange labour and render mutual aid in the course of pro-duction, they become more friendly towards each other. (5) The army complains less often about the government authori-ties and the relations between them have improved. (6) The people's widespread campaign for increasing production is stimulated. Once the army engages in production, the government organisations will find it all the more imperative to engage in production and will be more enthusiastic about it; the whole people will, of course, also find it all the more imperative to start a widespread campaign for increasing production and will be more enthusiastic about it.

Started in 1942 and in 1943 respectively, the two widespread campaigns for the rectification of the style in work and for increasing production have played and are still playing a decisive role in both our spiritual and material life. If we do not grasp these two links in time, we shall not be able to grasp the whole chain of the revolution, and consequently our struggle will cease to forge ahead.

As we know, of all those who joined our Party before 1937, only a few scores of thousands are left, and most of the 1,200,000 of the present membership are from the peasantry and other sections of the petty bourgeoisie; such comrades have a revolutionary fervour which is very valuable, and are willing to undergo Marxist training, but they have brought with them into the Party their original ideology conforming little or not at all to Marxism. The same is true even of some of the members who joined the Party before 1937. This constitutes a serious contradiction, a great difficulty. Things being so, can we advance smoothly if we do not start a widespread campaign for Marxist education, *i.e.* a campaign for the rectification of the style in work? Obviously not. But as we have solved and are solving this contradiction among large numbers of cadres—a contradiction in the Party between proletarian ideology and non-proletarian ideologies (mainly the ideology of the petty bourgeoisie, also including that of the bourgeoisie and even of the landlord class), *i.e.* a contradiction between Marxist ideology and non-Marxist ideologies, our Party can achieve an unprecedented (though not perfect) ideological, political and organisational unity, and advance with swift, firm strides. Our Party can and must go on growing and we can, guided by the principles of Marxist ideology, still more effectively direct its further growth.

The second link is the campaign for increasing production. At the beginning of the eight-year War of Resistance we could still get food and clothes. But later on the situation grew more and more difficult until it became a conglomeration of difficulties: we are short of food, of cooking oil and salt, of bedding and clothes and money. This great difficulty, this great contradiction, has arisen with the enemies' big offensive of 1940-3 and the three large-scale anti-popular drives (the "anti-Communist upsurges") launched by the Kuomintang government. Can our anti-Japanese struggle forge ahead if we do not overcome the difficulties, solve the contradictions and grasp this link? Obviously not. But we have learnt and will continue to learn how to develop production, and thereby we have regained our full strength and vigour. In a few years we shall have no fear of any enemy whatever and we shall overwhelm all our enemies.

Thus it is evident that the two great campaigns for rectifying the style in work and for increasing production are of historic importance.

Let us further broaden these two campaigns everywhere so as to lay the foundation for the fulfilment of other fighting tasks. If we can do so, the complete liberation of the Chinese people will be ensured.

Now is the season for spring ploughing, and I hope that the leading comrades, the army, Party and government workers and the masses of the people in all the liberated areas will not miss the opportunity to grasp this link of production and strive for even greater achievements than in the last year. In the coming year greater efforts should be made, particularly in areas where skill in developing production has not yet been acquired.

April 27, 1945

THE HURLEY-CHIANG DUET IS A WASHOUT

This is a comment written for the Hsinhua News Agency.

Convoked for the purpose of whitewashing Chiang Kai-shek's dictatorial régime, the Fourth People's Political Council opened on July 7 in Chungking. Never was attendance at the People's Political Council so small as at the first session of this one. Not only did no representatives of the Chinese Communist Party attend, but many from other quarters were also absent. Out of a total membership of 290, only 180 were present. At the opening of the session, Chiang Kai-shek held forth. "The government", he said, "is not going to submit any specific programme on questions relating to the convocation of the national assembly; thus you can discuss these matters fully. The government is ready, in all sincerity and candidness, to listen to your opinions on them." The whole business of "convoking the national assembly on November 12 this year" will probably end up like this. It has also something to do with the imperialist Patrick J. Hurley. It turns out that it was only because this imperialist did all he could to egg Chiang Kai-shek on to play this hand, that Chiang Kai-shek dared to stiffen his back a little, as in his New-Year's Day speech,[1] and a great deal more, as in his March 1 speech,[2] in which he declared his determination to "return the state power to the people" on November 12. As to the proposal made by the Chinese Communist Party voicing the Chinese people's universal wish for convening a conference of all parties and groups and establishing a coalition government, Chiang Kai-shek in his March 1 speech rudely repulsed it. Beside himself with glee, he trumpeted the so-called three-man committee with an American participant for the "reorganisation" of the army of the Chinese Communist Party. He had the audacity to say that the Chinese Communist Party must hand over its troops to him before he would graciously grant it a "legal status". In all this, the support of his patron Patrick J. Hurley played a decisive role. On April 2, Hurley made a statement in Washington, in which, besides playing up such hackneyed imperialist stuff as denying the role of the Chinese Communist Party, libelling its activities and declaring America's non-co-operation with the Chinese Communists, he did his best to boost Chiang Kai-shek's "national assembly" and other disgraceful things. In this way, the duet between Hurley in America and Chiang Kai-shek in China, with the sacrifice of the Chinese people as the common objective, reached its highest pitch of noise. After this, however, the show seems to have flagged. Among the Chinese as well as foreigners, inside the Kuomintang as well as outside it, among people belonging to various parties and groups as well as non-party people, countless voices are being raised in protest. There is only one reason for this: the Hurley-Chiang racket, no matter how it has advertised itself, aims invariably at sacrificing the interests of the Chinese people, disrupting still more the unity of the Chinese people, and laying mines as it were to touch off a large-scale civil war, thereby damaging the common cause of the anti-fascist war as well as the prospects of peaceful co-existence after the war, in which the American people as well as those of other allied countries are all interested. Hurley is now busy about no one knows what; in any case, he seems to be lying low for the time being and Chiang Kai-shek had therefore to take the trouble of talking lamely and irrelevantly to the People's Political Council. On March 1, Chiang Kai-shek said: "The conditions of our country differ from those of other countries: until the convocation of the national assembly, we have no responsible organisation which is representative of the people and through which the government can consult the people for their opinions." If so, then we wonder why our Generalissimo should "listen" to "the opinions" of the People's Political Council. According to the Generalissimo, there is not within the boundaries of China any "responsible organisation through which one can consult the people for their opinions". Therefore the People's Political Council is an "organisation" which lives merely to eat, and therefore his "listening" to it has no legal basis. But in any case, if the People's Political Council says even a single word against the convocation of that bogus "national" assembly, it will be regarded as having done a good deed and merited divine grace, though that would mean flying in the face of His Majesty's decree of March 1 and violating

His Majesty's law. Of course, it is still too early to make any comment on the People's Political Council, for we have yet to wait a few days to know what it will let the Generalissimo "listen" to. One thing, however, is certain: ever since the Chinese people rose in protest against the "national" assembly, even those who were enthusiastic about the "constitutional monarchy" have begun to get worried about our monarch, to caution him not to put his neck into the noose of the so-called "Piglings Parliament" and warn him against the fate of Yuan Shih-k'ai.[3] Who knows but that His Majesty may hold his hand in consequence of this? But our "monarch" and his retinue will never lightly part with even a single hair so that the people could obtain the smallest rights. The immediate proof of this is that His Majesty has described the people's judicious criticism as "wilful attack". It is said that "under war conditions, there is no possibility of holding any general election in the Japanese-occupied areas". Consequently two years ago the Plenary Session of the Kuomintang's Central Executive Committee resolved to convoke the national assembly within a year after the conclusion of the war for the realisation of a constitutional government. At that time, however, certain people made "wilful attacks", because they regarded this as too late. These people, quite unexpectedly, again indulged in "wilful attacks", when our "monarch" came to "understand that it would take quite a long time for the war to be completely concluded, and that even after the war ends order might not be restored everywhere in a short while, and therefore advocated the convocation of the national assembly as soon as the war situation is stabilised". And this has thrown His Majesty into a terrible fix. But the Chinese people must teach Chiang Kai-shek and his crowd this: whatever you say or do, absolutely no deceitful trick in violation of the people's will is allowed. What the Chinese people demand is the immediate introduction of democratic reforms, such as releasing the political prisoners, abolishing the secret service, granting freedoms to the people and legal status to various parties and groups. Doing none of these things, you juggle only with the date of the "national assembly"; but even a three-year old tot will not be taken in by you. Without a minimum of democratic reform in earnest, all your assemblies, big and small, are fit only for the rubbish heap. Call this a "wilful attack" if you like, but all such deceitful tricks must be exploded resolutely, thoroughly, utterly and completely and not a trace of them should be allowed to remain. The reason is simply that they are deceitful tricks. It is one thing whether there is a national assembly and another whether there is the minimum of democratic reforms. For the time being we can dispense with the former but we cannot do without the latter. Since Chiang Kai-shek and his crowd are willing to "return the state power to the people sooner", why are they unwilling to introduce "sooner" the minimum of democratic reforms? Gentlemen of the Kuomintang: you have to admit, while these concluding lines are being written, that the Chinese Communists are not in any sense indulging in "wilful attacks" on you, but are only putting to you one question which can hardly be considered improper or brushed aside unanswered. The question you have to answer is: Why are you willing to "return the state power to the people" but not willing to introduce democratic reforms?

July 10, 1945

ON THE DANGER OF THE HURLEY POLICY

This is a comment written for the *Hsinhua News Agency*.

It becomes more and more obvious that the policy of the United States towards China as represented by its ambassador Patrick J. Hurley is leading China to a crisis of civil war. The Kuomintang government, sticking to its reactionary policies, has devoted itself to the making of civil wars ever since its formation eighteen years ago; and only at the juncture of the Sian Incident in 1936 and the Japanese invasion of China Proper[1] in 1937, was it compelled to abandon for a time a civil war which spread through the whole country. Since 1939, however, civil war on a local scale has again been waged without interruption. The Kuomintang government has a mobilisation slogan for internal consumption: "The foremost task is to combat Communism"; resistance to Japan is relegated to a position of secondary importance. At present the centre of gravity in all its military dispositions is not placed on resisting the Japanese invaders but on "recovering lost territory" from the liberated areas of China, and on exterminating the Chinese Communists. In envisaging both victory in the Anti-Japanese War and peace-time reconstruction after it, we must fully take stock of this situation. The late president Roosevelt did take this into account, and consequently in the interest of the United States he refrained from adopting the policy of helping the Kuomintang to undertake armed attacks on the Chinese Communist Party. In November 1944, Hurley, visiting Yenan as Roosevelt's personal representative, agreed to the plans proposed by the Chinese Communist Party for the abolition of the Kuomintang's one-party dictatorship and the establishment of a democratic coalition government. But later he changed his tune and went back on what he had said in Yenan. This change of tune was sharply indicated in the statement he made at Washington on April 2, in which, from the lips of the selfsame Hurley, the Kuomintang government represented by Chiang Kai-shek suddenly became a Beauty while the Chinese Communist Party was a Monster; he even bluntly declared that the

328

United States would co-operate only with Chiang Kai-shek but not with the Chinese Communist Party. This, of course, is not only Hurley's personal opinion but the opinion of a group of people in the U.S. government; it is however an erroneous and dangerous opinion. At this juncture Roosevelt died and Hurley, beside himself with jubilation, returned to the U.S. Embassy in Chungking. The danger of the U.S. policy towards China as represented by Hurley consists in its encouraging the reactionary trend of the Kuomintang government and increasing the danger of civil war in China. If Hurley's policy continues, the U.S. government will fall hopelessly into the deep, stinking cesspool of Chinese reaction; it will place itself in opposition to the hundreds of millions of awakened or awakening Chinese people, and become a hindrance to the Anti-Japanese War at present and to world peace in the future. Isn't it clear enough that this policy can lead only to such a result? A section of the U.S. press which, on the question of China's future, has clearly perceived that the irresistible forces of the Chinese people demanding independence, freedom and unity will burst forth and supplant both foreign oppression and feudal oppression, feels acutely worried about such a dangerous policy towards China as Hurley's and has requested that it be changed. But whether or when the policy of the United States will be changed, we cannot say at present. But one thing is certain: if such a policy as Hurley's, a policy which aids and abets the anti-popular forces in China in opposition to the Chinese people whose number is so immense, is to continue, it will place a crushing burden on the government and people of the United States and plunge them into endless woes and troubles; this is a point that should be brought home to the people of the United States.

July 12, 1945

TELEGRAM TO
COMRADE WILLIAM Z. FOSTER

Comrade William Z. Foster and the National Committee of the Communist Party of the United States of America:

We are glad to learn that the special conference of the Communist Political Association of the United States has resolved to abandon Earl Browder's revisionist-capitulationist[1] line, reaffirmed Marxist leadership, and re-established the Communist Party of the United States. We hereby extend to you our warm greetings on account of this great success of the working class and the Marxist movement in the United States. Browder's whole revisionist-capitulationist line (fully expressed in his book *Teheran*) essentially reflects the influence of the U.S. reactionary capitalist bloc on the U.S. labour movement. This bloc is now endeavouring to extend its influence in China too, supporting the erroneous anti-national and anti-popular policies of the reactionary clique in the Kuomintang, thereby bringing to the Chinese people the grave danger of civil war and jeopardising the interests of both the Chinese and American peoples. The victory of the working class of the United States and its vanguard, the Communist Party of the United States, over Browder's line will beyond all doubt contribute signally to the great cause to which the Chinese and American peoples are dedicated, the cause of carrying on the war against Japan at present and of reconstructing the world on a peaceful and democratic basis after it.

July 2, 1945

THE LAST ROUND WITH THE
JAPANESE INVADERS

The Chinese people heartily welcome the Soviet government's declaration of war on Japan on August 8. The Soviet Union's action will very much shorten the duration of the war against Japan. The war is already in its last stage and the time has come for us to defeat finally the Japanese invaders and all their jackals. Under such circumstances, all the forces in China engaged in the struggle against the Japanese invaders should launch a nation-wide counter-offensive in close and effective co-ordination with the operations of the Soviet Union and other Allied countries. The Eighth Route Army, the New Fourth Army and all other people's troops should seize every chance to launch extensive offensives against all invaders and their jackals who refuse to surrender, annihilate their forces, capture their arms and *matériel*, put forth the most energetic efforts to expand our liberated areas and reduce the areas under enemy occupation. They must boldly form armed squads which, by hundreds and by thousands, should penetrate deep into the rear of the enemy-occupied areas to organise the people for the wrecking of the enemy's communication lines and to support the operations of the regular armies. They must boldly rouse the tens of millions of the people in the enemy-occupied areas, and immediately proceed to organise underground forces, prepare armed uprisings and annihilate the enemy in co-ordination with the regular forces attacking at the front. The consolidation of the liberated areas should not be overlooked. Among the 100 million people there, and among the people in all areas to be liberated by us, we should universally carry out this winter and the coming spring campaigns to reduce rent and interest, to develop production, to build up the political power and armed forces of the people, to intensify the militia work, to strengthen army discipline, to persist in the united front of all sections of the people and to guard against waste of man-power and material resources. All these measures are taken with a view to putting more force into the offensives our troops are making against the enemy. All the people in our country must make efforts to prevent civil war and expedite the formation of a democratic coalition government. A new stage in China's war of national liberation has arrived; all our people should strengthen their solidarity and struggle for the final victory.

August 9, 1945

NOTES

PREFACE AND POSTSCRIPT TO "RURAL SURVEY"

1. The first directive refers to the *Resolutions of the Central Committee of the Chinese Communist Party on the Current Situation and the Party's Policy*, and the second to the article *On Policy*, Vol. III of the *Selected Works*.

2. A person who has passed the first grade of the imperial examination held in his own county.

3. J. V. Stalin, *Foundations of Leninism*.

4. The earlier period of the ten-year civil war lasted from late 1927 to late 1928, and is generally known as the period of the Chingkang mountains; the middle period lasted from early 1929 to the autumn of 1931, *i.e.* from the establishment of the Central Red base area to the victorious conclusion of the campaign against the Kuomintang's third "encirclement and annihilation"; the final period lasted from the end of that campaign to the enlarged meeting of the Central Political Bureau held in Tsunyi, Kweichow. The Tsunyi meeting of January 1935 put an end to the "Left" opportunist line that had dominated the Party during 1931–4 and steered the Party back to the correct line. *Cf. Resolution on Some Historical Problems* (appendix to *Our Study and the Current Situation*), Sec. III, in this volume.

REFORM OUR STUDY

1. About fifty miles south of Yenan.

2. The border region currency was issued by the Bank of the Shensi-Kansu-Ningsia Border Region Government, and the national currency was first issued in 1935 by the four big Kuomintang banks of bureaucratic capital, with the backing of Anglo-American imperialism. Here Comrade Mao Tse-tung refers to the problem of the fluctuations in the rate of exchange between these two currencies.

3. Karl Marx, *Capital*, Preface to the Second Edition. In this Preface Marx wrote:
   ". . . The latter [the method of inquiry] has to appropriate the material in detail, to analyse its different forms of development, to trace out their inner connection. Only after this work is done, can the actual movement be adequately described."

4. *Cf.* J. V. Stalin, "Style in Work", *Foundations of Leninism*.

EXPOSE THE MUNICH PLOT IN THE FAR EAST

1. Referring to the campaign of the Chungtiao mountains. In May 1941, a Japanese force of 50,000 strong attacked the region of the Chungtiao mountains

to the north of the Yellow river in southern Shansi. There were seven Kuomintang armies in that region and four Kuomintang armies in the Kaoping area to the north-east, making a total of 250,000 men. But as the Kuomintang troops north of the Yellow river had always regarded anti-communism as their main task and never thought of fighting the national enemy, they tried not to engage the Japanese. Although the Eighth Route Army fought actively in co-ordination, the Kuomintang troops met with a crushing defeat, with 50,000 casualties in three weeks. The remainder scuttled to the south of the Yellow river.

RECTIFY THE PARTY'S STYLE IN WORK

1. *Cf.* Note 34 to *Strategic Problems of China's Revolutionary War*, Vol. I of the *Selected Works*. The "eight-legged essay" is an extremely formalised manner of composition in which phrases and paragraphs are arranged in a rigid pattern, and even the number of words is prescribed. The writer spins out his empty discourse by expatiating on the signification of each word in the theme set by the examiner or the tutor. The Party "eight-legged essay" refers to the kind of writing produced by certain people within the revolutionary ranks, which, like the "eight-legged essay", contains no analysis of things but only heaps of revolutionary words and phrases.

2. Referring to the December 1939 resolution of the Central Committee of the Chinese Communist Party, *Draw in Large Numbers of Intellectuals*, which appears in Vol. III of the *Selected Works*.

3. J. V. Stalin, *Foundations of Leninism*.

4. The opening sentence of the *Analects* of Confucius.

5. J. V. Stalin, *Report on the Work of the Central Committee to the Eighteenth Congress of the C.P.S.U. (B)*.

6. *Cf.* J. V. Stalin, *Report on the Work of the Central Committee to the Eighteenth Congress of the C.P.S.U. (B)*, Sec. III.

7. The means frequently adopted by the Chinese people to fight against Japanese imperialist aggression in the first half of the twentieth century. Witness the campaigns to boycott Japanese goods during the patriotic May 4 Movement of 1919, after the Incident of September 18, 1931, and during the Anti-Japanese War.

OPPOSE THE PARTY "EIGHT-LEGGED ESSAY"

1. *See* Note 1 to *Rectify the Party's Style in Work*, and also Note 34 to *Strategic Problems of China's Revolutionary War*, Vol. I of the *Selected Works*.

2. Title of an essay included in *Northern Dialect with a Southern Accent (Complete Works of Lu Hsun*, Vol. V).

3. The name in Shanghai dialect for those who have no legitimate occupation and live on beggary or theft. Such people look generally underfed and emaciated.

4. The *Great Dipper* was a monthly published from 1931 to 1932 by the League of Chinese Left-Wing Writers. This letter is included in *The Divided Mind*, the *Complete Works of Lu Hsun*, Vol. IV.

5. See *Confucian Analects*, Book V, "Kung-ye Ch'ang". (*Cf. The Chinese Classics*, Vol. I, p. 180, translated by James Legge, Oxford, 1893.)

6. Han Yu, famous Chinese writer who flourished between the late eighth century and the early ninth century. In his *Apology for the Scholar*, he wrote: "A deed is accomplished through thought and ends in failure through lack of thought."

TALKS AT THE YENAN FORUM ON ART AND LITERATURE

1. See V. I. Lenin, *The Party's Organisation and the Party's Literature*, in which the characteristics of proletarian literature are described as follows:

"This will be a free literature, because neither covetousness nor careerism but rather the idea of socialism and feelings for the working people will draw ever fresh forces into its ranks. This will be free literature, because it will serve millions and tens of millions of working people who constitute the strength and future of the country. This will be free literature because it will fructify the latest events in the revolutionary thought of mankind with the experience and daily work of the socialist proletariat, creating a permanent inter-relationship between the experience of the past (scientific socialism, which completed the development of socialism from its primitive, utopian forms) with the experience of the present (the present day struggle of our worker comrades)."

2. A member of the counter-revolutionary National Socialist Party, he has for years propagated the literary theories of the reactionary U.S. bourgeoisie, stubbornly opposed the revolution and denounced revolutionary literature.

3. Both capitulated to the Japanese invaders upon their occupation of Peking and Shanghai in 1937.

4. See "My View on the Alliance of Left-Wing Writers", *Complete Works of Lu Hsun*, Chinese edition, Vol. IV.

5. See "Death", *Complete Works of Lu Hsun*, Chinese edition, Vol. VI.

6. A popular Chinese operetta with a cast of only two characters, a cowherd and a village girl, carrying on a dialogue in songs. With its songs reworded for the purpose of anti-Japanese propaganda, it enjoyed much popularity in the early days of the War of Resistance.

7. In Chinese, these are characters of a few strokes, usually given in the first lessons of old primers.

8. This and "The Spring Snow" were songs of the third century B.C. sung by people of Ch'u, one of the largest states in ancient China. They represented respectively music of a lower and a higher order. Sung Yu's "Answer to the King of Ch'u" relates that, in the capital of the state, when a singer sang "The Spring Snow" only a few dozens would join in the chorus, but when he sang the "Pa Emigrants in the Poor Quarters", thousands of people joined in.

9. *See* V. I. Lenin, *The Party's Organisation and the Party's Literature*, in which he says: "The cause of literature should form a part of the entire cause of the proletariat and become one of the 'cogs and screws' in the great united, social-democratic machine operated by the whole awakened vanguard of the working class."

10. In Shanghai, in those days, the impecunious artists, writers, intellectuals, and sn all office employees mostly lived in such quarters for the sake of the low rent.

11. Referring to the Kuomintang-controlled areas. During the Anti-Japanese War, people used to call the vast areas in South-west and North-west China, which were free from Japanese occupation and were under the Kuomintang control, the "big rear", as distinguished from the "small rear"—the anti-Japanese base areas in the enemy rear under Communist leadership.

12. In this novel, published in 1927, the famous Soviet writer describes how in Siberia a guerrilla unit composed of workers, peasants, and revolutionary intellectuals fought the gangs of the counter-revolutionaries. It was translated into Chinese by Lu Hsun.

13. *See* "In Mockery of Myself", *Complete Works of Lu Hsun*, Chinese edition, Vol. VII.

AN EXTREMELY IMPORTANT POLICY

1. This refers to Japan's policy of killing all, burning all, and looting all in the liberated areas of China.

2. *See* the Chinese fantasy *Pilgrimage to the West* (entitled *Monkey* in Arthur Waley's abridged English translation), Chapter 59. The Princess of the Iron Fan is also known as Raksha.

3. Liu Tsung-yuan (A.D. 773–819), a great Chinese writer of the T'ang dynasty. *The Donkey in Kweichow* is one of his "Three Parables". It relates how a tiger in Kweichow, never having set eyes upon a donkey before, was scared when he saw one for the first time. But having realised that all the donkey could do was to bray and kick, the tiger fell upon it and ate it up.

ECONOMIC AND FINANCIAL PROBLEMS DURING THE ANTI-JAPANESE WAR

1. These are the totals paid in agricultural tax ("public grain") by the peasants of the Shensi-Kansu-Ningsia border region.

2. *Cf. An Extremely Important Policy*, in this volume.

ON METHODS OF LEADERSHIP

1. *Cf.* J. V. Stalin, *The Prospects of the Communist Party of Germany and the Question of Bolshevisation*, *Collected Works* Vol 7.

2. *See* Georgi Dimitrov's concluding speech at the Seventh World Congress of the Communist International: *Unity of the Working Class Against Fascism*.

SOME QUESTIONS PUT TO THE KUOMINTANG

1. In his *China's Destiny* Chiang Kai-shek openly announced his frantic opposition to both communism and liberalism.
2. Meaning something like "director-general", Chiang Kai-shek's official title as the top leader of the Kuomintang.

SPREAD IN THE BASE AREAS THE CAMPAIGN FOR RENT REDUCTION, FOR PRODUCTION, AND FOR THE ARMY'S SUPPORT OF THE GOVERNMENT AND PROTECTION OF THE PEOPLE

1. *See* Note 4 to *Let Us Get Organised*, in this volume.

A COMMENT ON THE ELEVENTH PLENARY SESSION OF THE KUOMINTANG'S CENTRAL EXECUTIVE COMMITTEE AND THE SECOND SESSION OF THE THIRD PEOPLE'S POLITICAL COUNCIL

1. Referring to those Kuomintang generals and officers who had once been instructors or cadets at the Whampoa Military Academy. They were Chiang Kai-shek's devoted followers in the Kuomintang Army.
2. Yeh T'ing and Hsiang Ying were respectively the commander and deputy commander of the New Fourth Army.

LET US GET ORGANISED

1. Quoted from "Kung-sun Ch'au, Part I", Book II of *The Works of Mencius. Cf. The Chinese Classics*, translated by James Legge, Vol. II, pp. 180–208, Oxford, 1895.
2. That is, the article *Spread in the Base Areas the Campaign for Rent Reduction, for Production, and for the Army's Support of the Government and Protection of the People*, in this volume.
3. *Cf.* V. I. Lenin. *On Co-operation.*

4. Both being mutual-aid organisations in agricultural production in the Shensi-Kansu-Ningsia border region. "Work-exchange" is a means by which the peasants adjust labour-power as well as ox-power among themselves. They may exchange man-power for man-power, ox-power for ox-power, or man-power for ox-power, etc. Members of a work-exchange team contribute their own labour-power or ox-power to till collectively and by rotation the land which belongs to each of the member-families. The work-day, of both men and cattle, is taken as the basis to balance the accounts, and those who have contributed more are paid for the difference. "Labour-for-hire teams" are usually formed by peasants who do not have enough land. Their members, besides exchanging labour-power among themselves on a mutual-aid basis, generally hire themselves out collectively to families which are short of labour-power.

5. See Note 2 to Our Economic Policy, Vol. I of the Selected Works.

6. Chukeh Liang, a symbol of resourcefulness and wisdom in Chinese folklore, was a statesman and strategist in the period of the Three Kingdoms (221–65).

7. The New Year's Day in the lunar calendar.

8. The Shensi-Kansu-Ningsia border region was divided into these five sub-regions.

OUR STUDY AND THE CURRENT SITUATION

1. The plenary session of the Central Committee of the Chinese Communist Party which was the fourth held since the Sixth National Congress. See the third part of the appendix to this article.

2. See the third part of the appendix to this article.

3. See Note 8 to Strategic Problems of China's Revolutionary War, Vol. I of the Selected Works.

4. See Note 31 to On the Tactics of Fighting Japanese Imperialism, Vol. I of the Selected Works.

5. The plenary session of the Central Committee of the Chinese Communist Party held in January 1934. It was the fifth session since the Sixth National Congress. Cf. the third part of the appendix to this article.

6. The session reviewed the Party's political lines in the past, especially that during the Second Revolutionary Civil War.

7. This means a cliquish tendency arising during the protracted guerrilla war, when the revolutionary bases were scattered over the countryside and cut off from each other. Since most of these revolutionary bases were first established in isolated mountain regions, comrades in each of them naturally tended to band themselves into a close-knit group. Thus this erroneous tendency became known as the "sentiment of the mountain-stronghold".

8. In the relatively consolidated base areas the people paid taxes only to the anti-Japanese democratic government. But in the guerrilla zones or on the borders of the base areas, which were constantly harassed by the enemy, the people were often forced to pay additional taxes to the enemy's puppet government.

9. A measure adopted by the Japanese imperialists after the failure of their large-scale offensives on the anti-Japanese base areas. Instead of "gobbling

up" our territory, they would now "nibble it up" over a long period of time. They attempted to reduce the anti-Japanese base areas and expand the areas under their occupation by taking sure steps to cut up the base areas into smaller and smaller pieces.

10. The campaign was set afoot in March 1941 by the Japanese aggressors and Chinese collaborators in North China. Aiming at the suppression of anti-Japanese forces, it actually meant raiding the people's houses, establishing the *pao-chia* system (*cf.* Note 5 to *On Coalition Government* in this volume), making a census and expanding the puppet army.

11. Namely, subjectivism in study, sectarianism in the Party and the Party "eight-legged essay" in writings and speeches. *Cf. Rectify the Party's Style in Work*, in this volume.

12. Now the Peking-Hankow railway.

13. A campaign which the Japanese aggressors launched in March 1944 with a strength of 50,000 to 60,000 men. The 400,000 Kuomintang troops under Chiang Ting-wen, T'ang En-po and Hu Tsung-nan collapsed before the Japanese invaders. Consequently thirty-eight counties, including Chengchow and Loyang, fell one after another, and T'ang En-po lost 200,000 of his men.

14. A large-scale war of the warlords waged along the Kansu-Haichow and Tientsin-Pukow railways. It lasted for six months from May to October 1930. Casualties on both sides reached 300,000.

15. This refers to Kuo Mo-jo's *In Memory of the Peasant Uprising of 1644*, written to commemorate the 300th anniversary of the downfall of the Ming dynasty under the impact of the peasant uprising led by Li Tzu-ch'eng. The essay explains that the peasant forces finally met with defeat in 1645 because, once they entered Peking, a number of their commanders began to be lapped in luxury and wage factional struggles among themselves. The essay first appeared in the *New China Daily* in Chungking, and was subsequently published in book form in Yenan and other liberated areas.

16. Quoted from "Kao Tsze, Part I", *The Works of Mencius*, Book VI. (*Cf. The Chinese Classics*, translated by James Legge, Vol. II, p. 418, Oxford, 1893.)

APPENDIX: RESOLUTION ON SOME QUESTIONS IN THE HISTORY OF OUR PARTY

1. *See* Note 1 to *Problems of War and Strategy*, Vol. II of the *Selected Works*.

2. *Cf.* Note 2 to "Strategic Problems of China's Revolutionary War", Vol. I of the *Selected Works*.

3. Member of the Chinese Communist Party in its early days who later became a renegade. About the time of the Central Committee's plenary session of January 1931 (the fourth since the Party's Sixth National Congress), Lo Chang-lung, growing pessimistic about the future of the Chinese revolution, openly supported the counter-revolutionary views of the Trotskyite Ch'en Tu-hsiu clique, opposed the line of the Sixth National Congress of the Party, denounced the Red Army and the Red base areas, and even disclosed the identity of Communist cadres to Chiang Kai-shek's bandit gang by mentioning

their names in the leaflets he prepared for distribution. To undermine the revolutionary struggles led by the Party, he carried on disruptive activities, setting up organisations like the "Central Emergency Committee", "Second" provincial committees, "Second" district committees, and "Second Party fractions" in Trade Unions. He was expelled from the Party in January 1931.

4. *Cf.* Note 23 to *On the Tactics of Fighting Japanese Imperialism*, Vol. I of the *Selected Works*.

5. The First Front Army of the Red Army launched its second offensive on Changsha, capital of Hunan, in September 1930. As the enemy forces put up a stubborn defence behind well-built fortifications and made use of airplanes and warships, the Red Army failed to capture the city in spite of a long siege. With the gradual increase of the enemy reinforcements, the Red Army found itself placed in an unfavourable situation. Comrade Mao Tse-tung persuaded the senior cadres in the First Front Army to withdraw the troops and abandon the attempt to seize Kiukiang, northern Kiangsi, and other metropolitan cities. The Front Army thus divided its forces to attack the counties of Chaling, Yu, and Liling in Hunan and of Pingsiang and Kian in Kiangsi, and scored great successes.

6. Veteran member and one of the earliest leaders of the Chinese Communist Party, Comrade Ch'u Ch'iu-pai was elected member of the Central Committee from the Third to the Sixth National Congresses, held in the years 1923–8. During the First Revolutionary Civil War he actively fought against the anti-Communist and anti-popular "Tai Chi-t'ao-ism" of the Kuomintang's Right wing and the Right opportunism represented by Ch'en Tu-hsiu in the Chinese Communist Party. After the Kuomintang's betrayal of the revolution in 1927 he called the emergency conference of the Central Committee on August 7, which put an end to the rule of Ch'en Tu-hsiu-ism in the Party. But from the winter of 1927 to the spring of 1928 he committed the mistake of "Left" adventurism when directing the work of the Central Committee. In September 1930 Comrade Ch'u Ch'iu-pai called the Central Committee's plenary session (the third since the Sixth National Congress), and stopped the execution of Li Li-san's line that was doing harm to the Party. At the next plenary session of the Central Committee held in January 1931, however, he was attacked by the "Left" doctrinaire-sectarians and excluded from the Party's central leading body. Thenceforth he devoted himself to the revolutionary cultural movement, working in co-operation with Lu Hsun in Shanghai. In 1933 he arrived in the Red base area in Kiangsi and served as commissioner of people's education of the Workers' and Peasants' Democratic Central Government. When the main forces of the Red Army embarked on the Long March, he was left in the Kiangsi base area. He was arrested by Chiang Kai-shek's bandit gang in the Fukien guerrilla area in March 1935, and died a martyr on June 18 in Changting, Fukien.

7. Member of the Chinese Communist Party and one of the early organisers and leaders of the Chinese trade union movement, Comrade Lin Yu-nan was once director of the Wuhan office of the Secretariat of the Chinese Associated Labour Unions and a member of the Executive Committee and secretary-general of the All-China Federation of Trade Unions. In 1931 he was arrested by Chiang Kai-shek's bandit gang in Shanghai and died a martyr at Lunghwa.

8. Member of the Chinese Communist Party, Comrade Li Ch'iu-shih served in 1928 as member of the Central Committee of the Chinese Communist Youth League, as head of its Propaganda Department, and chief editor of *Chinese*

Youth, organ of the C.C. of the C.C.Y.L. In 1931 he was arrested by Chiang Kai-shek's bandit gang while working in the Propaganda Department of the Chinese Communist Party, and died a martyr at Lunghwa.

9. Member of the Chinese Communist Party, one of the early organisers of the trade union movement in North China, and founder of the Railwaymen's Union on the Peking-Suiyuan Line. After the Kuomintang's betrayal of the revolution in 1927, Comrade Ho Meng-hsiung worked in Shanghai and served as a member of the Party's Kiangsu Provincial Committee and as secretary of its Peasant Department. In 1931 he was arrested by Chiang Kai-shek's bandit gang and died a martyr at Lunghwa.

10. From September 1931 to January 1935, Comrade Ch'in Pang-hsien headed first the Chinese Communist Party's Provisional Central Political Bureau in Shanghai and then its Central Political Bureau in the Red base areas. During this period he committed serious mistakes of a "Left" character. He worked in the Southern Bureau of the Party's Central Committee during the early period of the Anti-Japanese War. After 1941, under the guidance of Comrade Mao Tse-tung, he founded and directed the *Liberation Daily* and the *Hsinhua News Agency* in Yenan. He was re-elected member of the Central Committee at the Seventh National Congress of the Party in 1945. In February 1946 he arrived in Chungking to take part in the negotiations with the Kuomintang. He died in April in an airplane crash on his way back to Yenan.

11. In autumn 1935 Comrade Chu Li-chih, a follower of the erroneous "Left" line, arrived in the revolutionary base area in northern Shensi (including the borders of Shensi and Kansu) as a representative of the Central Committee. In collaboration with Comrade Kuo Hung-t'ao, another follower of the erroneous "Left" line, he thoroughly carried out the line of "Left" opportunism in political, military and organisational work, and excluded from the leadership comrades like Liu Chih-tan and others who had pursued the correct line and built up the Red Army and the revolutionary base area in northern Shensi. Then, in a campaign to comb out counter-revolutionaries, Comrades Chu and Kuo wrongly arrested a great many cadres who were carrying out the correct line, and thus created a serious crisis in the northern Shensi revolutionary base area. Arriving in Northern Shensi in November after the Long March, comrades of the Central Committee redressed the wrong done by the followers of the "Left" line, released Liu Chih-tan and other comrades from jail, and thus saved the situation.

12. *Cf.* J. V. Stalin, "Problems of the Chinese Revolution" and "On the Perspectives of the Revolution in China", included in *Stalin on China*, Bombay, 1951, and Part II of "The Chinese Revolution and the Task of the Communist International".

13. *Cf. Report of An Investigation into the Peasant Movement in Hunan*, Vol. I of the *Selected Works*.

14. *Cf.* the section entitled "The Problem of the Character of the Revolution" in *The Struggle in the Chingkang Mountains*, Vol. I of the *Selected Works*.

15. From the letter of the Front Committee in the Chingkang mountains to the Central Committee in April 1929, as quoted in *A Single Spark Can Start a Prairie Fire*, Vol. I of the *Selected Works*.

16. *Cf. Why Can China's Red Political Power Exist?* and *The Struggle in the Chingkang Mountains*, Vol. I of the *Selected Works*.

17. In its declaration of January 1933, the Chinese Communist Party offered to conclude on three conditions a cease-fire agreement with all Kuomintang

troops attacking the Red Army and the revolutionary base areas and to ally with them for resisting Japan. The conditions were: (1) Stop attacking the revolutionary base areas and the Red Army; (2) Grant freedoms and rights to the people; and (3) Arm the people.

18. *Cf.* Note 16 to *On the Tactics of Fighting Japanese Imperialism*, Vol. I of the *Selected Works*.

19. J. V. Stalin, "On the Perspectives of the Revolution in China", English translation published in the *Political Affairs*, New York, December 1950, p. 29.

20. *Cf. Why Can China's Red Political Power Exist?* and *A Single Spark Can Start a Prairie Fire*, Vol. I of the *Selected Works*.

21. From *Why Can China's Red Political Power Exist?* Ibid.

22. From *A Single Spark Can Start a Prairie Fire.* Ibid.

23. Quoted from J. V. Stalin's "Comments on Current Affairs", *Stalin on China*, Bombay, 1951, p. 59. *Cf.* J. V. Stalin, *The Foundations of Leninism*, Part VII, "Strategy and Tactics".

24. From *The Struggle in the Chingkang Mountains*, Vol. I of the *Selected Works*.

25. Ibid.

26. Ibid.

27. From the letter of the Front Committee in the Chingkang mountains to the Central Committee in April 1929, quoted in *A Single Spark Can Start a Prairie Fire*, Vol. I of the *Selected Works*.

28. From "General Resolution of the Central Committee of the Chinese Communist Party on the Fight Against the Enemy's Fifth Campaign of 'Encirclement and Annihilation'" (adopted at the Tsunyi meeting).

29. From Chapter III of *Strategic Problems of China's Revolutionary War*, Vol. I of the *Selected Works*.

30. *Cf. On Policy*, Vol. II of the *Selected Works*.

31. From Comrade Liu Shao-chi's *Eliminate Closed-Door Sectarianism and Adventurism*.

32. From Comrade Liu Shao-chi's *Letter to the Central Committee on the Work in the White Areas*.

33. From Comrade Liu Shao-chi's *Eliminate Closed-Door Sectarianism and Adventurism*.

34. Lo Ming, once member of the Chinese Communist Party, was the acting secretary of the Fukien Provincial Committee of the central Red base area in 1933. He was attacked by the "Leftists" in the Party because he held that, as the Party was confronted with a quite difficult situation in Shanghang, Yungting and other places on the western border of Fukien, its policy should be different from that in the consolidated areas. The "Leftists" erroneously exaggerated his viewpoint as representing "an opportunist-liquidationist line of flight and retreat, stemming from pessimism and despair about the future of the revolution", and resorted to organisational measures and waged a so-called "struggle against the line of Lo Ming".

35. Both are the disciplinary rules which Comrade Mao Tse-tung laid down for the Chinese Workers' and Peasants' Red Army during the Agrarian Revolutionary War, and which were later adopted by the Eighth Route and New Fourth Armies and the present People's Liberation Army. As the army units stationed at various places adopted slightly different formulations of these

rules, the General Headquarters of the People's Liberation Army issued in October 1947 the standard version as follows:

The Three Cardinal Rules of Discipline:
   (1) Obey orders in all actions.
   (2) Do not take a single needle or piece of thread from the people.
   (3) Turn all booty over to H.Q.

The Eight Reminders:
   (1) Talk to people politely.
   (2) Be fair in all business dealings.
   (3) Return everything you have borrowed.
   (4) Pay for anything you have damaged.
   (5) Don't beat or bully people.
   (6) Don't damage crops.
   (7) Don't flirt with women.
   (8) Don't ill-treat prisoners of war.

36. From the letter of the Front Committee in the Chingkang mountains to the Central Committee in April 1929, as quoted in *A Single Spark Can Start a Prairie Fire*, Vol. I of the *Selected Works*.

37. *Cf.* Chapter V of *Strategic Problems of China's Revolutionary War*, Vol. I of the *Selected Works*.

38. From *The Summing-Up of the Central Committee of the Chinese Communist Party on Smashing the Enemy's Fifth Campaign of "Encirclement and Annihilation"*, February 1935.

39. *On the Rectification of Incorrect Ideas in the Party*, Vol. I of the *Selected Works*.

40. V. I. Lenin, *What Is To Be Done?*

41. From J. V. Stalin's *The Work of the April Joint Plenum of the Central Committee and Central Control Commission*, a report at a meeting of the activists of the Party organisations in Moscow, delivered on April 13, 1928. *See* J. V. Stalin, *Collected Works*, Vol. 11.

42. From *Our Study and the Current Situation*, in this volume.

43. Referring to followers of the revolutionary adventurism represented in France by Auguste Blanqui (1805–81). The Blanquists fancied that capitalist exploitation could be ended by the intrigues of a handful of intellectuals rather than by the class struggle of the proletariat.

44. From *Our Study and the Current Situation*, in this volume.

SERVE THE PEOPLE

1. A soldier in the Guards Regiment of the Central Committee of the Chinese Communist Party and a Party member serving the people with great devotion. He joined the revolution in 1932, took part in the Long March and was wounded in service. On September 5, 1944, when making charcoal in the mountains of Ansi county, northern Shensi, he was killed by the sudden collapse of a kiln.

2. From "Letter to Jen Shao-ch'ing" by Szuma Ch'ien (*fl.* second century B.C.), famous Chinese writer and historian, author of the *Historical Records*.

3. An enlightened member of the gentry in northern Shensi, once elected Vice-Chairman of the Shensi-Kansu-Ningsia Border Region Government.

4. This was the total of the population of the Shensi-Kansu-Ningsia border region and that of all other liberated areas in North, Central and South China.

ON CHIANG KAI-SHEK'S SPEECH ON THE DOUBLE TENTH FESTIVAL

1. October 10, anniversary of the rising in Wuhan which set off the Revolution of 1911.

2. Kuomintang generals who openly capitulated to the Japanese invaders.

3. An anti-Japanese armed force of the people in Shansi which developed under the leadership and influence of the Communist Party in the early days of the Anti-Japanese War. *Cf.* Note 3 to *Unite All Anti-Japanese Forces and Combat the Anti-Communist Die-Hards*, Vol. III of the *Selected Works*.

4. From the early months of 1944, the demand for ending the Kuomintang dictatorship, for bringing about democracy and for protecting the freedom of speech became the common cry of the people in the Kuomintang-controlled areas. To parry the people's urgent request, the Kuomintang promised in April 1944 so-called "greater latitude for the voicing of opinions". In May, the Twelfth Plenary Session of the Central Executive Committee of the Kuomintang again declared that it would "protect freedom of speech". But the Kuomintang never fulfilled these promises wrung from itself. On the contrary, measures for suppressing the people's voice multiplied as the movement for people's democracy broadened.

THE UNITED FRONT IN CULTURAL WORK

1. An old-style opera of Shensi province, so named because the province formed the main part of the state of Ch'in in ancient times.

2. A folk-dance with songs popular among the Chinese peasants.

3. A Confucian saying. *See Confucian Analects*, Book XIII, "Tsze-Lu". (*The Chinese Classics*, Vol. I, translated by James Legge, Oxford, 1893.)

PRODUCTION IS ALSO POSSIBLE IN THE GUERRILLA ZONES

1. A *liang* is approximately one ounce.

2. Sixteen *liang* (see note above) make a catty, which, according to the *market system*, is about 1·1 lb.

CHINA'S TWO POSSIBLE DESTINIES

1. Referring to Chiang Kai-shek's *China's Destiny*, published in 1943.
2. Referring to Comrade Mao Tse-tung's report, *On Coalition Government*, at the Congress.

ON COALITION GOVERNMENT

1. This was a revolutionary youth organisation formed under Communist leadership in September 1936 by the progressive youth in the December 9 Movement of the previous year. After the outbreak of the Anti-Japanese War, many of its members went to the front and took part in establishing the base areas in the enemy rear. In the Kuomintang-controlled areas the organisation was forcibly dissolved by Chiang Kai-shek's government in 1938. In the liberated areas it was later merged into the Association of Youth for National Salvation, an even broader youth organisation.

2. For an account of the facts, see *A Comment on the Eleventh Plenary Session of the Kuomintang's Central Executive Committee and the Second Session of the Third People's Political Council*, in this volume.

3. This refers to the offensive launched by the Japanese army designed to seize the Hankow-Canton railway and thus secure an uninterrupted land link between North and South China.

4. A market picul is 1/20 of a metric ton.

5. *Pao chia*—a system founded on collective responsibility, which formed the lowest link in the chain of the administrative organs and through which the Kuomintang reactionary clique maintained its fascist rule. On August 1, 1932, Chiang Kai-shek proclaimed in Honan, Hupeh and Anhwei the "Regulations for the Organisation of *Pao* and *Chia* and for Population Census in the Counties", which provided that "the *pao* and *chia* are to be organised on a household basis; the household, the *chia* (made up of ten households) and the *pao* (made up of ten *chia*) each with a head of its own". Thus a system of collective responsibility was established. The regulations also required neighbours to keep watch on each other and to report to the authorities on each other's activities, and all were punishable when one was found guilty. In addition, these regulations provided for various counter-revolutionary measures for compulsory labour. On November 7, 1934, the Kuomintang government officially announced that this fascist system was to be established in all provinces and municipalities under its rule.

6. This refers to the feudal-comprador fascist education carried out by the Kuomintang government.

7. An international conference held in November 1943 between China, the United States, and Great Britain in Cairo, capital of Egypt. The Cairo Declaration issued by these three countries clearly stipulated that Taiwan and certain other territories were to be returned to China. But in June 1950 the U.S. government openly violated this agreement by placing Taiwan under the control of its naval forces in an attempt to deprive China of her sovereignty over it.

8. A famous mountain in the south-western section of Szechwan province. Comrade Mao Tse-tung refers to it here as a symbol of the whole mountainous region of Szechwan, last refuge of Chiang Kai-shek's ruling clique in the Anti-Japanese War.

9. *Cf. The Reactionaries Must Be Punished, Unite All Anti-Japanese Forces and Combat the Anti-Communist Die-Hards,* and *Ten Demands to the Kuomintang,* Vol. III of the *Selected Works.*

10. From Dr. Sun Yat-sen's *Statement on My Departure for the North,* dated November 10, 1924.

11. This refers to the absurd theory of pan-Hanism which Chiang Kai-shek advanced in his counter-revolutionary pamphlet, *China's Destiny.*

12. The Atlantic Charter was issued jointly by the United States and Great Britain upon the conclusion of their Atlantic Conference of August 1941. The Moscow conference was held in October 1943 by the foreign ministers of the Soviet Union, the United States and Great Britain. The Teheran conference was held by the Soviet Union, the United States and Great Britain in Teheran, capital of Iran, from November to December, 1943. The Yalta conference was held in February 1945 by the Soviet Union, the United States and Great Britain at Yalta on the Crimean Peninsula. All these international conferences resolved to defeat fascist Germany and Japan through common endeavour and, after the war, to prevent the revival of the forces of aggression and the remnants of fascism, maintain world peace and help the peoples of various countries to realise their aspirations for independence and democracy.

13. In accordance to the decisions of the Moscow and Teheran conferences, representatives of the Soviet Union, the United States, Great Britain and China met from August to October 1944, in Dumbarton Oaks, U.S.A., and proposed a draft constitution of the United Nations' Organisation. A conference of the United Nations was held in San Francisco in the U.S.A. from April to June 1945, with delegates from fifty countries. Comrade Tung Pi-wu attended the conference as the representative of the Chinese liberated areas.

14. After the Seventh National Congress of the Chinese Communist Party, the "Preparatory Committee of the People's Congress of the Chinese Liberated Areas" was formed in Yenan and held its inaugural meeting with representatives from all the liberated areas participating. After the Japanese surrender, the proposal for the convocation of this congress was dropped because of changes in the situation.

HOW YU KUNG REMOVED THE MOUNTAINS

1. Referring to Comrade Mao Tse-tung's political report, Comrade Chu Teh's military report and Comrade Liu Shao-ch'i's report on the revision of the Party Constitution.

2. The story is taken from "The Questions of T'ang" in *The Book of Lieh Tze. Cf.* Lionel Giles' translation entitled *Taoist Teachings,* pp. 86–8, London, 1912.

3. Meaning "Foolish Old Man".

4. Meaning "Wise Old Man".

5. Patrick J. Hurley of the U.S. Republican Party, was appointed ambassador to China towards the end of 1944. Because of his support for Chiang Kai-shek's anti-Communist policy, he was resolutely opposed by the Chinese people and compelled to resign in November 1945. His open declaration of non-co-operation with the Chinese Communist Party was made on April 2, 1945 at a press conference given by the U.S. State Department in Washington. *Cf. The Hurley-Chiang Duet Is a Washout,* in this volume.

6. *Cf.* J. V. Stalin, *Foundations of Leninism,* Part I, "The Historical Roots of Leninism".

THE HURLEY-CHIANG DUET IS A WASHOUT

1. This refers to Chiang Kai-shek's radio speech on New Year's Day, 1945. In this speech he did not even mention the Kuomintang troops' ignominious defeats at the hands of the Japanese invaders in the past year. On the contrary, he outrageously calumniated the people, insisted on continuing the Kuomintang's one-party dictatorship and opposed the proposal to abolish it in favour of a coalition government and a united supreme command, a proposal supported by all the people and the anti-Japanese parties and groups in the country. By way of shielding himself against the people's criticism, he put forward the proposal of preparing to convene the so-called "national assembly", which was monopolised by the Kuomintang and denounced by the whole people.

2. This refers to the speech Chiang Kai-shek delivered in Chungking on March 1, 1945, at the Association for the Realisation of Constitutionalism. In addition to the reactionary views expressed in his "New-Year's Day Speech" (*see* note above), he openly demanded that the U.S. imperialists intervene in China's domestic affairs by proposing to set up a three-man committee with a U.S. participant to "reorganise" the Eighth Route Army and the New Fourth Army.

3. *See* Note 2 to *On the Tactics of Fighting Japanese Imperialism*, Vol. I of the *Selected Works*.

ON THE DANGER OF THE HURLEY POLICY

1. *See* Note 6 to *On the Tactics of Fighting Japanese Imperialism*, Vol. I of the *Selected Works*.

TELEGRAM TO COMRADE WILLIAM Z. FOSTER

1. Earl Browder was the Central-Secretary of the Communist Party of the United States from 1930 to 1944. During World War II, the Rightist ideas in the Communist Party of the U.S.A., with Browder as their exponent, developed into an anti-Marxist revisionist-capitulationist line. From December 1943 onward, Browder advocated this line in a number of speeches and articles, and in April 1944 he published *Teheran* as a programme for his Right opportunism. Revising the basic theoretical principle of Leninism that imperialism is monopolistic, decadent and moribund capitalism, and denying the imperialist nature of U.S. capitalism, he declared that U.S. capitalism "retains some of the characteristics of a *young* capitalism" [Browder's italic] and that there is a "common interest" between the proletariat and the big bourgeoisie in the U.S.A. Thus he pleaded for the safeguarding of the trust system and dreamed about saving U.S. capitalism from inevitable crises by means of "class collaboration". With this absurd appraisal of U.S. capitalism and following a capitulationist line of class collaboration with monopoly capital, Browder brought about in May 1944 the dissolution of the party of the U.S. proletariat, the Communist Party of the U.S.A. and the formation of a non-Party organisation, the Communist Political Association of the U.S.A. From the very beginning many U.S. Communists, headed by William Z. Foster, opposed Browder's

erroneous line. Under the leadership of Comrade Foster, the Communist Political Association in June 1945 passed a resolution denouncing Browder's line. In July the Association held a special national convention and decided on a thorough rectification of Browder's line and the reinstitution of the Communist Party of the U.S.A. Browder was subsequently expelled from the Party in February 1946 because he insisted on his stand, which was tantamount to a betrayal of the proletariat, openly supported the imperialist policy of the Truman administration, and carried out factional activities against the Party.